Libraries and Archives in the Digital Age

Susan L. Mizruchi
Editor

Libraries and Archives in the Digital Age

palgrave
macmillan

Editor
Susan L. Mizruchi
Department of English
Boston University
Boston, MA, USA

ISBN 978-3-030-33372-0   ISBN 978-3-030-33373-7 (eBook)
https://doi.org/10.1007/978-3-030-33373-7

© The Editor(s) (if applicable) and The Author(s), under exclusive licence to Springer Nature Switzerland AG 2020

This work is subject to copyright. All rights are solely and exclusively licensed by the Publisher, whether the whole or part of the material is concerned, specifically the rights of translation, reprinting, reuse of illustrations, recitation, broadcasting, reproduction on microfilms or in any other physical way, and transmission or information storage and retrieval, electronic adaptation, computer software, or by similar or dissimilar methodology now known or hereafter developed.

The use of general descriptive names, registered names, trademarks, service marks, etc. in this publication does not imply, even in the absence of a specific statement, that such names are exempt from the relevant protective laws and regulations and therefore free for general use.

The publisher, the authors and the editors are safe to assume that the advice and information in this book are believed to be true and accurate at the date of publication. Neither the publisher nor the authors or the editors give a warranty, expressed or implied, with respect to the material contained herein or for any errors or omissions that may have been made. The publisher remains neutral with regard to jurisdictional claims in published maps and institutional affiliations.

Cover illustration: Getty Images, TonisPan

This Palgrave Macmillan imprint is published by the registered company Springer Nature Switzerland AG.
The registered company address is: Gewerbestrasse 11, 6330 Cham, Switzerland

In Honor of James Anderson Winn (1947–2019), Scholar, Musician, Teacher, and Tireless Advocate for the Humanities

Acknowledgments

This book began as a forum at Boston University, "Recording Lives: Libraries and Archives in the Digital Age," October 5–7, 2017. The forum was co-sponsored by the Boston Public Library and the Boston Athenæum and took place over three days at BU, the BPL, and the Athenæum. Most of our contributors agreed to turn their papers into full-fledged chapters, and for that I am very grateful. I am also grateful to Alan Liu for his willingness to contribute when I reached out to him. I want to thank Tamzen Flanders and Chris Loken-Kim, administrators at the BU Center for the Humanities who worked so hard on the forum logistics, which included bringing many participants from overseas. I also want to thank the BU College and Graduate School of Arts & Sciences and Office of the Provost for their generous support of the forum. Thanks to Alison Paddock whose design for our forum catalog helped to inspire our book cover. She made our "Brochure" design, not our "Catalogue". And many thanks to my son, Sascha Bercovitch, whose work on the Bolivar Archive renewed my interest in the subject. Let me end by saying that we were all saddened by the death, on October 26, 2019, of our contributor, Rudolf G. Wagner.

Contents

1 Introduction: Libraries and Archives in the Digital Age   1
 Susan L. Mizruchi

Part I   Access   11

2 Libraries, Books, and the Digital Future   13
 Robert Darnton

3 From Open Access to Maximal Access   27
 Daniel J. Cohen

4 A National Library in the Digital Age   35
 Alberto Manguel

5 Discovery, Access, and Use of Information in a "Digital Ecosystem"   43
 Jack Ammerman

Part II   Preservation and Community   51

6 Supporting Manuscript Translation in Library and Archival Collections: Toward Decolonial Translation Methods   53
 Ellen Cushman

7   Radical Recordkeeping: How Community Archives
    Are Changing How We Think About Records   69
    Jeannette A. Bastian

8   Digital Archives for African Studies: Making Africa's
    Written Heritage Visible   83
    Fallou Ngom

Part III   Archival Politics   109

9   Nambiquaras in Paris: Archival Images, Appearances,
    and Disappearances   111
    Beatriz Jaguaribe

10 Future Memory: Preserving Diverse Voices from
    and About China in a Time of Unification of Thought   141
    Rudolf G. Wagner

11 Cold War Archives and Democratic Aspirations in Latin
    America   149
    Kirsten Weld

12 Globalism, Transparency, and Loss   171
    Maurice S. Lee

Part IV   Digital Practice   179

13 Building from the Inside Out: Librarians as Nodes
    in Digital Scholarship Collaboratories   181
    Harriett E. Green

14 On Librarianship and/with Digital Scholarly Practice   195
    Vika Zafrin

15 Data Moves: Libraries and Data Science Workflows   211
    Alan Liu

Index   221

Notes on Contributors

Jack Ammerman is the Associate University Librarian for Digital Initiatives & Open Access (retired). In libraries at Boston University, Hartford Seminary, and Emory University, he led numerous projects to create digital collections for research and pedagogical use. Among his research interests are the future of libraries and the impact of digital collections on how students perceive information.

Jeannette A. Bastian is Professor Emerita of the School of Library and Information Science, Simmons University, Boston where she directed their Archives Management program. Her books include *Owning Memory, How a Caribbean Community Lost Its Archives and Found Its History* (2003), *Community Archives, The Shaping of Memory* (2009), *Decolonizing the Caribbean Record, An Archives Reader* (2018). She is a fellow of the Society of American Archivists.

Daniel J. Cohen is the Vice Provost for Information Collaboration, Dean of the Library, and Professor of History at Northeastern University. Prior to his tenure at Northeastern, he was the founding Executive Director of the Digital Public Library of America, which brought together the riches of America's libraries, archives, and museums and made them freely available to the world. He was an inaugural recipient, in 2006, of the American Council of Learned Societies' Digital Innovation Fellowship, and in 2011, he received the Frederick G. Kilgour Award from the American Library Association. He is the co-author of *Digital History: A Guide to Gathering, Preserving, and Presenting the Past on the Web* and author of *Equations from God: Pure Mathematics and Victorian Faith*, among other publications.

Ellen Cushman is Dean's Professor of Civic Sustainability and Associate Dean of Academic Affairs, Diversity, and Inclusion in the College of Social Sciences and Humanities at Northeastern University. She is author of *The Cherokee Syllabary: Writing the People's Perseverance* (2011) and *The Struggle and the Tools: Oral and Literate Strategies in an Inner City Community*. Her publications include two edited collections: *Literacies: A Critical Sourcebook*, 2nd edition, with co-editors Christina Haas and Mike Rose (forthcoming Macmillan) and *Landmark Essays on Rhetorics of Difference*, with co-editors Damian Baca and Jonathan Osborne (2019). She serves as Chair of the Coalition for Community Writing.

Robert Darnton is the Carl H. Pforzheimer University Professor and Director of the University Library, Emeritus of Harvard University. His books include *The Great Cat Massacre and Other Episodes in French Cultural History*, *Censors at Work: How States Shaped Literature*, and *A Literary Tour de France: the World of Books on the Eve of the French Revolution*. He has served as president of the American Historical Association and the International Society of Eighteenth-Century Studies. Among his awards are a MacArthur Prize Fellowship, a National Book Critics Circle Award, and a National Humanities Medal conferred by President Obama.

Harriett E. Green is Associate University Librarian for Digital Scholarship and Technology Services at Washington University in St. Louis. Her research focuses on scholarly communication and digital publishing, curation of humanities data, and the use and users of digital humanities resources. Her publications include articles in *College & Research Libraries*, *Journal of the Association of Information Science and Technology (JASIST)*, *D-Lib Magazine*, *Library Quarterly*, *EDUCAUSE Review*, and *portal: Libraries and the Academy*. Her research has been supported by grants awarded from the Institute for Museum and Library Services, the National Endowment for the Humanities, The Extreme Science and Engineering Discovery Environment, and the Andrew W. Mellon Foundation.

Beatriz Jaguaribe has a Ph.D. in comparative literature from Stanford University. She is a professor at the School of Communication of the Federal University of Rio de Janeiro. Her fields of research are literature, urban studies, and media studies with a particular emphasis on Latin American cultures. She has been a visiting professor at Stanford University, Princeton University, New York University, and The New School for Social Research, among other institutions. She has been awarded a Guggenheim Fellowship, The Robert

F. Kennedy Visiting Professorship, International Centre of Advanced Studies Fellowship, and RioArte Grant and is a researcher with the Brazilian National Council for Scientific and Technological Development. Her publications include the books *Rio de Janeiro: Urban Life Through the Eyes of the City* (2014), *O choque do real* (2007), and *Fins de século* (1998).

Maurice S. Lee is Professor of English at Boston University, where his work focuses on nineteenth-century American literature. His most recent book is *Overwhelmed: Literature, Aesthetics, and the Nineteenth-Century Information Revolution* (2019). He has received awards from the Melville Society, Poe Studies Association, and the Association of College and Research Libraries, as well as fellowships from the National Endowment for the Humanities, American Council of Learned Societies, and Radcliffe Institute for Advanced Study.

Alan Liu is Distinguished professor in the English Department at the University of California, Santa Barbara. He has worked in the areas of digital humanities, Romantic literature, and literary and cultural theory. His books include *Wordsworth: The Sense of History*, *The Laws of Cool: Knowledge Work and the Culture of Information*, *Local Transcendence: Essays on Postmodern Historicism and the Database*, and *Friending the Past: The Sense of History in the Digital Age*. He leads the 4Humanities.org "WhatEvery1Says" (WE1S) project, a digital humanities big-data initiative funded by the Andrew W. Mellon Foundation to understand public discourse about the humanities.

Alberto Manguel is an Argentinian-Canadian writer, translator, and critic. He has published both fiction and non-fiction and received numerous international awards, among others the Guggenheim, the Formentor, and the Gutenberg Prize. He was selected to deliver *The Massey Lectures* in 2007, and he has edited a number of anthologies on subjects ranging from erotica and gay stories to fantastic literature and mysteries. His many books include *A History of Reading* (1996); *The Library at Night* (2007); *Homer's Iliad and Odyssey: A Biography* (2008), and the novel, *News From a Foreign Country Came* (1991). Until August 2018, he was the Director of the Argentine National Library. He has been a regular contributor to journals and magazines including *The Globe and Mail; TLS; The Village Voice; The New York Times*, and *Geist*.

Susan L. Mizruchi is the William Arrowsmith Professor in the Humanities, Director of the Humanities Center, and Professor of English at Boston

University. Her books include *Brando's Smile* (2014); *The Rise of Multicultural America* (2008); *Religion and Cultural Studies* (2001), *The Science of Sacrifice* (1998); *The Power of Historical Knowledge* (1988). She has received many academic honors, including fellowships from the Guggenheim; the Huntington Library; the Fulbright Foundation, and the NEH.

Fallou Ngom is Professor of Anthropology and Director of the African Studies Center at Boston University. He has held Fulbright, American Council of Learned Societies (ACLS), and Guggenheim fellowships. His recent research has been supported by the British Library Endangered Archives Programme and the National Endowment for the Humanities. His book, *Muslims beyond the Arab World: The Odyssey of Ajami and the Muridyya* (2016), won the 2017 Melville J. Herskovits Prize for the best book in African studies.

Rudolf G. Wagner Senior Professor of Chinese Studies at Heidelberg University and a research fellow at the John K. Fairbank Center for East Asian Research at Harvard, had a long and distinguished career as a sinologist and was a leading scholar on the politics and culture of China. He received the Gottfried Wilhem Liebniz Prize, the highest German award for academic work, was a member of the Berlin-Brandenburg Academy of Sciences, and President of the European Association of Chinese Studies. He used his Liebniz Prize money, together with a grant from the Alfried Krupp von Bohlen und Halbach Foundation, to develop the library and digital research collection at the Heidelberg Institute of Chinese Studies. He died on October 26, 2019.

Kirsten Weld is Professor of History at Harvard University, where she researches and teaches the modern history of the Americas. She is the author of the award-winning book *Paper Cadavers: The Archives of Dictatorship in Guatemala* (2014) and articles in venues such as *Hispanic American Historical Review*, *Journal of Latin American Studies*, *Radical History Review*, and *NACLA Report on the Americas*. She is writing a book about the Spanish Civil War's impact and afterlives in Latin America.

Vika Zafrin is Boston University's Digital Scholarship Librarian and serves as the Executive Secretary of the Association for Computers in the Humanities. Her professional interests include open access to scholarship and cultural heritage, computationally meaningful digital collections, and the expansion of opportunities for knowledge creation to underrepresented groups and citizen contributors. Zafrin holds a Ph.D. in digital humanities from Brown University.

List of Figures

Fig. 2.1	The author posing with a friend at a point where students used to climb into St John's College, Oxford University, in 1961. (Source: Private photo (David Winter))	15
Fig. 2.2	Barriers that kept outsiders outside college libraries in Oxford. (Source: Private photo (Richard Ovenden))	16
Fig. 2.3	Inscription carved over the main entrance to the Boston Public Library. (Source: DPLA)	19
Fig. 2.4	DPLA's website. (Source: DPLA)	21
Fig. 2.5	An artist's rendering of ideas suggested during a public meeting about what should be included in the DPLA. (Source: DPLA)	22
Fig. 6.1	B22 F1843 Letter to Dollie Duncan on Oklahoma Penitentiary stationery IID15533005. Kilpatrick Collection of Cherokee Manuscripts. Yale Collection of Western Americana, Beinecke Rare Book and Manuscript Library	61
Fig. 6.2	Interlinear translations of first four lines of letter from Walter Duncan to Dollie Duncan	62
Fig. 8.1	Excerpt from the petition of the inhabitants of Rufisque, Senegal, sent to the colonial Governor of French West Africa in 1882 with signatures in Arabic and Wolof Ajami script. (Source: Lettre des habitants de Rufisque, 6 avril 1882, Sénégal, XVI, 1a, Archives Nationales d'Outre Mer, Aix-en-Provence, France)	85
Fig. 8.2	Wooden boards used in traditional Quranic schools in Senegambia. (Picture taken in Ziguinchor, Senegal, by Fallou Ngom in January 2018)	89
Fig. 8.3	A sample bilingual Arabic-Hausa Ajami document from Mustapha Kurfi's collection illustrating dual literacies in Northern Nigeria. (Source: https://open.bu.edu/handle/2144/11722)	91

List of Figures

Fig. 8.4	Most common Wolofal (Wolof Ajami) letters used to write Wolof consonants that do not exist in Arabic. (Source: Fallou Ngom (2010, 14–15))	93
Fig. 8.5	Mixed Arabic and Mandinka Ajami manuscripts from Casamance, Senegal. According to the current owner (Abdou Karin Thiam), some of the manuscripts in this archive are over 200 years old as he is the sixth-generation heir. He inherited them from his father, Nimbaly Thiam, who died in the Mina stampede that occurred in the 2015 pilgrimage in Mecca, Saudi Arabia. (Source: Picture taken by Fallou Ngom in January 2018)	96
Fig. 8.6	Excerpt from Muusaa Ka's popular Wolof Ajami poem called *Xarnu bi* (The Century) written in 1929 during the Great Depression	97
Fig. 9.1	The second photograph is a portrait of the guide Matias Toloiri, Expedition of 1907. Photograph by Luiz Leduc. (Source: This image is part of the collection of the Société de Géographie)	119
Fig. 9.2	Photograph by Thomaz Reis, Album of 1922. Rondon distributing gifts to the Paresis. (Source: Museu do Índio)	124
Fig. 9.3	Photograph by Tomaz Reis, Album of 1922. Rondon with Paresis at the waterfall of Utiariti. (Source: Museu do Índio)	125
Fig. 9.4	Photograph by José Louro. Olga Higgins with two of her Paresi students. (Source: *Índios do Brasil*, vol 1, p. 107. Museu do Índio)	128
Fig. 9.5	Photographs by José Louro, Album of 1922. Chief Nuchilaitê and his wife. (Source: Museu do Índio)	128
Fig. 9.6	Photographs by José Louro, Album of 1922. Portrait of Cavaignac posing as a Nambiquara and dressed in uniform. Only the photograph of Cavaignac as a Nambiquara was donated to the Société de Géographie. In the collection given to the Société de Géographie, the portrait of Cavaignac dressed in uniform is absent. There is only his image with his arrows and posing as a Nambiquara. (Source: Museu do Índio)	129
Fig. 15.1	A Wings workflow for a data analysis related to drug discovery. (From Garijo et al., "Common Motifs in Scientific Workflows: An Empirical Analysis"; © 2012 IEEE; reprinted with permission)	212
Fig. 15.2	Combinations of "moves" or "motifs" in folk narratives from Vladimir Propp, *Morphology of the Folktale*, 2d ed., translated by Laurence Scott, revised and edited with a preface by Louis A. Wagner, University of Texas Press, 1968; reprinted with permission. (Original work published in 1928)	214

1

Introduction: Libraries and Archives in the Digital Age

Susan L. Mizruchi

This book originated in a 2017 forum that was organized by Boston University's Center for the Humanities and held at the *Boston Athenaeum*, at the *Boston Public Library* (BPL) and at Boston University from October 5 to 7. By invoking the term "forum," rather than the more typical "conference," we were thinking deliberately about creating a public space to facilitate communication among various audiences that rarely come together to share questions, ideas, and solutions. These included academic, philanthropic, and public institutions, like the *BPL* and the *Athenaeum*, which both co-sponsored our forum.

In conceptualizing forum in the broadest classical sense—as an open place for addressing issues common to the citizenry—we were not unmindful of the fact that the traditional Roman forum was confined to men of the wealthiest class, and excluded almost everyone else. Our forum was designed to be inclusive, bringing together people from a variety of institutional and professional backgrounds, with very different relationships to libraries and archives. Our contributors come from all over the world, and the subjects of their chapters are just as diverse, covering territories from the Americas—the US, South America, and indigenous America—to Africa, Asia, and Europe. The divergent life experiences, professional training, and approaches of our contributors will, we hope, result in a volume that is unique to the field.

S. L. Mizruchi (✉)
Department of English, Boston University, Boston, MA, USA
e-mail: mizruchi@bu.edu

The role of archives and libraries in our digital age is one of the most pressing concerns of humanists, scholars, and citizens worldwide. Questions of what to keep and how to keep it touch the very core of who we are as individuals, cultures, nations, and humankind. Now, more than ever, the accessibility of curated historical information, the sharing of resources, and the uses of digitization raise questions central to democratic societies. This edited book brings together specialists from academia, public libraries, governmental agencies, and nonprofit archives to pursue common questions about value across the institutional boundaries that typically separate us.

The very existence of a library or archive signals a value judgment—that someone has declared a collection of materials worthy of preservation. Sometimes these declarations are made by public agencies, such as *The Library of Congress* or *The Boston Public Library*. Sometimes they are made by community groups whose collections are defined by and also help to define their political identities and purposes. Sometimes they are made by academic institutions where such judgments are dictated by the needs of scholars and by standards of professional research.

Everyone working in libraries and archives today must make decisions about how much to retain in physical form while embracing the opportunities afforded by digital methods, and such decisions inevitably raise questions about what it means to preserve things and also what significance we attribute to the things we preserve. Moreover, the matter of *how* we preserve has critical epistemological and ethical implications. Just as importantly, access to materials determines what we as scholars and citizens can know. As those who study politically embattled nations have revealed, libraries and archives hold secrets, and the recuperation of their contents can both expose the violence of authoritarian regimes and recover the memories of their victims. Regimes destroy collections as expressions of power, and their restitution can be tantamount to redressing injustices and identifying lost peoples.

While our book is focused broadly to encompass the political urgency of archival decision-making in a global context, it also attends to more local institutional considerations, particularly issues of professional status and economic compensation that arise among the staff, faculty, public servants, and administrators in various academic, governmental, and philanthropic settings. While a common commitment to libraries and archives and to innovative methods unites us, these same commitments can divide us. The frictions that arise from educational and professional as well as personal and experiential differences have to do above all with the ways in which the distinct kinds of labor performed by practitioners and scholars are valued.

Of equal concern is the goal of making the wealth of global information widely available. While pioneering organizations such as the Digital Public Library of America have succeeded in bridging institutional barriers, the next frontier is the development of new users. The pursuit of open access must be joined to the pursuit of maximal access in order for our libraries and archives to realize their ultimate aim of enlightening a world citizenry.

We hope that this book will initiate a broader global conversation among representatives of a wide range of institutions, disciplines, and professional capacities, on subjects of profound cultural and political importance. The notably diverse specialists contributing to this book represent five different continents.

The book is organized according to four major areas of analysis. **Part I, Access**, describes the innovative efforts being pursued by leading institutions and organizations to democratize access, making ever-expanding resources available on a global scale. **Part II, Preservation and Community**, explores the role of preservation methods in recuperating lost communities, strengthening existing communities, and creating new ones. **Part III, Archival Politics**, considers the practical, moral, and legal implications of destroying and restoring archives in places where the status of archives has particular political urgency. **Part IV, Digital Practice**, takes up methodological imperatives highlighting the myriad ways in which librarians and scholars can collaborate in the name of more holistic institutional understandings of digital work.

The four chapters in the first section of the book, "Access," focus on the various problems that have arisen over time in making collections widely available. Robert Darnton's chapter, "Libraries, Books, and the Digital Future," describes the goals of the New Digital Public Library, invoking its chief purpose—extending access to a vast global community—as a guide to changing conceptualizations of libraries through the ages. Noting that libraries are typically considered communal, national, and even international assets, Darnton points out that their intellectual wealth has not always been viewed as shareable. In ancient Greece and China, for instance, libraries were used primarily to store precious materials and reflect dynastic power. Where library holdings were deemed subversive of governing institutions—for example, in the eighteenth-century Ching Dynasty and Stalin's Great Terror of 1938–1939—their contents were destroyed. Elite universities contributed greatly to civilization by building up their collections but kept them behind locked doors.

During the Enlightenment, however, a counter-tendency developed, which viewed the diffusion of knowledge as a positive historical force. Articulated by

European philosophers like Condorcet and US statesmen like Thomas Jefferson, this Enlightenment ideal of open access to information depended on the printing press. Our era of digitization has given rise to a new ideal of openness. Today, Darnton asserts, we have open universities, open-source software, open metadata, and the beginnings of an open information highway. But still a darker side persists, and the final section of the chapter describes efforts by the Digital Public Library of America (DPLA) to negotiate greater access with major publishing monopolies, from conglomerates such as Reed Elsevier, Wiley-Blackwell, and Springer that control 42 percent of the academic market to Google. In conclusion, Darnton points out that the DPLA is not simply a digital version of the Library of Congress, but an ever-expanding collection designed to function at personal, local, national, and international levels, and to seek out new functions over time, along with new populations to utilize them.

Daniel J. Cohen's chapter, "From Open Access to Maximal Access," notes the importance of the Open Access movement in articulating how digital media and technology, especially the web, can democratize the availability and use of primary sources that were formerly difficult to reach. Such sources were physically embedded in libraries and archives and thus mostly accessed by professional researchers with the time and ability to visit collections, rather than by the general public. The movement has had significant success in opening these collections to a wider array of readers over the last 20 years.

However, it is now clear that open access on its own is not enough. Digitized materials from libraries and archives may exist on the web in growing numbers, but these materials are largely inert, waiting for potential researchers and the public to somehow find them, rather than actively participating in the dynamism of the modern web and taking advantage of the energy and interactions of diverse communities. Thinking instead of "maximal access," and the mechanisms—both technical and social—whereby primary sources can be curated, synthesized into larger aggregate collections, and more directly engaged with audiences, is essential for the next phase of digital libraries and archives. This more ambitious goal of maximizing access has implications for scholarly and institutional practice.

Alberto Manguel's chapter, "A National Library in the Digital Age," starts with the proposition that a library exists always in potentia; it is never merely a physical construction but represents a possibility of knowledge extending beyond its own space and time. Electronic technologies have helped libraries overcome these two ancestral obstacles by offering unprecedented possibilities of access. A national library, in particular, must establish means by which all citizens become aware of these possibilities, and of the importance of reading, both as a basic skill and as a way to stimulate and free the imagination. A national library carries a projected communal identity both for those who are, in practical terms, familiar with them and for those who are not.

The chapter raises questions such as, how is a national library to become capable of serving readers and non-readers alike; how can it convert non-readers into readers; and how can it transform the perception that most non-readers have of libraries as alien places and books—printed or digital—as alien instruments? Perhaps, he suggests, a national library can become a place where new readers are formed and old readers reaffirmed.

Jack Ammerman's chapter, "Discovery, Access, and Use of Information in the 'Digital Ecosystem,'" explores the impact of a new digital ecosystem on traditional library services and collections. For over a quarter of a century, libraries and archives have responded to changes in an increasingly digital information ecosystem while still adhering to traditional analog models for collecting and managing information. More recently, the shift from scarcity to abundance of information has resulted in the replacement of discovery and close reading by newer methods of filtering, scanning, and computational analysis. Similarly, notions of copyright and ownership have given way to emerging patterns of sharing and remixing information. Thus, the ways we think and construct knowledge evolve as new communities embrace epistemologies that challenge dominant epistemological models.

The chapters in the second section of the book, "Preservation and Community," focus on the impact of preservation and preservation methods on different communities. Ellen Cushman's chapter, "Supporting Manuscript Translation in Library and Archival Collections: Toward Decolonial Translation Methods," explores ongoing efforts to decolonize the archive, in order to build alliances between scholars, archivists, and the peoples represented in archival materials. She charts the important advances in creating protocols for working with communities to identify culturally sensitive materials and to select metadata categories for those materials.

The next step involves separating from the imperialist legacy of translation by developing decolonial translation methods and practices, which begin with an understanding of the instrumental, historical, and cultural importance of the Cherokee syllabary as an indigenous form of archiving knowledge in and on Cherokee terms. For scholars, decolonial translation methodologies help to ensure the creation of knowledge that is conversant with indigenous interpretations and representations of the past. For indigenous peoples, decolonial translation methods help to ensure that archival materials can be meaningfully integrated into ongoing language preservation efforts in indigenous communities.

Jeannette A. Bastian's chapter, "Radical Recordkeeping: How Community Archives Are Changing How We Think About Records," analyzes the functions of community archives, which have proliferated in recent years both as global and as social movements that allow diverse groups of people in a wide variety of locations—both analog and virtual—to document themselves outside of traditional archival venues. Community archives, she suggests, are markers of community-based activism. This participatory approach exemplifies the ongoing evolution of "professional" archival (and heritage) practice and is integral to the ability of people to articulate and assert their identity. Defining community archives, she describes the community archives movement, exploring it as a social phenomenon, its activist role, and its potential impact on traditional archives. She then discusses specific examples of community archives, noting by way of these examples how this radical approach to records and recordkeeping helps to capture society broadly in all of its diversity.

Fallou Ngom's chapter, "Digital Archives for African Studies: Making Africa's Written Heritage Visible," challenges the academic overemphasis on African oral traditions that began in the colonial era and has been perpetuated ever since. Creating the false impression that only oral traditions exist in sub-Saharan Africa, this scholarly misconception has obscured local forms of literacy that have endured for centuries, and also led to the complete neglect of the voluminous holdings in non-European languages contained in archives across Africa. Major collections of documents written in Arabic, *Ajami* (African languages written with enriched forms of the Arabic script), and other locally invented writing systems have existed in sub-Saharan Africa for centuries. These documents feature varied contents and forms and provide new insights into precolonial, colonial, and postcolonial Africa that will enhance the work of students and scholars in the humanities, social sciences, and professional fields. Ngom's chapter shows how digital technology helps to correct the scholarly record, by creating access to a previously overlooked African cultural heritage contained in written archives.

The chapters in the third section of the book, "Archival Politics," focus on archives that have been censored or hidden, preventing the peoples they represent from accessing their cultural history, political identities, and, in some cases, evidence of family members who were disappeared. Beatriz Jaguaribe's chapter, "Nambiquaras in Paris: Archival Images, Appearances, and Disappearances," offers a case study of a photographic archive made by the Rondon Commission and stored in the Map and Cartography Section of the National Library of France. Issuing from a 1925 gift by an anonymous donor to the Société de Géographié in Paris, these 120 images of the expeditions of the Rondon Commission provide invaluable records of the many Indian tribes inhabiting these regions, giving rise to an exploration of the relationships among archives, historical contexts, and the politics and poetics of remembrance.

Although the feats of the military officer Candido Rondon (1865–1958) were discussed in some of the issues of the journal *La Géographie*, the images themselves have never been analyzed. In 1953, the Museum of the Indian was created in Rio de Janeiro, and when the archives of the Rondon Commission were integrated into the museum's collection, the images were digitized. Tracing the material and symbolic trajectory of these photographs, she offers a contextualized reading of their roles in different archives, historical moments, and cultural contexts. From the heady atmosphere of Paris in the 1920s with its assortments of colonial exhibits, ethnographic displays, and avant-garde appropriations of "primitive" art to a contemporary Rio de Janeiro beset by economic crisis, social conflicts, and turbulent politics, these images evoke a past of scars, legacies, and aspirations.

In his chapter, "Future Memory: Preserving Diverse Voices From and About China in a Time of Unification of Thought," Rudolf G. Wagner describes the 30-year effort of the Heidelberg Institute of Chinese Studies to develop a hybrid Chinese Studies library of books, films, TV recordings, music scores and recorded performances, and digital resources (subscribed and locally curated). Launched in 2001, The Digital Archive of Chinese Studies (DACHS) is part of this effort. Designed to counter government censorship, and the consequent loss of Chinese public discussions as well as academic work in Chinese Studies journals, the goal of DACHS is to preserve the conflicts and tensions in the national discourse by downloading political controversies and archiving voices silenced by Chinese officialdom. By documenting the widest possible range of voices in the public sphere, from the Chinese government to social groups, public intellectuals, and individuals who have been directly at odds with it, DACHS (and the library as a whole) seeks to make this cacophony of perspectives available to professional humanities and social science research.

In "Cold War Archives and Democratic Aspirations in Latin America," Kirsten Weld explores efforts to secure citizen access to the archives of formerly repressive Cold War regimes in Latin America. The opening of such state records, especially the records of security and intelligence services, has come to be considered essential to processes of transitional justice in postwar and post-dictatorship societies like Guatemala, El Salvador, Argentina, and Chile, and civil society movements have fought ardently for their release. Yet the greatest social value of such records may extend beyond their potential evidentiary use in court, to their role in what some analysts have called an "ecological approach to social repair." Along the way of her analysis, she asks about the benefits and costs of applying a narrowly juridical logic to the opening of such files; whether there might be other uses to which such files might fruitfully be put, and how the framework of "human rights archives" enables grappling with these issues. Her ultimate concern is to assess how the opening of Cold War state security archives relates to the work of concretizing democratic aspirations in Latin America.

Maurice S. Lee's chapter, "Globalism, Transparency, and Loss," reflects on the complex and contradictory aspirations of our "digital age," which cleaves on the one hand to the promise of total information, while acknowledging on the other the historical and cultural contexts in which such promises are foiled. National barriers, epistemological limits, the opacity of physical bodies do not simply undermine dreams of total information, but prompt a more modest, more necessary set of claims that digital archives can pursue. The possibilities of reclaiming information, whether in the service of political justice or scientific objectivity, remain haunted by the specter of loss, even as facts and knowledge are gained. Assuming a classically skeptical stance, the chapter traces the power and limits of digital archives in our increasingly disenchanted information age.

The chapters in the fourth and final section of the book, "Digital Practice," examine the prospects and limits of this moment from the perspective of library and information professionals and the research collaborations they seek in their effort to retool scholars in the humanities and social sciences. In her chapter, "Building from the Inside Out: Librarians as Nodes in Digital Scholarship Collaboratories," Harriett E. Green offers an overview of the challenges and possibilities for librarians to partner with humanities and social science scholars in data-driven research. She then explores the recent training initiatives she and others have led that seek to expand the scope of librarians' research capacities. She proposes strategies that involve recalibrating methods to meet the data-driven needs of users, as well as reframing the role of librarians in the research lifecycle today. Such changes, she concludes, should lead to new understandings of the scholarly end product of research as well as greater appreciation for the interdependence of different knowledge producers.

In her chapter, "On Librarianship and/with Digital Scholarly Practice," Vika Zafrin explores the role of library professionals as information management specialists in a politically fraught information age. Taking an institutional perspective, she notes how assessments of the intellectual contributions of library professionals can be distorted by dated ideas about what librarians do, and by institutionalized inequity between faculty and staff. Widely acknowledged by the fields involved, and largely unacknowledged by institutional structures, is the fact that librarians are engaged in digital scholarly work that generates new knowledge. In order to truly innovate, she asserts, librarians must be given the space and time for their work to evolve. Invoking the example of Boston University's Digital Scholarship Services' contributions to the African Ajami Library (discussed above in Fallou Ngom's chapter), she highlights the economic, relational, and labor issues that arise with the institutionalization of digital scholarship. Addressing the internal political dimensions of translating knowledge among digital project participants with different fields of expertise, she assesses what libraries can offer in the current global political context. Her ultimate purpose is to challenge the image of library professionals as service providers; they are instead intellectual collaborators whose unique ability to mediate varieties of knowledge should be recognized as central to the university's research mission.

In his chapter, "Data Moves: Libraries and Data Science Workflows," Alan Liu seeks to bridge disciplinary approaches to data, by identifying common goals and stressing the value of certain methods across disciplinary enterprises. Thus, for example, the precedent set by in silico science models, which have annotated and visualized data-analysis workflows for reproducibility and compared data workflows in different fields, would be applicable to data analysis in the humanities and social sciences. Citing shared goals of making data scholarship open and reproducible, and enabling a meta-level analysis of such scholarship, he suggests that the digital humanities, digital arts, and digital social sciences would derive great benefit from borrowing such scientific data paradigms. Such borrowings, Liu argues, work both ways, for the sciences also have something to learn from the storytelling methods of the humanities. In particular, a twentieth-century tradition of literary and ethnographic analysis, the idea of the narrative "motif" or "move," might prove valuable to scientific analysis of data workflows. For no matter how one is analyzing data, it is always necessary to *tell the story* of that workflow and its results.

Part I

Access

2

Libraries, Books, and the Digital Future

Robert Darnton

Despite a lot of loose talk about the death of the book and the obsolescence of libraries, books and libraries are more important than ever in the current digital environment; and their importance will increase as we design the digital future—if only we can get it right.[1] I want to develop this argument by looking backward into history and forward into the prospects for a new kind of library, the Digital Public Library of America.

The historical importance of libraries may seem obvious. Take a tour of a typical American university, and you will immediately get the point: the library stands at the center of the campus, and it occupies a corresponding place at the heart of the university's intellectual life. It pumps intellectual energy into every sector of the university, including laboratories where scientists download electronic journals and databases without suspecting that they come from the library.

At Harvard, the university owes its name to its library, a collection of 400 books left to the College in 1638 by one John Harvard, and it grew up around that original core of learning. Today, nearly four centuries and 20 million volumes later, we recognize that the university's greatness has derived above all from the intellectual riches built up over many generations and stored in the largest library system of any university in the world. But I don't mean to indulge in institutional bragging, which is an occupational disease among librarians ("How many incunabula do you have in your collections?" "How

R. Darnton (✉)
Harvard University, Cambridge, MA, USA
e-mail: robert_darnton@harvard.edu

many e-books do you have in yours?"). Instead, I want to ask a question: Shouldn't Harvard's library and those of other research universities be considered as a national and even an international asset? Shouldn't their intellectual wealth be shared?

For most of history, that wealth was restricted to a privileged few. And contrary to common belief, the history of libraries does not follow an uninterrupted, upward trajectory leading to the democratization of access to knowledge.

From what little we know about the ancient library of Alexandria, it functioned primarily to store texts, not to make them available to readers. It admitted a few scholars, but its main purpose probably was to embody the magnificence of the Ptolemaic dynasty. The same principle applied to the Chinese attempt to create a library that would contain all the books in the world—that is, the Chinese world. The Ching emperor Ch'ien-lung set out to do so by confiscating books from his subjects on a gigantic scale from 1772 to 1778. He kept everything that glorified the Ching Dynasty and burned everything that was critical of it or favorable to the Mings—at least 2320 books produced between 1550 and 1750. The Communist regime in Czechoslovakia exploited the country's libraries in the same way—that is, to purge literature rather than to preserve it. In 1954, it ordered all local librarians to cleanse their shelves of works that fit into categories that ranged from the expected ("fascism" and "pornography") to the bizarre ("formalism," "ruralism," and "snobbism"). They got rid of 7500 works. And that was little compared with the 51 million books destroyed by the Soviets in Ukraine.

The history of libraries has a dark side in the United States as well as in other countries. The African-American author Richard Wright was not permitted to borrow books from the public library in Memphis, Tennessee, when he was a young man, because the color of his skin was black. The only way he could take out books was by pretending he was a servant fetching them for a white man.

To be sure, the oldest universities contributed greatly to civilization by building up their libraries. But they kept their books behind locked doors and thick walls, which removed them from outsiders. When I was a student at Oxford, the massive gate of my college slammed shut at 10:00 in the evening, and if you hadn't made it inside, you had to climb over one of the walls—a daunting experience, as the walls were ten to fifteen feet high and bristled at their top with spikes and shards of glass. A few secret passes existed, but even they were treacherous—as you can see in this photo from 1961, which shows me posing with a friend at one of my favorite entry points, where you had to slip between rows of fixed and revolving spikes (Fig. 2.1).

2 Libraries, Books, and the Digital Future   15

Fig. 2.1 The author posing with a friend at a point where students used to climb into St John's College, Oxford University, in 1961. (Source: Private photo (David Winter))

Oxford's walls still keep its libraries closed inside its colleges, and the Bodleian or university library has a fortified appearance with spikes and crenellations, although it welcomes researchers from the outside world (Fig. 2.2).

But I want to discuss the invisible barriers to the knowledge stored in libraries. They frequently keep outsiders outside by all sorts of measures: restrictive qualifications for entry, payment to obtain a readers' card, and an atmosphere of intimidation. Ordinary folk hesitate to brave these barriers. They are kept at a distance by the learned elite, who wear an air of effortless superiority, which corresponds to the social sifting that the French sociologist Pierre Bourdieu identified as "distinction."

Fig. 2.2 Barriers that kept outsiders outside college libraries in Oxford. (Source: Private photo (Richard Ovenden))

A counter-tendency gathered force in the age of Enlightenment, when philosophers like Condorcet understood the diffusion of knowledge to be the most important force in history, one that would extend everywhere, destroying prejudice and promoting progress. That faith was shared by the Founding Fathers of the United States, notably Condorcet's friend, Thomas Jefferson, who declared that "The field of knowledge is the common property of mankind." As the Founders understood it, the health of the republic depended on a well-informed citizenry, and the spread of light was commensurate with the reading of books.

In retrospect, that vision looks utopian. But it helped inspire the opening up of libraries. Ordinary readers were allowed inside the French Royal Library in 1692 and the British Museum in 1759. In the United States, the first large public library, established in Boston in 1848, allowed any citizen to borrow books and take them home to read. The New York Public Library opened its great collections in 1911 to anyone who walked in from the street. It served as an informal university for generations of immigrants who wanted both instruction and access to the literature in their native languages.

Of course, this kind of access to knowledge depended on a limited technology: the printing press. Most people in the eighteenth century could not read, and most of those who were literate could not afford to buy books. Today we have the Internet. We now have it in our power to realize what was a utopian vision in the age of Enlightenment. As an example of what can now be accomplished, consider the difference between two great encyclopedias. The *Encyclopédie* edited by Diderot was the bible of the Enlightenment and a marvel of intellectual production 250 years ago: 17 volumes of text by about 200 contributors. But it cost 980 *livres*, the equivalent of two and a half years' income for a common laborer. Wikipedia now contains 30 million articles by 77,000 "active" contributors, and it reaches 365 million readers free of charge.

A new ideal of openness is transforming the world of knowledge. Its origins go back to the Enlightenment ideal of a republic of letters—that is, in principle, a free, intellectual realm with no police force, no boundaries, and no exclusiveness. But in practice, only a tiny elite enjoyed citizenship in this republic during the eighteenth century. Today we have open universities, open-source software, open metadata, open-access journals, and the beginnings of an open information highway.

Unfortunately, however, this tendency also has a darker side, because in some ways access to knowledge is being closed.

What is the cost of an average subscription to a chemical journal today? $4773 a year. What was it in 1970? $33 a year. Inflation accounts for only a small part of the increase. During the last 25 years, the price of academic periodicals went up at four times the rate of the consumer price index. One year's subscription to the *Journal of Comparative Neurology* in print and online costs $44,832—the equivalent of 900 monographs. Three giant publishers—Reed Elsevier, Wiley-Blackwell, and Springer—now publish 42 percent of all academic articles, and they make giant profits from them. In 2017, Elsevier's profit came to 913 million pounds sterling, a margin of 36.8 percent, on its revenue from science, technology, and medical journals.

The ruinous increase in journal prices cannot simply be explained by greed on the part of the publishers. They are doing their job: returning the largest possible profit to their shareholders. Perhaps they should be congratulated for doing it so well, but their success should give us pause, because it illustrates the negative counterpart to the trend toward openness—namely, commercialization, a trend toward closing access to knowledge.

The output of articles in medical science doubles every three to four years. So yes, more knowledge is constantly being produced, but an increasingly small proportion of it is available to the public. Why? Libraries can no longer afford to pay the prices. The average price for a medical journal was $12 in 1970; it was $1736 in 2017. All over the country, libraries are canceling subscriptions to academic journals, because they are caught between decreasing budgets and increasing costs. The logic of the bottom line is inescapable, but there is a higher logic that deserves consideration—namely, that the public should have access to knowledge produced with public funds.

Congress acted on that principle in 2008, when it required that articles based on grants from the National Institutes of Health be made available from an open-access repository, PubMed Central. But lobbyists for the publishers blunted that requirement by getting the NIH to accept a 12-month embargo to prevent public accessibility long enough for them to cream off the demand. Not content with that victory, the lobbyists tried to abolish the NIH mandate in the so-called Research Works Act, a bill introduced in Congress in November 2011 and championed by Elsevier. The bill was withdrawn four months later following a wave of public protest, but the lobbyists are still at work, trying to block the Fair Access to Science and Technology Research Act (FASTR), which would give the public free access to the publication of all research funded by federal agencies with research budgets of $100 million or more. It was introduced unsuccessfully to Congress in 2013, 2015, and 2017. Will it make it through Congress in 2019? Not likely.

The battles over journal prices illustrate a conflict between two tendencies that will determine the digital future: democratization versus commercialization. However, I don't mean to reduce a complex situation to a simplistic formula. We have to find some way in a real world of wealth and power to find an equitable balance between private interests and the public good. We therefore face a fundamental question: Have we got the balance right in the world of books and libraries?

Consider Google. In 2004, Google set out to digitize the collections of our greatest research libraries. It intended to use the data in a search service, which would make available snippets or short passages from the books for users seeking information about a specific subject. Authors and publishers sued Google for infringing their copyrights; and after four and a half years of strenuous negotiations, they reached a settlement, which transformed the search service into a gigantic commercial library. As a consequence, the research libraries that had originally supplied the books, free of charge, to Google would have to buy back access to the digital copies of the same books at a price that Google would determine. The cost they would have to pay for subscribing to Google's database could have escalated as disastrously as the price of subscriptions to academic journals, because the settlement had no provision for oversight or control by public authorities. In fact, the public was never consulted, and its interest was never considered. Fortunately, a New York federal court refused to authorize the settlement on the grounds that, among other things, it would create a monopoly in violation of the Sherman Anti-trust Act.

Google was actually proposing a monopoly of a new kind, a monopoly of access to information in digital form. It would have privatized a vast stretch of the public domain and collected a toll from anyone who tried to enter its

Fig. 2.3 Inscription carved over the main entrance to the Boston Public Library. (Source: DPLA)

fenced-off territory. It was an audacious and in some ways a thrilling project, and it raised the prospect of finding a democratic alternative to a commercial speculation.

In the era of print, this open-access tradition goes back to the founding of the Boston Public Library in 1848. The inscription carved over its main entrance says, "Free to All" (Fig. 2.3).

Now that we have entered the digital age, we can do better. We can make all of the material in all of our research libraries available to everyone free of charge. That is the basic idea behind the Digital Public Library of America.

On October 1, 2010, long before Google Book Search was rejected by the court, a group of leaders from foundations, libraries, and computer science met at Harvard to discuss the possibility of creating a Digital Public Library of America or DPLA. The foundations would combine forces to provide the funds; the libraries would cooperate to furnish the books. We created a steering committee, a secretariat with a small staff, and work groups scattered across the country.

Thousands of people participated, and everything was discussed openly—in large meetings in San Francisco, Chicago, and Washington; and also through e-mail, LISTSERVS, websites, wikis, and blogs. There was streaming, texting, tweeting—a running debate about every aspect of the plans in which everyone had a chance to be heard. At the same time, there was enough coordination from the Berkman Center at Harvard for the DPLA to be launched successfully online on April 18, 2013.

Now that it has celebrated its eighth anniversary, its collections include over 17 million books and other objects, five times the amount that it offered when it first went online. They come from more than 2000 institutions located in all 50 states, and they are being widely used: millions of visitors have consulted the DPLA's website (dp.la), and they come from every country in the world, except three: North Korea, Chad, and Western Sahara. The DPLA's collections include material in 500 languages (Fig. 2.4).

By clicking on the website, you can call up the texts of books, but you can do much more. You can browse through all the collections by place and by time period; you can wander through virtual exhibitions, which are particularly popular in secondary schools; and you can make use of all sorts of apps, which are constantly being grafted onto the system by independent innovators.

How should you envisage the DPLA? Not as a grand edifice with an imposing dome erected over a gigantic database but rather as a "distributed" system—that is, a horizontal network that links up digital collections in libraries, archives, and museums in such a manner that users can get access to a document with a click or two on an electronic device. Now incorporated as a nonprofit enterprise, the DPLA has headquarters with a small staff in Boston, but it is not a top-down organization. Its horizontality corresponds to its democratic spirit and its basic goal—namely, to make the cultural heritage of America available, free of charge, to all Americans and to everyone in the world.

Moreover, it belongs to a worldwide movement to promote the democratization of access to culture. The DPA's technical infrastructure was designed to be compatible with that of Europeana, a digital network that includes libraries in all the countries of the European Union. La Referencia is a similar organization, which aims to integrate digital collections throughout Latin America.

Fig. 2.4 DPLA's website. (Source: DPLA)

Digital networks like SNR (Sistema Nacional de Repositorios Digitales) in Argentina are being built in many countries. It is only a matter of time before they all will be linked in a world digital library.

Equality of access means that library services will extend deep into the countries united by the electronic interfaces. For its part, the DPLA is designed to meet the needs of many different publics—students of all ages, seniors in homes for the elderly, researchers without institutional affiliation, readers of every kind, including those who merely want to deepen their enjoyment of literature. It is organized in "hubs" that extend its services like spokes of a wheel.

"Content hubs," such as Harvard, the Smithsonian Institution, and the New York Public Library, provide digitized material from their enormous collections. "Service hubs" aggregate other collections and develop networks at the state level. So far, they exist in 25 states; they are being completed in six more states, and soon they will be active everywhere in the country. The service hubs make special efforts to reach people in small communities, working with local public libraries. The libraries invite everyone in a town or an urban neighborhood to bring in diaries, letters, family photographs, and other items stored in attics or trunks. The material is digitized, supplied with metadata, curated, and preserved. In this way communities sharpen their awareness of their own culture and history, and at the same time their local collections are integrated into a national network, which grows organically day by day. A new program has just been funded to develop community-based digital repositories and advanced software for the "back end" connective tissue that unites the system.

Of course, the DPLA cannot reach every town in the United States. It relies on volunteers, including a small army of "Community Reps" who stimulate activities within designated areas. There now are 600 Community Reps scattered through all 50 states, and the DPLA is also developing a program to train librarians in public libraries to acquire the special skills that will be needed to launch digital projects in their communities. Proposals for such functions often originated at public meetings where artists provided sketches to illustrate them as they occurred (Fig. 2.5).

Many of these services are aimed at schools. The DPLA recently formed a partnership with the Public Broadcasting System to provide specially-designed and curated materials to teachers and students. It also makes available 120 "course sets," or collections of primary source materials, for use in the classroom, and they have been adopted everywhere in the country. In another

Fig. 2.5 An artist's rendering of ideas suggested during a public meeting about what should be included in the DPLA. (Source: DPLA)

program (announced by President Obama on April 30, 2015), it is cooperating with publishing houses to provide free e-books to children in low-income families. The DPLA has therefore developed an important pedagogical mission.

Of course, all these new programs depend on the most advanced technology. I won't attempt to describe the DPLA's technological infrastructure, but I should emphasize that it, too, was a volunteer effort conducted on a national scale. For two and a half years, 1100 computer scientists submitted ideas, which were combined and integrated by a team of experts in the Berkman Center at Harvard University. When the system went online in 2013, it functioned flawlessly, and it turned out to have special appeal because of the API (Application Programming Interface) built into its structure. We have been surprised at the enormous use of the API, which gets millions of hits every month.

The API provides a way for anyone to develop a particular tool or collection, which then can be used by everyone connected to the system. One such tool, "Book Shelf," creates the possibility of digital browsing. When consulting a particular book, users can see a row of related books whose spines appear on the computer screen as if they were physical books aligned on a shelf. One can click on the image of any spine, search through the book's table of contents and text, and construct an individualized collection of material on a certain subject. One example of the apps developed independently by DPLA users is a database of maps of Chicago, which makes it possible to study urban space on macro- and micro-levels. In these and other "outreach" projects, the DPLA hopes to engage with its readers. Instead of simply making material available and waiting for them to use it, it seeks to interact with them and to enlist them in shaping its growth.

Of course, the DPLA faces plenty of problems. Having depended on support from foundations since 2010, it needs to develop a long-term business plan. Its technology requires constant maintenance and improvement. And as it increases in size and scope, it must resolve issues of governance and administration.

But the biggest problem, strange as it may seem, is legal. The DPLA must respect copyright, but copyright now covers books for the life of the author plus 70 years—that is, in most cases, for more than a century. Most literature from the twentieth century—everything after 1964 and most books published after 1923—is therefore excluded from the DPLA's collection. There may be ways around this difficulty as case law evolves in American courts. Some recent court decisions favor a broad construction of "fair use"—that is, digital lending for certain non-commercial purposes in accordance with clause 107 of the copyright act of 1976. Another possibility is an extended collective licensing agreement based on Scandinavian models such as Copyswede and Kopinor. Kopinor makes all Norwegian literature available to all Norwegians while paying compensation to the rights holders, but that kind of project would require legislation by Congress.

For the moment, the DPLA is hoping that authors and publishers will voluntarily turn over the use of their copyrights after the commercial viability of their books has been exhausted. Authors, in general, derive little income from a book a year or two after its publication. Once its commercial life has ended, it frequently dies a slow death, lying unread, except for rare occasions, on the shelves of a few libraries, inaccessible to the vast majority of readers. At that stage, authors generally have one dominant desire—for their work to circulate freely through the public. Except for a small minority of writers who live from royalties, their interest coincides with the goals of the open-access movement. A new organization, Authors Alliance has launched a campaign to persuade authors to make their books available online at some point after publication through the DPLA and Creative Commons licenses. So far, the response is encouraging. It may sound naïve, but I think it is possible for the DPLA to satisfy authors and readers alike by bringing them together digitally.

Despite the pressure of commercialization, therefore, the DPLA has tapped a vein of public spirit that is both idealistic and pragmatic. It draws inspiration from the age of the Enlightenment, but it is designed to serve the needs of the twenty-first century; and at a time of disgust at the dysfunction of Washington, it has proved that it can get things done by independent initiative.

You should not think of it as a digital version of the Library of Congress. It's a new kind of library altogether, not just in its technology but also in its organization and spirit. It will operate simultaneously on many levels—personal, local, national, and international. It is already functioning successfully, and it will continue to acquire new functions, with ever-expanding collections, for many generations.

Technology will also continue to change, and the DPLA will have to change with it far into the future. But if we can get it right now, we can help shape that future. For the first time in history, we can make the cultural heritage of humanity available to all humans. We have the technology, the know-how, the resources, and the will. We have taken the first steps, and now we have to get the job done.

Note

1. This chapter derives from a lecture delivered at the Boston Public Library on October 5, 2017, to inaugurate the conference on Libraries and the Archives in the Digital Age held at Boston University during the following two days. Because of its original format, it does not include footnotes and is relatively informal in tone.

3

From Open Access to Maximal Access

Daniel J. Cohen

The term "open access" is almost as old as the web itself. The idea of using the Internet to provide remote and broad access to library and archival collections, especially within the frame of the easy-to-use graphical interface of the browser, was—and is—a compelling one. Moreover, it is clear that using digital media and technology in this way has beneficially extended the reach of, and democratized access to, our shared cultural heritage. As a historian, librarian, and technologist, I grew up in the open access movement, and have enthusiastically echoed its clarion call for the wide availability of resources.

However, we are now three decades into the era of the web—and its subsequent forms on new devices beyond the desktop and laptop computer—and the term is showing its age. Indeed, it may very well be inadequate for what we must now ask of "access."

When we think in the present day about open access, and look carefully at how it has developed over time, it feels more inert than it should be. In reality, open access has often operated under the assumption that digitizing and putting materials online will be action enough. It does not conceive of much *interactivity* or *permeability* between the digital library and the public. It rarely involves the public in the process of creating or curating archives, participating in these collections, or deciding what goes into them. It generally fails to engage in an active program that constantly increases visibility and use.

D. J. Cohen (✉)
Northeastern University, Boston, MA, USA
e-mail: d.cohen@northeastern.edu

© The Author(s) 2020
S. L. Mizruchi (ed.), *Libraries and Archives in the Digital Age*,
https://doi.org/10.1007/978-3-030-33373-7_3

In its historically fairly circumscribed character, open access doesn't provide us the methods or tools to bring libraries and archives to multiple, large audiences. Indeed, those who have taken the greatest advantage of open access have been people like me—traditionally trained historians who were delighted that we suddenly didn't have to get on an airplane to go visit a remote archive. Most other researchers and students, and the public in general, do not even know where to find these materials, even if they are now online. Many people do not know how to create new ad hoc collections from what they find online, or to analyze and use them in robust ways. They likely do not understand what "metadata" is, or what it implies for these collections.

"Maximal access" is an attempt to think about how we can maximize the availability and use of these materials, not just make them "open." Bringing resources online is undoubtedly advantageous, but that must be merely the first step. What are steps two, three, and four? How can we truly bring digital library items to the audiences who could most benefit from them? How can we have audiences fully engage with library and archival materials, including collections of greatest relevance to their communities?

I have been a historian and a librarian in my career, but in thinking about maximal access, one needs to think like an economist—examining the "supply side" and the "demand side" of the materials we bring online. Open access has largely focused on the former to the detriment of the latter. We now need to focus on the demand side, how we stimulate demand for the use and the creation of these materials. How do we get a much larger audience interested in, and deeply involved with, digital collections?

The library I currently oversee at Northeastern University received over two million visits last year. We have days in which our turnstiles turn over 10,000 times, as students, staff, and faculty swipe their ID cards to enter the library. We are not alone in this tremendous foot traffic; many other libraries have seen their gate count rise in recent years, a nice affirmation of the value the public still places on libraries. It's also a terrific opportunity, because it's possible to put in front of visitors, in the high-visibility spaces of the library, what we hold and share with students, staff, and faculty, such as the unique riches of our archives and special collections.

Of course, even at an extraordinarily busy library like ours, we have many more visitors to the library's resources online. Indeed, we have an order of magnitude greater traffic to library.northeastern.edu than through our front doors. Northeastern has students and researchers and faculty all across the country and around the world, and we have many other people who want to visit our collections virtually. For many of those people, the library at Northeastern *is* its digital presence, period.

In short, the library is an ecosystem of collections and services, including physical and digital elements, and at this point many library patrons do not even make a distinction between these realms. By bringing together and sharing common resources, the library provides a critical social and civic service.

When I was executive director of the Digital Public Library of America (DPLA), I would often say that DPLA was as much a social project, a political project, as it was a technical project. Yes, DPLA had a large technical infrastructure and data about library holdings—metadata—and so it seemed on the surface like a technological initiative. But it began and flourished as a social project because at heart it connected cultural heritage institutions across the country. DPLA sought to combine all kinds of library materials that were in disparate locations to place them in a common, virtual shared space. The organization created the connective tissue between thousands of different institutions, synthesized their collections together by taking records and materials that existed in multiple places, and presented a unified window into those items for the public.

We thus created a *social* library, one that brought into dialogue many different libraries, making them interactive with each other. When I would go to a new city or town to give a talk about DPLA, I would always search on the DPLA website for items we made available about that place I was visiting. I would then click on a button at the bottom of the DPLA site that would show the audience the institutions that contributed one or more digitized items from their city. Invariably, there would be hundreds of institutions from across the country that had donated materials. For example, DPLA has well over 100,000 items about Boston, but they come from hundreds of widely distributed libraries, archives, and museums, not just local New England institutions. The idea of a "Boston collection" in this context suddenly becomes clear: it must today be a synthesis of hundreds of collections that exist across the country and world because materials about Boston are housed almost everywhere.

So DPLA created an incredible "supply side" to the equation of open access, a powerful network model involving many nodes feeding into the complete collection of DPLA—which ended up being tens of millions of items. We partnered with many institutions to create what we called "service hubs" in each state, and these hubs assembled regional metadata, and often stored the digitized copies of items, from smaller institutions. The Minnesota Digital Library, for instance, aggregated and stored the digital collections of almost 200 community libraries, archives, and historic sites into a single statewide project. Then those digitized items flowed seamlessly into the national-scale

Digital Public Library of America. From small ponds—local collections—to lakes—state digital libraries—to the ocean—that was DPLA.

As extensive as this supply network was, however, we quickly realized it was insufficient as a platform for open access, since an aggregation of items alone could not guarantee broad and deep use. Even in the early stages after the launch of the DPLA, when the collection was only a few million items rather than tens of millions of items, we would hear from users of the website that they couldn't find materials they wanted, either in the giant sea of the combined collection or because those items hadn't yet been added. Audiences wanted help connecting to the collection in different ways, and understanding how to use and contribute to it.

After we started to hear these critiques, DPLA began to set up focus groups to ask and answer questions such as, "What can we be doing better to *maximize* the access? How can we actually get it into diverse and broad communities? How can we have communities feed into it?" One of the first groups we started to work with was in education. The educational world was of course from the start a primary user of the giant DPLA collection, but many educators and students weren't necessarily encountering our resources on the web, much less integrating it into their courses. Classrooms from kindergarten through graduate school were clearly missing out because we hadn't done enough on the demand side of access.

So we created a dedicated educational division and hired educators to help expand our offerings. We brought in teachers at all levels, media specialists, and librarians, and had them think through with us what we could improve to maximize—not just provide—access to America's combined cultural heritage collections. All agreed that we couldn't just have a site with millions of items and hope that people would find what they needed. They required multiple venues and ways to make these remarkable materials more discoverable and usable.

Our best idea was empowering these communities and involving them in the creation and curation of "primary source sets." If you wanted to study Reconstruction or the Civil Rights Era, we would now make prominently available a small set of hand-picked, extremely compelling items from different institutions to integrate into courses, easily found on our site but also portable to other contexts. As soon as we launched the primary source sets part of the DPLA site, our traffic surged by about 50%. Educators from a wider range of institutions more readily came to us, and they discovered new ways of using our materials. They also initiated other education-related curation, leading to a permanent community of instructors at all levels who would advise us on the access and use of our digital library. This blossoming was essential to the next stage of DPLA. Instructors would often add additional items, frequently from their state or town, to the pre-existing sets—enhancing and personalizing them so that they would connect with their local students better.

We also thought anew about *distribution channels* for DPLA materials, ways of marketing our digital content to a much wider audience by disseminating these millions of items to places beyond our website. To maximize access, we would need to proactively bring DPLA to where audiences already were. We asked our focus groups, for instance, for the top websites they visited to find educational resources for the classroom. Most students and educators had a handful of trusted providers, like PBS, to which they returned frequently. So we started talking to PBS and similar nonprofits to see how we could port the DPLA to their platforms, thus shortening the connection to students, teachers, and researchers.

Through some modest additional technology, we were able to import DPLA's new primary source sets to PBS's LearningMedia website, engaging a massive new audience who could encounter and then make use of our materials. PBS helped to tag our items with information about the appropriateness of sets for different classes, ages, and topics. As a significant additional advantage, our materials now comingled with educational PBS television shows and related classroom resources that PBS developed. By letting DPLA live in other locales like this, by giving it a much greater distribution spectrum, we were able to stir demand to meet the supply of our shared culture.

We also had from the inception of DPLA an Application Programming Interface, or API, the technical means for anyone with a bit of programming knowledge to import DPLA materials into another site or app on their own. Early on, for instance, a software developer in the United Kingdom created a site called Culture Collage, which automatically pulled materials from DPLA and brought them into conversation with other digitized items from around the world. When you clicked on a Culture Collage thumbnail, it would take you straight to the library, archive, or museum that digitized and made the work available. DPLA, in this case, acted as a kind of cultural broker, as a middleman, in the distribution of these items.

Another software developer created an embeddable web widget that allowed you to search the entire DPLA collection seamlessly from within any other online library website. The New York Public Library actually made this bidirectional: you could look at a digitized scan from NYPL's collections, hop over to DPLA to find similar images, and then return to NYPL's website. Once again, libraries were becoming more closely bonded together, strengthening connections between various institutions and collections, and thus connecting to audiences wherever they might be.

Other groups used our API to retrieve large slices of DPLA's unified library to forge new topic-based search engines. The University of Minnesota, for example, created Umbra Search using their own collections and knowledge about African American history and culture, plus hundreds of thousands of items from other US archives, libraries, and museums, largely pulled from DPLA's combined database. Now, through a single search box, audiences can scan a vast array of materials on this subject.

Maximizing access also can entail connecting physical places with digital resources about those places. The recently renovated Johnson Building of the Boston Public Library's Central Library helps to capitalize on the foot traffic that comes into the library and alert them to digital materials. They installed a set of screens in the lobby that show all of the scanned items from Digital Commonwealth, DPLA's Massachusetts hub (and which BPL manages). As patrons come into Johnson Building, they can summon an old map of the immediate area (which used to be a marsh) or buildings that have come and gone. It greatly enriches these local interactions and the experience of visitors—a terrific service from a DPLA hub.

The same thing can be done by leveraging the GPS signal on our modern smartphones to show us DPLA photographs and maps of our surrounding area. Indeed, the rise of the smartphone over the last decade has provided a major new channel through which to maximize access to cultural heritage content. While there are many locations across the world with poor access to desktop and laptop computers, the smartphone revolution has actually reached an incredibly broad population. There are over a billion smartphones in Africa, for instance, that can act as a portal to digital libraries—but only if we tailor our interfaces and think about the projection of our digital content in this way.

In addition, we need to pay more attention to the rights that are attached to digitized library, archive, and museum resources. Another aspect of our self-reflection at DPLA had to do with how rights can help—or hinder—maximal access to shared collections. When we launched, we had thousands of different rights statements attached to items, often drafted by lawyers from the thousands of donating institutions. But this complexity made it hard for our audience to comprehend what they could and could not do with DPLA items, often on a case-by-case basis. Strongly worded language in these rights statements often repelled potential users, since lawyers are usually seeking to minimize institutional risk rather than to maximize use.

While we obviously need to respect copyright, there are many things we can do around these rights statements, however, that can expand the landscape of possible use of cultural materials, which in turn can stimulate demand for such use. Institutions can work together to create and promulgate more liberal rights statements to attach to digitized metadata and content where possible.

From the start, DPLA used the extremely permissive CC0 license from Creative Commons for all of its metadata, allowing anyone to take that data and use it in whatever way they wanted. In addition to the API, we even had a bulk download page for all of our metadata from all of our contributing institutions. Furthermore, we worked with those institutions to clarify the rights surrounding the items themselves (not just their metadata), to ensure that the most permissive license was applied to each object. In concert with Europeana, our sister project that brought together the combined digital collections of the 28 member states of the European Union, we established a clear, concise, and small set of rights statements that could signal to the public what they could do with each item found through our websites and APIs.

Although the DPLA was in part conceived as a reaction to the Google Books project, it soon (indeed even at its inception) took on a much more expansive scope, to share the riches of America's libraries, archives, and museums well beyond books. It has always had an aspiration to provide special services around books, of course, but the collections of which I speak were seen as most amenable to the project's launch at the start (largely for copyright issues), and digitized books are a significant portion of the DPLA collection too.

This attention to rights led to wonderful, expansive uses of the DPLA aggregate collection. For example, after a thawing in US-Cuba relations, Cuba's national library took all of our metadata and integrated it with their online catalog. Since they haven't digitized their own books yet, this connection meant that they could link their digital library with ours, and let their patrons easily find digital facsimiles of hundreds of thousands of works that had already been scanned in America. Many other projects used the liberal rights around our metadata and the more permissive use structure around the works themselves to improve their own collections virtually, and to encourage new forms of access and engagement.

Finally, we focused on community involvement, and how the modern online library has to be bidirectional—not just the source of a supply of digitized cultural heritage content. "Open access" always had that unidirectional feel—delivering content from an institution to an online patron—but in focusing on maximal access and on the demand side—the side of our patrons and what they can do to improve our collections—we can have interactions that enhance our digital libraries and archives and even fill in gaps.

Trove, Australia's national digital library, has done this for years. After digitizing their country's newspapers, and providing open access to them (up to the latest possible year under their copyright law), they also enabled the public to add context and make millions of corrections to the automated transcription of articles. Families have found pieces about their ancestors and corrected proper names, for instance, or jotted down the final score of a big football game in their town's history. These additions and corrections by the public in turn make Trove more accurate and searchable, which maximizes discovery and overall access.

At Northeastern University, we have pursued similar bidirectional activities related to the community archives of the neighborhoods near our Boston campus. In the Lower Roxbury Black History Project, we connected with community groups to solicit and record oral histories, providing digital infrastructure and other services while letting the major activities be driven by the community, including selection and curation. This has worked well as a partnership.

Maximal access ultimately involves all of these methods in concert: bidirectional archiving work, allowing the public to annotate and correct our data and metadata, the projection of those digital materials as far and wide as possible through new channels, and the curation of millions of items for the easy and immediate use of educators and students from kindergarten through retirement. The infrastructure of the Digital Public Library of America had to have the social and technical features to allow its platform to connect with audiences as widely as possible in this way, and to make sure that our enormous record of history and culture was full and complete—and also maximally used.

4

A National Library in the Digital Age

Alberto Manguel

I've been Director of the National Library of Argentina for the past two years. I'm not a librarian. I accepted the position under false pretenses. I realize now, after two years, that my entire job is to try and help librarians do the real work. I am trying my best, but an institution like the National Library is daily confronted with huge obstacles (as librarians know better than anyone else), which in a country such as Argentina are multiplied by a thousand. When I accepted the position, I imagined that I could apply certain ideas to the running of the library, ideas that I had developed over the past few decades in different books. I felt like somebody who has been writing recipes for ages and finds himself for the first time in the kitchen cooking.

I believe, and I still believe, that a public library is what Susan Mizruchi has defined as a social space, the library as a social space, a forum. Dan Cohen affirms this claim when he refers to the library in his essay as a political and social project. I too believe that the library is that, among other things. Every human act is a political act, and a public library is a political space. By political I don't mean sectarian, which was the characteristic of the National Library of Argentina for a number of years. Unfortunately, the position of director of the National Library is seen in Argentina as a political position and I've tried

---

Transcription of Presentation by Alberto Manguel at "Recording Lives: Libraries and Archives in the Digital Age" Forum, October 6, 2017. Hosted by the Boston University Center for the Humanities at the BU Law School Alumni Auditorium.

A. Manguel (✉)
Independent Scholar, New York, NY, USA

© The Author(s) 2020
S. L. Mizruchi (ed.), *Libraries and Archives in the Digital Age*,
https://doi.org/10.1007/978-3-030-33373-7_4

my best to distance myself from any political party. That is not to say that our activity is not political. It is of course. We've made several decisions that must be seen as political decisions. For instance, when President Putin closed the Ukrainian library in Moscow and imprisoned the director of that library, we immediately opened a Ukrainian library in the National Library of Argentina. We understand that no act of censorship such as the one which Putin committed can go unanswered, and our reaction was to set up a Ukrainian library in Argentina not only because Argentina has an important Ukrainian community but simply because a library, especially a national library, has to be universal and respond humanely to such acts of barbarism. Also, it was important for us politically to understand the national library not as a library of Buenos Aires, where it physically stands, but as a library of the rest of the country, and also as an international library, and also especially representing the different communities about which Jeannette Bastian writes so eloquently.

So for instance, a hidden community that we brought to light in the Library, one of the many hidden corners, was the section for the blind. The librarians there received blind high school students and helped them with their studies. They received older people who had lost their sight and wanted still to read and be aware of the news. And we awarded a Medal to 'The Eldest Reader at the Library,' to a woman who had been coming to the library for decades. We gave her the medal on her 103rd birthday. She said that she came to the library three times a week because she needed to be aware of the latest news. She was absolutely right.

David Ferriero, the Tenth National Archivist of the United States, asserts that the three main acts of faith for a library should be a belief in the past, a belief in the future, and a belief in the present so that we can make use of the learning of the past in order to build our own future.[1] I think that encapsulates the mission of the library. This is a mission of justice, of social justice. The idea that Robert Darnton writes about, that everyone should have access to the experience of the past, that what we have done and what we have thought about and what we have written about should be for everyone, is of the essence. There is an apocryphal quotation attributed to Don Quixote (it sounds very much like something the old knight might have said) that to change the world is neither a utopia nor an act of madness; it's simply an act of justice. I think the function of a library can be that. Now, saying that, I'm very much aware of a number of stumbling blocks on the path to this goal. Robert Darnton's ambitious project, the DPLA, of trying to bring together all the digital libraries in America, is in that vein. We are trying to do something similar in South America and Spain, collect the digital libraries of the Spanish-speaking world—La Referencia. This kind of ambition is a very old ambition;

it's the ambition of Alexandria to have everything known and everything recorded. However, collecting everything was for Alexandria, from the little we know, the assembly of a multi-media collection: the Library of Alexandria must have had clay tablets, papyrus scrolls, perhaps parchment volumes, slabs of stone on which texts were inscribed, maps, all kinds of objects. A library has never been an exclusionary repository. Every technology needs to be represented in a library. This is obvious.

Nowadays, a digital library allows us to collect these various representations of text in ways that can be easily shared, but this must not allow us to neglect other containers of the text. This also is an old ambition. There is a wonderful book written in the third century (there are versions of it all the way up to the ninth century) called *The Life of Adam and Eve*. If it were written today, we would call it a postmodern book because in the end, after the lives of Adam and Eve have been fully chronicled, Eve speaks to her son Seth and says to him: "Now you will write the lives of your parents." (This is the book which we have just read, that's the postmodernist twist.) "And you will write it both on stone and on bark because if the Lord has the world end in water, the bark will survive and if it ends in fire the stone will survive." We need to preserve our texts in every technology available, stone and bark and all the other supports that we have now. And of course, we have to collect material from what Jeannette Bastian describes as the different communities in our different societies.

Now I have a bone to pick with Jeannette about this, because I don't know how we define these communities whose material a library is supposed to collect. At least, my experience in Canada and then in Argentina and then in France has been that communities are largely defined from outside. There is some kind of racist impulse to define those who are not you as "a community." In Canada, a self-defined multicultural city such as Toronto for instance, there are neighborhoods that are known as the Greek neighborhood and the Portuguese neighborhood and so on. With the best will in the world to allow foreigners who come and become Canadian, to continue with their traditions, Canada gives them a label. For example, I, as someone born in Argentina but having lived abroad for most of my life, was expected more or less to put on a Mexican hat and a Chilean poncho and enjoy Mexican food. So what do we call communities? I think we need to allow for great elasticity, ask people how they define themselves, and apply something like the mathematical theory of groups to the notion of community, where circles overlap. I, for example, could at the same time belong to some part of the Argentinian community, certainly not to all, and also to the gay community, and to the community of people having lived abroad for a very long time, and many others.

I am trying to set up at the National Library of Argentina collections for several self-defined communities that are not fairly represented or are not represented at all—for instance, the native communities, the LGBTQ communities, and several others. We are trying to obtain material from these sections of society, but we have to be enormously careful not to impose our definition or label. For instance, I have not yet been able to find someone to organize the native community material because, first of all, there are many indigenous communities in Argentina and there are political rifts among them. And there are different identities within even one community: the Mapuches, for instance, who now have a very strong political presence in Argentina. So, how do you go about it? I have been speaking to Canadian and Australian librarians who have indigenous material that they decided to give back to the communities in digital form; the communities identify these materials, label them, and send them back explaining that this is not a cup, this is a ritual vase, this can be shown, this can only be shown to people from this family or tribe, and so on. At the National Library of Argentina, we have not yet managed to see how we can organize what would be a "native collection" or various native collections. We need what Dan Cohen called permeability. I think that's a very useful term. I don't know how we can put it into practice but perhaps from the essays in this collection I can learn more.

Returning to Robert Darnton's idea of collecting everything for everyone, we can recall once again that this was what the Alexandrian kings wanted to do. Their purpose was, as Darnton pointed out, the prestige that the collection gave them. You were as powerful as what you had collected. The problem is, as we find out constantly at the National Library, that there is always something missing. I remember that G.K. Chesterton, talking about book reviewers, said that there is always someone who will review *Martin Chuzzlewit* and say, "Well it's a fairly good novel; unfortunately, it sheds no light on the marital customs in Norway." As in a library, there's always something missing.

And then we come to the greater problem: a large collection requires a large staff. We collect what we can afford to collect, but we must keep on collecting. In 2015, under the previous administration, about 10,000 items entered the national library. In the first year of this administration, 100,000 items entered the library, and in 2017, almost 200,000. So we are increasing our collections at an amazing rate. But because of budget restrictions and the dearth of qualified personnel, we don't know what to do with the bottleneck in the departments of inventory and cataloging. We need more cataloguers: if anyone reading this wants to come to work at the National Library, you're welcome to! But I warn you: we have no money to pay you.

Now: What happens with all this material? How do you access readers? How do you let the common readers, the readers who commonly come to the library, know what you have? How do you get readers who never come to the library to use that material? And the most important question of all—how do you get readers, people who are not yet readers, to read? Christopher Ricks raises a truly important point, when he notes that we can provide access but that is not enough.[2] John Rawls makes a useful distinction between freedom and freedom's worth. It's one thing to tell everyone that you are free but if you don't have a salary, if you don't have a job, if you don't have access to health care, if you don't have food, if you don't have housing, then you are not free, or at least that freedom is totally worthless. And in Argentina this is true of the majority of the population, who are struggling to put bread on the table. And literally I mean bread.

I am convinced that reading can open the world for us. I am convinced that a reader has more tools to survive in the world than someone who can't read. And I am convinced that anyone can become a reader. But how do you go from the fulfillment of basic vital needs to opening those library doors? I am not convinced by Brecht's "first comes the food, then come the morals." They have to come at the same time, because if there are no morals, you will kill one another at the trough. I think that I want to believe that the National Library can provide a source for a sort of civic education to teach people what it means to be a citizen, what are their responsibilities and rights, and more importantly, how to go about obtaining those rights, the effective rights, not just the nominal rights.

Whatever strategy we come up with, we have, in Argentina at least, a number of almost insurmountable obstacles. I will name three.

1. **Bureaucracy**. For everything that we want to do, whether it is to buy a pencil or to send someone to offer a technical course at some provincial town, or to bring students in, there is so much paperwork, useless paperwork, that it consumes both time and money. To bring books into Argentina, which you would think is the obvious job of the library, I have to go through a tangled bureaucracy at customs, at huge cost, which is a legacy of the previous government. This is a problem that has not been solved despite the promises of the present government. And so we have to pay middle-persons at customs to help us bring the books out, and sometimes this costs more than the book itself. I am going to write an essay in my very old age called "Bureaucracy Leads to Crime," because I am committing crimes every day. I am breaking the law. I am smuggling books into Argentina in my suitcase to avoid the customs bureaucracy, because

this is for the library and I don't think the library should pay anything to bring a book in. I am forced, for instance, to buy tickets out of our petty cash, if I need to send someone to a training course somewhere. We are supposed to buy them through a state agency that charges us ten times more than the price that I would pay with Expedia, for instance. So I buy the tickets from Expedia, which I am not allowed to do. So at some point I will be taken to prison for this and I will go gladly.

2. **Unions**. I believe strongly in the need for unions. I believe strongly in the defense of the workers, but the unions in Argentina are immensely corrupt and I have daily proof of this. They don't defend their workers; they simply try to collect points for themselves and make money out of certain measures. And I have to deal with this every day.

3. **Politics**. The Argentinian government today is not interested in culture. This will not come as a surprise to anyone. So they see the position of the director of the national library as a political position. And when I accepted the position, I warned that I would not be photographed beside any politician. I am an administrator of the library; I have nothing to do with politics. But every time we do something, and we've managed to do very many things, some politician will come and have his or her picture taken in front of what we have done. In the section for the blind, where I was able to secure donations for a number of machines that enable electronic reading and so on, the vice president came and had her picture taken. Well, this creates obstacles because donors and people who work as volunteers might not want to be identified with these politicians, and so as you can imagine, this creates problems.

I am trying to change some of these things but you should only know how long a legal process takes in Argentina. There are laws that need to be changed. The ISBN for some bizarre reason goes through the book chamber and the publishers' association not to the national library. We don't have what libraries around the world have: "fair use" of our material. So we collect but we cannot allow researchers to quote the material in their work.

What might our strategies be, in spite of all these obstacles, to achieve some of our dreams, of what we might simply term social justice, which would involve enabling anyone to make use of these rights? I believe that a library, a museum, an archive can have an exemplary, a cautionary role. In the *Satyricon* in the first century, one of the protagonists wanders into a museum and sees the images of the gods in love and identifies with those images and says even the gods have pangs of love and suffer from unfaithfulness. I believe that we can have readers and non-readers alike learn to see in the stories and pictures and everything we have to offer mirrors of their own condition and inklings of how the world can change for the better and be a little happier and a little more just. I don't believe in national plans for the promotion of reading. I have looked at very many and I don't think any of them work. No one is convinced by a picture of Madonna or Maradona holding a book and saying "I read, you should too." That doesn't work.

What might work is something that I'm trying to implement. Some time ago, a teacher with 30 years' experience in the slums of Buenos Aires came to see me with a reading project that encourages teachers to become enthusiastic about reading. Her name is Roxana Levinsky. She discovered something very, very obvious. If you don't like reading, if you're not passionate about reading, you can't teach reading. Kids are not stupid. They are not convinced by somebody who simply says you should read. So she has developed a system that worked in several places and so I'm trying to extend that first to the province of Buenos Aires and then to the rest of the country. I got the OEI to give us a large amount of money for this project and in this way shame the government into putting a little bit of money into it.

I had a very important experience some 20 years ago with my son when he was a young adolescent. He was a fan of video games. And once he asked me to accompany him to a video arcade. I said, do we need to buy a ticket? He said, no we just walk in. So I walked in and there were all these machines and I said, do we queue? How do we select what machine? How do we know what games are played on each machine, and so on? I had to learn the rituals of the place. As readers, we don't often realize up to what point the rituals of reading have to be learned. How to use a book, how to use a library, how to open a book? Whether it is digital or physical, there is a ritual to be learned. So I am trying to implement workshops for teachers so that they take them to schools to teach how to read.

Unfortunately, this does not reach the majority of the population. Many kids don't go to school; many kids are not interested when they're in school because they're concentrating on where their next meal is coming from, and also because school lacks prestige as does the entire intellectual realm, and not only in Argentina but in the world as a whole. It's not surprising that today an academic discourse, rational, logical, clear, that sets out a contemporary problem appears much less trustworthy than the grunts and squeals of a president on twitter—because it feels sincere, because it feels as if it comes from the gut. I don't know how the process can be reversed, but the intellectual word has lost the prestige that it had. We need to restore the confidence in common sense, in grammar, in the logical argument, in dialogue.

Let me end by returning to Robert Darnton's cautionary wisdom about collecting, that there will always be more material than a library, however large, can store. A valid definition of a library is a place that always exceeds the space you give it. In this sense, there is a story by Borges that might perhaps be illuminating. It's a short apocryphal tale that he imagined. He says that in the Empire of Cartographers, mapmaking had developed to such a degree that not only could they map a neighborhood or a city but they could map the empire itself on a scale of one-to-one. In the outer limits of the empire, says Borges, there remained a few ruins that were all that was left of that colossal map.

I think that we are tending toward that all-comprehensive map of the universe in digital form, at least in our wishful imagination. The material that we are collecting will never hold everything, but I believe it will approach if not infinity then at least something that cannot be measured. And therefore it becomes essential (as Darnton and others have mentioned) to find a practical search instrument, to guide us through the maze of the ever-expanding digital universe. In Alexandria they realized this. Callimachus, the librarian, invented the *Pinakes*, what came to be known as the canon, which consisted of annotated bibliographies of the titles he thought were the most important in a certain field, because he realized that if you said to someone who wanted to consult Greek philosophy, here you have 5000 volumes, the person would not know where to start. And yet, with any search tool, be it a canon or an electronic program, one must be aware of implied censorship in any choice. You can't guide someone to one section, selecting certain titles, without neglecting others. And so, in this act, whether involuntarily or not, you are omitting things and closing off possibilities for understanding. This, I think, is the main problem facing librarians in all times and places, from Alexandria to the present, how to guide without being dictatorial. I have no idea what the solution is. And I'm hoping that librarians will have an answer.

Notes

1. David Ferriero, the Tenth National Archivist of the United States, delivered a paper at our 2017 Humanities Center Forum on Libraries and Archives in the Digital Age, but was not able to develop his paper into an essay for this collection.
2. Christopher Ricks was the respondent to Robert Darnton's paper for the opening night of the Humanities Center Forum at The Boston Public Library, October 5, 2017.

5

Discovery, Access, and Use of Information in a "Digital Ecosystem"

Jack Ammerman

In analyzing the failure of some well-managed companies, Clayton M. Christensen distinguishes between "sustaining technologies" and "disruptive technologies."[1] Sustaining technologies improve the performance of established products. Sustaining technologies enable incremental improvement of products and services. Disruptive technologies, however, while initially underperforming established products, "bring to market a very different value proposition than had been available previously."[2] They enable radically new products and services that have the potential to make obsolete more established products and services.

Computers and high-speed data networks are disruptive technologies that have radically transformed our information ecosystem from physical to digital. Even well-managed publishers and libraries struggle to understand the impact on their business and service models though they have been working at this for decades. Many have focused on utilizing these technologies to improve established products and services. The impact of becoming digital, however, is much more far-reaching.

In 1995, Nicholas Negroponte wrote "The information superhighway is more than a short cut to every book in the Library of Congress. It is creating a totally new, global social fabric."[3] Critiquing the notion that high-speed networks are simply improved information delivery systems, he recognized their potential to radically alter our interactions not just with information but with all of society. Today, the Internet is the means by which we publish,

---

J. Ammerman (✉)
Boston University, Boston, MA, USA

discover, and access information. We also use it to engage in rituals, communicate, transact business, establish and attempt to secure our identities, seek entertainment, receive education, do research, find community, experience bullying and harassment, propagate misinformation, wage war, and commit crimes. In short, there are few parts of our lives that are not affected by our digital environment. Yet many libraries continue to treat the Internet as a high-speed delivery system. The e-books and e-journal articles that libraries provide are largely electronic facsimiles of the same information in print. Their formats remain unchanged. Discovery and access systems are now available online, but the models used to organize digital information are often only slightly tweaked models for organizing print materials.

David Weinberger in his book *Everything Is Miscellaneous* describes the move from analog to digital formats as a move from atoms to bits. Atoms occupy physical space.[4] They require physical arrangement and discovery systems designed for physical objects. Their physicality imposes constraints on how the content can be reused. Bits remove many constraints for how we organize, discover, and reuse information. The digital world thereby allows us to transcend the most fundamental rule of ordering the real world: Instead of everything having a place, it's better if things can get assigned to multiple places simultaneously.

In 2000, the Library of Congress published *LC21: A Digital Strategy for the Library of Congress.* It begins by asserting

> No stereotype of libraries as quiet, uneventful places could survive the 1990s. Whatever stability and predictability libraries once had as ordered storehouses of the treasures of the printed world were shattered by the digital revolution. The intellectual function of libraries—to acquire, arrange, and make accessible the creative work of humankind—is being transformed by the explosion in the production and dissemination of information in digital form, especially over global networks.[5]

The Library of Congress strategy, of course, foresees the use of digital networks and formats not just for dissemination of information, but also for triggering a rapid escalation in the rate of production of information in a vastly expanding variety of formats. The information ecosystem is rapidly expanding, at least in part due to the impact of high-speed networks and digital methodologies on the production of knowledge. While there is variation by academic discipline, the number of scholarly journals published in the sciences, for example, increases by about 3.25% every year. In other words, the number of journals published doubles every 20–25 years.[6] The rate of increase in the number of books published each year increases at a similar rate.

This, of course, has a major impact on the traditional role of libraries in collecting and preserving information. Libraries emerged in an era of information scarcity. Local library collections were carefully curated to ensure both quality and access to appropriate materials for their clientele. One couldn't assume, for example, that materials to support the curriculum would be available or accessible to students beyond the walls of the library.

In an era of information abundance, and particularly with high-speed digital access, the role of collecting for most libraries must change. The resources available to collect at a research or comprehensive level in even narrowly defined areas quickly become insufficient with such rates of expansion of knowledge. Clearly, we want to preserve our intellectual heritage and cultural life. For most traditionally published material, perhaps collecting and preservation should be the role of national libraries, and/or of a relatively small number of special "preservation" libraries. Most libraries, on the other hand, would take responsibility for collecting and curating truly local, unique materials. The tasks of organizing digital objects for discovery and access seem to be enormous and vastly different from organizing physical objects. These tasks should become major priorities for most libraries in a digital age.

Like the Library of Congress, the National Archives and Records Administration's 1997–2007 strategic plan (updated in 2000) identified electronic records as a significant trend requiring a solution. Now, NARA like the Library of Congress is becoming digital. NARA is guiding the transition of all federal government record-keeping from analog to electronic formats. Among the purposes identified in the 2011 Presidential Memorandum[7] was to promote openness and to reduce inefficiencies in government. With the draft 2018–2022 strategic plan, NARA proposes to make 500-million pages of records available online through the National Archives Catalog. Beyond government efficiency, the availability of federal records in digital formats enables new computational methodologies for analysis. Beyond simply tracking clicks or downloads, developing a metric that demonstrates the impact on government and society of making these documents available online would be an invaluable project with broader implications for understanding the impact of a variety of "open government data" policies (https://www.data.gov/open-gov/).

The shift to digital has become a drive to data, and a number of publishers have led the way. The production workflow for commercial publishers has been revolutionized by digital tools. More importantly, these platforms provide data on the use of the content they sell. This has enabled publishers like

Elsevier to make radical shifts in their business models. In addition to acquiring a number of workflow and preprint tools like SSRN, bepress, and Pure,

> Elsevier embarked on a cultural and business turnaround. Now, although they still produce the same world-renowned content in science, healthcare and humanities, they do it from the position of an analytics company that packages and sells "curated content" in all different forms, and through a number of innovative channels—rather than a traditional publisher of document-based materials.[8]

Most publishers claim these shifting business models are not a direct response to open-access efforts like institutional repositories, PlanS,[9] and more controversial projects like Sci-Hub that advocate for the cancelation of copyright and intellectual property laws for scientific and educational resources. Publishing in digital formats makes copying and sharing such documents much easier than is possible with analog formats. To do so, users must navigate an often confusing and/or opaque cloud of copyright and licensing to determine how they can access and employ digital materials. This can be a deterrent, but often, the regulations are ignored.

Dan Cohen rightly observes that simply converting an analog object to digital, or capturing a born-digital object, does not necessarily make it easy to use. At Boston University, we have many reports of our faculty, students, and even library staff being unclear about what they may legally do and not do with digital objects. What is the copyright status? Fair Use? Contractual/license agreements? When we catalog physical items, we rarely think about providing metadata to clarify how an item might be used. Use of physical texts primarily follows the model of a single concurrent reader. Conversion to a digital object makes copying, distribution, and reuse much easier. Embedding clear and standard indications of rights is essential for making digital content usable. Some argue, however, that copyright and intellectual property legislation designed for analog objects are simply outdated and need to be replaced with more workable solutions for today's digital ecosystem.

In his book, *Remix*, Lawrence Lessig describes an encounter between the late Jack Valenti and a Stanford student. In a debate between Valenti and Lessig, Valenti asked the students how many had downloaded music from Napster to which 90% of students admitted they had. Valenti asked the student to defend this "stealing." The student's response was, "Yes, this might be stealing, but everyone does it. How could it be wrong?"[10] Calling for new approaches to copyright, Lessig continues,

In a world in which technology begs all of us to create and spread creative work differently from how it was created and spread before, what kind of moral platform will sustain our kids, when their ordinary behavior is deemed criminal? Who will they become? What other crimes will to them seem natural?[11]

In this digital age, not only has discovery and access changed, but so have the social norms around use and reuse. Clarifying how digital objects can be used is important, but that does not really address the changing societal expectations for how we use information in digital formats. Digital technologies challenge more than just how we use and reuse information. They raise interesting epistemological questions as well.

What was not clear 25 years ago, or even at the turn of the century, was how living in a digital age would change the way we think and the way we construct knowledge. Several years ago, a professor at Boston University was lamenting Wikipedia's growing presence on the web, and particularly its creep into his classroom. At root, his real objection was the epistemological model that underlies Wikipedia. Encyclopedia Britannica uses a model in which "experts" function both as filters and as authorities. Accordingly, the stamp of approval given by such an expert assures both accuracy and the quality of information contained in an article. Wikipedia, on the other hand, assumes knowledge can be constructed, or at least encyclopedia articles can be written via a participatory process of social interaction, requiring no authorized "expert."

In his essay, Cohen poses the question, "How can an array of audiences involve themselves in the use, curation, and even production of these resources?" Allowing for such an engagement by diverse audiences introduces multiple voices, often with vastly different narratives about what we perceive to be reality. In contrast to the government records maintained by NARA, community archives and a wide range of public humanities projects provide opportunities for diverse publics to engage in the creation and curation of knowledge.

While community archives such as those described in Jeannette Bastian's essay are not always digital, and they are certainly very different from Wikipedia, they are epistemologically very similar. Both reject the assumption that there is one reality, one knowledge, one story. It is too much to claim a causal relationship between the Internet and community archives, but a highly networked digital environment makes the emergence of groups of people articulating their own identity more visible if not easier to facilitate. It also raises some interesting questions as we find ourselves navigating a vast sea of digital information. Who gets to select and organize documentary records?

What worldview guides retention decisions? When multiple stories emerge, by whom and how are they validated? In an age of "alternative facts" and "fake news," how do we discern the difference between disinformation, propaganda, and knowledge that is based on a different view of the world? Admittedly, these are not new issues that have emerged with the advent of digital technologies. They are, however, readily apparent and must not be ignored as we read or consume information. Consumption of information becomes formative for the consumer.

A library, as Alberto Manguel envisions it, plays an important role beyond simply being a repository of cultural heritage. In *A History of Reading*, Manguel says, "Reading ... comes before writing. A society can exist—many do exist—without writing, but no society can exist without reading.... For most literate societies ... reading is the beginning of the social contract..."[12] To read in such a way is to engage in a formative relationship not just with the book being read, but with the community in which it is read, and in the context of a library of books.

Imagining the library as a place where new readers are formed and old readers reaffirmed is a particularly important challenge in a digital environment. Research indicates that we read text onscreen differently than in print. Reading web pages in a browser or even a book on an e-book reader like a Kindle is a "rapidly interactive activity. Even new pages with plentiful information and many links are regularly viewed only for a brief period."[13] Katherine Hayles suggests with hyper-reading we are witnessing a shift in cognitive styles that

> can be seen in the contrast between deep attention and hyper attention. Deep attention, the cognitive style traditionally associated with the humanities, is characterized by concentrating on a single object for long periods (say, a novel by Dickens), ignoring outside stimuli while so engaged, preferring a single information stream, and having a high tolerance for long focus times. Hyper attention is characterized by switching focus rapidly among different tasks, preferring multiple information streams, seeking a high level of stimulation, and having a low tolerance for boredom.[14]

"Hyper-reading and hyper-attention are effective and appropriate techniques for discovering, organizing and accessing information in a media intensive environment. The challenge is to hold these techniques in balance with deep reading and deep attention. The hardware and software used for reading may aid in maintaining this balance. The task remains, however, to develop strategies to nurture both deep and hyper-reading."[15]

As different as they are, both deep reading and hyper-reading generally assume engagement with the text in a more or less linear fashion. Digital texts afford other possibilities. With the development of graph databases like Neo4j, network text analysis is possible. The text is normalized and loaded to a graph database where metrics for key concepts in the text are generated using network analysis. The network, with nodes representing these concepts and lines representing their relationships to other nodes, is then visualized and used to navigate the text in a networked mode rather than a linear mode.[16] Navigating the network of the text, then, allows the reader to ask questions of the text from different "locations" in the network, informed by the relationships between the nodes (concepts) that might have been transparent with a linear reading. Other approaches to analyzing digital texts include what Franco Moretti calls "Distant Reading," or the use of computational methodologies and tools to analyze an entire corpus of texts. Topic modeling, network analysis, distant reading, and other computational approaches allow the reader not only to discover patterns that would not have been observed otherwise, but to ask questions of a corpus of texts that might not have been otherwise imagined.

Engaging texts in these disparate ways clearly results in a range of reader experiences. Might we call them all "formative"? Probably not in the way Manguel envisions. But for academic libraries in particular, reading is taking on many new forms we would not have imagined 25 years ago.

Our digital information ecosystem is constructed using disruptive technologies that challenge traditional methodologies and workflows. User expectations shift rapidly as the affordances of digital formats make possible discovery and use of information in ways never imagined possible. And as Negroponte predicted, the social fabric within which we operate has been altered by the introduction of digital technologies. For libraries and other cultural heritage institutions, digital technologies introduce exciting possibilities for new ways to engage with information. They also challenge these institutions to assess changing user needs and expectations, to abandon those services that are no longer needed, and to develop and implement new services to address the emerging needs of their users.

Notes

1. Christensen, Clayton M. *The Innovator's Dilemma: The revolutionary book that will change the way you do business.* New York: HarperBusiness, 2003, p. xviii.
2. Ibid.

3. Negroponte, Nicholas. *Being Digital*. 1st ed. New York: Knopf, 1995, p. 183.
4. Weinberger, David. *Everything Is Miscellaneous: The Power of the New Digital Disorder*, New York: Macmillan, 2007.
5. National Research Council. Committee on an Information Technology Strategy for the Library of Congress. *LC21: A Digital Strategy for the Library of Congress*. Washington, DC: National Academy Press, 2000, p. 1.
6. Larsen, P.O. & von Ins, M. Scientometrics (2010) 84: 575. https://doi.org/10.1007/s11192-010-0202-z
7. Obama, Barak. *Presidential Memorandum – Managing Government Records*. Washington, DC: The White House, November 28, 2011. (https://obamawhitehouse.archives.gov/the-press-office/2011/11/28/presidential-memorandum-managing-government-records)
8. Harris, Esther. "Finally, Academic Publishing is Catching Up with the Future." *The BookSeller*, December 17, 2018, web: https://www.thebookseller.com/futurebook/finally-academic-publishing-catching-future-917536
9. Plan S is an initiative for open access publishing begun in 2018 and supported by a consortium of research funders that requires publications that result from research funded by public grants be made fully and immediately accessible in compliant Open Access journals and platforms beginning in 2020. Web: https://www.coalition-s.org/
10. Lessig, Lawrence. *Remix: Making Art and Commerce Thrive in the Hybrid Economy*. New York: Penguin Press, 2008, p. xvii.
11. Ibid, p. xviii.
12. Manguel, Alberto. *A History of Reading*. New York, NY; Toronto: Penguin Books, 1997, p. 7.
13. Weinreich, Harald, Hartmut Obendorf, Eelco Herder, and Matthias Mayer. 2008. "Not Quite the Average: An Empirical Study of Web Use." *ACM Transactions on the Web* 2 (1): 1–31.
14. Hayles, N. Katherine. 2007. "Hyper and Deep Attention: The Generational Divide in Cognitive Modes." *Profession*, 187.
15. Ammerman, Jack, "Reading in the 21st century; reading at scale." 2015 web: https://hdl.handle.net/2144/22850
16. Paranyushkin, Dmitry. "Identifying the Pathways for Meaning Circulation using Text Network Analysis." Berlin: Nodus Labs, 2011. Web: https://noduslabs.com/publications/Pathways-Meaning-Text-Network-Analysis.pdf

Part II

Preservation and Community

6

Supporting Manuscript Translation in Library and Archival Collections: Toward Decolonial Translation Methods

Ellen Cushman

Indigenous scholars from a range of disciplines and communities have suggested several ways to begin the process of decolonizing digital archives and museums (Lonetree 2012; Cushman 2012; O'Neal 2014 Respect and Right). These calls to action were occasioned by the need to redress the imperial legacy of archives and museums that may carry forward in archivists' decisions made when collecting, categorizing, and managing materials of cultural heritage—especially during the initial rush to digitize collections of documents written in indigenous languages. Initial efforts to digitize indigenous language documents sought to make these documents widely available to the broader public and to repatriate digital reproductions of these documents to their original communities. Though certainly well-intentioned, these efforts to digitize collections may have taken it for granted that the peoples represented in these documents would be comfortable with the material and content in these documents being made publicly available (Leopold). Also, architects of these early digital archives may have been a tad optimistic about the potential uses that visitors and native peoples might have for the digital reproductions.

Happily, recent efforts to decolonize archives have advanced the creation of protocols for working with communities to identify culturally sensitive materials and to select metadata categories that would help to cue relevant category systems that potential users may have in mind.[1] A next step in decolonizing the archive begins with the consideration of how community members might

---

E. Cushman (✉)
Northeastern University, Boston, MA, USA
e-mail: m.cushman@northeastern.edu

begin to translate these indigenous language manuscripts, particularly in keeping with their needs, purposes, and current practices. The process of building a digital archive to support the translation of indigenous language documents needs to begin with community members from the very inception of the project, while recognizing that community members themselves are not likely to be of one mind. This chapter briefly reviews the imperial legacies of archives and translation practices to frame a decolonial translation process for documents written in Cherokee housed in museums and libraries around the country. A decolonial archive should support and extend decolonial translation processes to ensure the ongoing creation of indigenous peoples' knowledges, interpretations, and representations of the past.

Imperial Legacy of Archives and Translation

As soon as the word "archive" is used, it evokes four imperialist tenets of imperial thought for indigenous scholars: Tradition. Collection. Artifacts. Preservation. I've described elsewhere the ways that these tenets of imperialist thought structure archives whether in material or digital forms (Cushman 2013). The notion of tradition, as a singularized concept, was created under the framing narrative of linear time. Western thinking creates and validates its singular tradition by pointing to itself along a timeline hatch-marked within and against a plurality of traditions. Often organized by Western notions of time, archives and museums train their visitors to be epistemologically obedient to Western modernity's concept of tradition. If the first move in decolonizing the archive is to challenge Western understandings of time as a necessary underpinning for tradition, the second move takes up the problem of collecting artifacts. The actions involved in the collection of artifacts damage them in three ways: (1) the item is taken from its context of use; (2) it is no longer understood in relation to the stories that place the item in its context and in relation to the people who use it; and (3) the people who would ostensibly have uses for the item are necessarily presumed to be no longer living. The third move in decolonizing the archive emerges directly from the second when trying to understand how these "artifacts" work to mediate knowledge for the people who use them. What does this object mean to the people who use it? This brings me to the fourth and final move that would be necessary to decolonize the digital archive: indigenous languages and decolonial translation methods. The language used to tell the stories in archives matters a great deal because English has been key to establishing Western thinking and histories.

Two questions emerge for those of us interested in building decolonial digital archives: How can digital libraries, scholars, and indigenous communities advance a decolonial vision of society? A vision that begins with epistemologies of peoples that features story, place, meaning, and perseverance? It strikes me that something can be said here for the important decolonial work of Dartmouth libraries and special collections in developing the Occom Digital archive and to shape the legacy which has attempted to honor the epistemologies of all peoples (Schweitzer and Henry 2019). We see this work also unfolding at Yale University in their Transcribe Yale project that features an area to translate Cherokee documents found in the Kilpatrick manuscripts. Scholars and archivists are on a good path, to be certain. An important next step in decolonizing the archive is to delink from the imperial legacy of translation and develop decolonial translation methods and practices.

Translation has been a cornerstone of imperial and settler agendas throughout the world. As Tejaswini-Niranjana (1992) has argued: "Translation … produces strategies of containment. By employing certain modes of representing the other—which it thereby also brings into being—translation reinforces hegemonic versions of the colonized" (3). Representing the other is necessary work to control subjects, to contain them within category systems, and to catalog their understandings as traditions against which a singular tradition might be defined. Translation used to control Cherokee people took place in several historical moments. Let me briefly point to two instances in order to suggest the instrumental value of translation as a key method used in imperialist agendas regardless of the target language. Employing certain modes of representing the other in Christianity and in disciplines, missionaries and academics have represented their civilizing missions and enunciations of superior knowledge through translation. Such was the translation work of the Bible into Cherokee, for example, first by John Pickering, who created an orthography to represent all American Indian languages in order to translate the Bible to them, and then by Worcester, whose first goal when entering Indian Territory was to learn Cherokee in order to preach in Cherokee. Both efforts were supported by the American Board of Foreign Commissioners in the early and mid-1800s.

And such was the imperialist tradition of translation work of anthropologists to preserve the language, manuscripts, and artifacts of indigenous others in order to create an imperial tradition from necessarily Othered traditions. James Mooney's rationale for his anthropological study of the Cherokee was clear in this vein. Mooney set his sights on the remote Carolina hills where "the *ancient things have been preserved*," rather than studying the Western Cherokee who are "so far advanced along the white man's road as to offer but little inducement for ethnologic study" (emphasis mine, 11–12). Mooney hoped to show the clearly visible differences of Cherokees in the Carolinas, who would warrant the considerable effort he undertook to translate their history, myths, and sacred formulas. Mooney totalizes the reality of Western man by translating the knowledge of Cherokees in North Carolina into English who were chosen precisely because they were less-civilized and showed that, "the heart of the Indian is still his own" (12). The greater the difference from white man's ways, the greater the anthropological interest in translating "primitive" knowledges to white outsiders.

These two instances of translation of Cherokee knowledge into and on Western terms illustrate a subtler point about the language itself as a medium of translation. It matters little if the target language for translation was Cherokee or English. The "target audience," purpose, and desired outcome are what matter most to the translation effort. In whatever direction the translation went (the Bible into Cherokee or Cherokee stories into disciplinary knowledge), translation served to produce containment of Cherokee subjects: on the one hand, the containment of Cherokee ceremonial knowledge into Christian theology; on the other hand, the containment of Cherokee stories into myths and legends (not knowledge, but quaint traditions and representations of the primitive oral culture). Regardless of the direction the translation went, in other words, it served to enunciate Western theologies and knowledge couched in narratives of conversion and representations of "primitive" people. Translation has been a tool useful in creating the imperial difference (Vázquez 2011), a difference that simultaneously disdains and recognizes, erases and makes visible, illuminates and obscures, in order to establish epistemic borders. This is the imperative for decolonial translation practices—how to work together to translate Cherokee-language manuscripts in ways that create alternatives to the imperial legacy of translation.

Three implications follow when engaging communities in decolonial translation practices. First, the practices developed with indigenous language documents housed in libraries and museums would bring to light suppressed epistemologies, stories, and practices chronicled in these documents. For Cherokee peoples, the 2000-odd pages of Cherokee-language manuscripts housed in museums and libraries around the country were created by knowledge holders of the Cherokee people who recorded their day-to-day lives, histories, observations of plants and land, and various practices. Second, understanding these documents through shared practices of translation promises to create connections across institutions, communities, and generations of peoples for the benefit of all, particularly as it gathers deep lexical knowledge of native speakers and linguists. Finally, decolonial translation practices ensure a collective building of knowledge together based upon the needs, purposes, practices, and exigencies of the various translators—be they archivists, scholars, language learners and teachers, or community members. These lessons are particularly needed at this crucial time.

The vitality of the Cherokee language, while comparatively strong among indigenous languages, has never been more precarious. As with most indigenous communities, Cherokees are experiencing a rapidly dwindling number of speakers in the adult generations to serve as "the middle ground between Elders, children, and youth within their communities" (Jenni et al. 2017, 1). Despite having a far-reaching mass of would-be learners, learners of Cherokee find few situations in which to practice the language. Everyday language transactions in Cherokee are few and far between. As King notes, most learners are "laboring under conditions that are radically different from the majority of world language learners…defined…by shortages of materials, limited domains of use, few proficient speakers, and wide dialectal variation" (1). In response, the Cherokee nations have developed programs that use digital tools to challenge some of these obstacles. Already, online learning communities are enabling Cherokee-language learners to connect with one another and establish support systems that are rooted in everyday contexts such as schools and bible study. Linguists working with the Cherokee Nation Foundation have also developed important digital resources including mobile apps, online dictionaries, and online tools to support reading comprehension. These initiatives demonstrate but do not fully realize the potential of digital tools to address the problems of critical mass and embedded, intergenerational language usage in supporting language perseverance.

Decolonial Translation

While Cherokee can be accessed across social media platforms and has a plethora of language revitalization resources (see for example those found on the Cherokee Nation website at https://language.cherokee.org/), Cherokee speakers and language learners still need a rhetorical situation in which to speak, read, and write: they need purposes, audiences, and reasons for their communicative transactions (King and Hermes). The contexts that language revitalization apps and social media outlets offer may not necessarily provide meaningful reasons to practice the language (perseverance) and to build lexical materials (preservation). What is needed is an archive that addresses the exigence of creating a digital platform where users and community members can come together to forward language perseverance and preservation as mutually sustaining activities. Doing so, the decolonized archive promises to **preserve and sustain** native languages by creating a digital archive around **the words and content in these manuscripts**. Since stories include an activist ethic of obligation and privilege, they enact a form of citizenship in their telling, hearing, and retelling. I remain hopeful that digital spaces like these might further the activist work of perseverance with our peoples by building relationships made possible through the collective translation of these manuscripts. Translation into and on indigenous people's languages (or any language Othered by those who wield imperial languages and displace others) is inescapable and is today more necessary than ever. But it is translation with different direction, purpose, exigency, and result. It is translation back to ourselves and for purposes defined by the people whose writing is being translated. Depending on the peoples, this translation can facilitate language perseverance efforts, the remembering of ceremonies in medicine, the relocating of landmarks and histories within the people's collective memory, or the reintroduction of plants and medicinal knowledge. It is translation to re-place peoples within a global earth, to help realize more fully human peoples, and to help create pluriversal options and knowledges. It's an exciting time to be an archivist, museum curator, or librarian. As parameters and protocols for interacting with indigenous peoples are being established (O'Neal 2015; Powell 2016), the reciprocal and collaborative relationships permit a different kind of interaction with manuscripts, material objects, images, and audio recordings. The next step is to understand ways in which the language presented in these materials can best facilitate the linguistic perseverance efforts already underway in many nations.

Decolonial translation is an epistemic method, a methodology, that seeks to reveal the gaps in knowing that were created by the colonial difference as it presents alternatives to these conversions of understanding into and on Western terms. Decolonial translation reveals the boundaries created by the imperial difference in an effort to include again the knowledges which have been lost or erased—to restore suppressed epistemologies.

With these goals in mind, the enterprise of decolonial translation becomes one quite apart from that undertaken by anthropologists and linguists who set their sights on the expansion of disciplinary knowledge in academe. To decolonize translation is to question discipline building altogether, to make connections across differences, to appreciate knowledges and languages as equally valuable while respecting and understanding the social injustices and hierarchical arrangements creating those differences, to find alternative ways of structuring being and knowing in this world. Decolonial translation works from a fundamental hope that through this work, we can imagine ways of being and being together on this earth without mining, pioneering, exploiting, taking, pillaging, differencing, but with localizing, exercising wonder, connection and healing, praising and working together, and understanding how deeply and fundamentally interconnected all beings and life are. In practice, decolonial translation begins by recuperating the instrumental logic of the original language.

Decolonial Translation in Practice

Decolonial translation methods begin with an understanding of the instrumental, historical, and cultural importance of the Cherokee syllabary as an indigenous form of archiving knowledge in and on Cherokee terms. These methods also pay close attention to the types of reading and writing practices currently in use in an effort to create online collaborative spaces for translation in support of these practices. For libraries and archives, the results would help to ensure fuller access to and interaction with manuscript collections. For scholars, decolonial translation methodologies help to ensure the creation of knowledge that is conversant with indigenous interpretations and representations of the past. For indigenous peoples, decolonial translation methods help to ensure that archival materials can be meaningfully integrated into ongoing language perseverance efforts in indigenous communities.

What this looks like in practice can take many forms depending on the communities' purposes, reasons, and practices for doing translation in the first place. During the five years of ethnohistorical research that contributed to my book, *The Cherokee Syllabary: Writing the People's Perseverance*, I had the opportunity to observe and learn more about the language translation team's work within the Cherokee Nation. I noted that the decoding of each phrase that was written in Sequoyan begins with transliteration into the roman alphabet. Developed by Sequoyah and accepted by the tribal council in 1821, Sequoyan is an 85-character writing system that has remained in use to the present. The instrumental, historical, and cultural legacy of this writing system has been central to the development of a literary canon of millions of pages of writings in print and manuscript form (Bender 2002; Cushman 2012; Parins 2013) and has facilitated language perseverance efforts (Nelson 2014; Montgomery-Anderson 2015). Following the Cherokee word written in Sequoyan, the character-by-character transliteration is presented alongside a rough translation into English. This translation practice privileges the Cherokee writing system first, then the sound of the words next, with meanings that might make sense to the English speaker last. A standard practice in many Cherokee Nation communications since the passing of the 2003 language preservation policy, this method of translation encourages the use of Cherokee language in public and business settings. This is also a standard practice for the Cherokee-language translation team that includes members from the Cherokee Nation based in Oklahoma as well as the Eastern Band of Cherokees based in North Carolina.

With an initial word-by-word decoding accomplished, the rough translation is triangulated against additional documents and all major and well-accepted dictionaries of Cherokee from Eastern and Western dialects. This triangulation of language resources lends additional semantic possibility to the translations provided and helps to correct for non-standardized spellings or dialectical differences that may emerge in the phrasings presented in the manuscript. Often times, there's discussion with colleagues or fellow translators on a translation team to try to make sense of the ways in which these words were related to or still are related to everyday practices of Cherokee people. This can also be a moment to trace the etymology of words to try to understand the ways in which some verb phrases are combinations of two or more morphemes. In these languages and texts, the enunciation of knowledge is centered on placing, locating, describing, and observing in Cherokee language, history, stories, and understandings. The focus of decolonial translation is to attempt to provide constellations of ideas clustered around longstanding ways of being. Below is an example of the types of translation possible through these practices. These are displayed as interlinear translations in concordance with best practices for publishing as established in recent publications of Cherokee-language linguists (see Feeling, Pulte, Pulte 2018; Montgomery-Anderson 2015).

Letter to Dollie Duncan on Oklahoma State Penitentiary Stationery

Cherokee-language documents from archival collections are being digitally disseminated by the American Philosophical Society, the Museum of the Cherokee Indian, the Gilcrease Museum, the Beinecke Library, the Smithsonian Institution, the University of Tulsa, West Carolina University, and a handful of other institutions. In general, documents in these collections are discoverable through standard search interfaces and viewable using document viewers that present the materials as digital renditions of literacy artifacts without semantic gloss, transcription, or translation (Figs. 6.1 and 6.2).

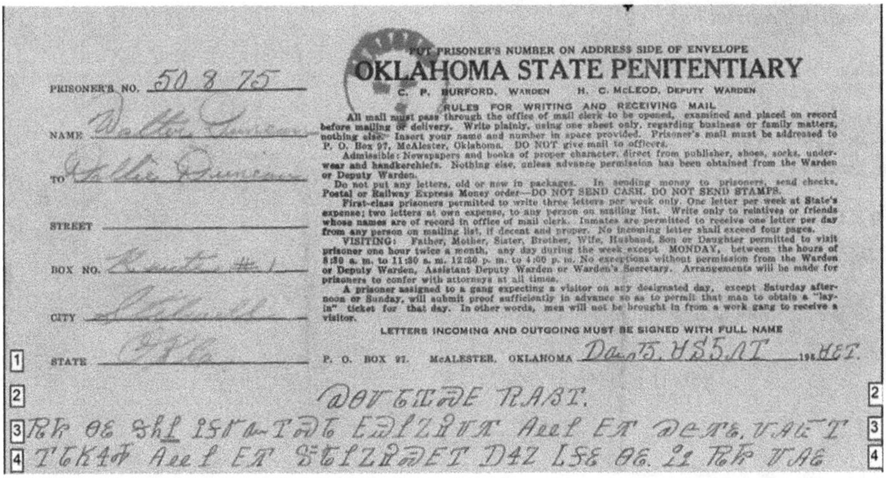

Fig. 6.1 B22 F1843 Letter to Dollie Duncan on Oklahoma Penitentiary stationery IID15533005. Kilpatrick Collection of Cherokee Manuscripts. Yale Collection of Western Americana, Beinecke Rare Book and Manuscript Library

The digital repatriation of these documents from the museums and archives where they're held often means a lack of contextualization from a specifically Cherokee perspective. Exceptionally, Yale's Digital Humanities Laboratory has established a public transcription interface (Transcribe@Yale) through which materials from the Beinecke collections (including Cherokee-language documents) can be either translated into English or transcribed into the Sequoyan syllabary to assist in making the documents searchable. A team from the United Keetoowah Band translators, led by Ernestine Berry (director of the John Hair Cultural Center & Museum), translated into English approximately 75 documents from this collection with the support of an Institute of Museum and Library Services Grant in 2017.

Working from a digital image of the source document, translators work as a team to provide several forms of information. First, they provide an **initial transcription** of the manuscript into Sequoyan, the Cherokee-language syllabary. The text is next **transliterated into the roman alphabet:** for instance, the word ᏣᎳᎩ ("Cherokee") could be transliterated as /jalagi/. This transliteration provides access to the document for those less familiar with the Sequoyan syllabary and can also be used for subsequent linguistic analysis that shows phonetic spellings of the words and morphemic information such as pronouns, verb forms, and tense. Finally, the text is **translated into English:** the user can select a sentence or phrase for translation and enter a free

English Translation

Name Walter Duncan #50875

To Dollie Duncan, Rt #1, Stilwell, OK

[1] March 11, 1951

[2] Sunday evening

[3] Mother, now I have prepared to talk with you a little on paper.

[4] We are really having a lot of trouble conversing with letters, but it will only be a short time longer.

1. DOᏬᏏ	ᏨᏏᏡᏗᎢ	195 ᏨᎬᎢ
anvhyi	sadusinei	195 sagwv?i
March	eleventh (?)	1951 (?)

2. ᎤᎾᎦᎷᏡᏬᎠᎬ	ᎡᎦβ[Ꮽ]Ꭲ	
unadodagwasgv[?i]	svhiye[yi]?i	
Sunday	evening	

3. RᎮ	ᎾᎬ [sc. -Ꮤ]	ᏚᏨᏢ [sc. -C for -P]	1ᏕᎶᎤᏭᎢᎤᎠᏝ	ᎬᏨᏢᏃᎮᎪᎶ [sc. -C- for -P-]	ᎠᏨᏢ	ᎬᎶ [sc. -Ꮤ]	ᎤᎬᎶᎢ	ᎡᎶᏣᎢ
eji	nagwv [-gwu]	gayoli [sc. gayohli]	vgadvnv?isda	gvyalinohehdohdi	gohweli	gvhdi [sc. -gwu]	ujatigwv dohiyu?i	
		gaayoŏ[h]li	vvgádvvnv́v́?isda	gvvyaliìnoohehdohdi		goohweeli	much (?) + just	ᎡᎶᏣᎢᎢ
ee-ji			vv-ga-advvnvv?isd-a	gvvy-ali-hnoo-heh-doh-di			ujati=gwu doohiyu?i	
1B.FAM -mother			ITER-1SG.A-prepare-PCT-IND	1/2SG-MID-converse-PRS-INST-INF			ujati=DT	

Fig. 6.2 Interlinear translations of first four lines of letter from Walter Duncan to Dollie Duncan

			'I have (just) prepared' (= 'arranged'?)	'for me to converse with you'			a little, a bit (< this with much)	really/very
Mother	now	a little				paper		
4. TLK4oƖ	AߪP	EЛ		SLPZPᏈET	D4Z	LᏚᏋ [sc. -Ꮢ]		ᎾᏋ [sc. -Ꮒ]
idajoseha	gohweli	gvhdi		dedalinohesgv?i	asehno	hlegagwv [sc. -gwu]		nagwv [sc. -gwu]
ìidajóóseha	goohweeli			dèèdaliinooheésgvv?i		hleẽgagwu		
iidii-ajoo?s-eh-a				dee-eedii-ali-hnoo-heésg-vṽ?i		hleẽga=gwu		
1PL.IN.A-be.troubled-PRS.IND				DIST1-1PL.IN>AN-MID-converse-IMPF-ASR/SH		for.a.while=DT		
we're having trouble		paper	with	'conversing (habitually), addressing each other'	but, probably, yet	'(only) for a while (longer)'		now

Fig. 6.2 (continued)

translation or offer a word-by-word literal translation as part of a more detailed linguistic annotation process. The goal of decolonial interlinear translation processes such as these is to provide for a **collaborative effort to translate, review, and study** in which learners and mentors, translators, and scholars can revisit difficult passages, examine transcriptions and translations in relation to the document images, and consult learning resources such as online lexicons and annotations. In other words, decolonial translation processes seek to develop meaningful interactions with text from a variety of perspectives, honoring equally the knowledge of the language speaker, translator, learner, scholar, and archivist. It can also support **administrative review** where language experts and project editors can read, edit, and comment and respond to queries.

These decolonial translation practices will work from documents that have been donated to an online repository of linked objects from across museums and libraries in the spirit of creating a next generation of digital archive. The decolonial digital archive I have in mind is one in which previously digitally curated documents like these have been donated from partner museum and libraries to facilitate the collective endeavor of decolonial translation described here. Throughout every iteration of design of this digital archive, community members representing the three federally recognized nations of Cherokee people have been involved. The initial idea for this collective space for translation originated as part of an IMLS sponsored grant by individuals from the Cherokee Nation translation team and individuals working with the Anishinaabemowin language. In that project, we conceptualized a digital archive and designed features of a user interface based on desiderata outlined for us by our respective nations. We outlined a workflow for selecting and incorporating particular documents paying particular attention to the need to identify and provide differential access to culturally sensitive documents. Finally, we proposed a process whereby documents would be incorporated into a future digital archive with memoranda of understandings agreed to by all to ensure that provenance and credit for digital documents linked through the digital archive were established beforehand. All of this work takes into account the needs of the various users we have to date partnered with and who form our advisory board as we seek funding to support the creation of the Digital Archive for American Indian Language Preservation and Perseverance (DAILP).

Implications

The methodology and method of decolonial translation presented here has been an exercise in border thinking—a process that reveals both the creation of difference, and the means by which those dwelling on the borders might begin to engage in the "rewriting of geographic frontiers, imperial/colonial subjectivities, and territorial epistemologies" (Tlostanova and Mignolo 72–3). Decolonial translation projects like this, offer the possibility of revealing the colonial differencing that has happened, while also forging connection across these differences to create pluriversal possibilities for recuperating suppressed epistemologies.

With these goals in mind, the enterprise of decolonial translation enters into discipline building by making connections across differences, seeing knowledges and languages as equally valuable, respecting and understanding the social injustices and hierarchical arrangements producing those differences, and finding alternative ways of structuring being and knowing in this world. Through everyday acts of translation, we can encourage pluriversal knowledges, concepts, and discourses that help all peoples persevere (Mignolo). And we can help to sustain the important recuperative and restorative rhetorical analyses of all peoples.

Developing decolonial translation processes for digital archives, particularly around the Cherokee language, is an attempt to bring together language learners, linguists, and community-based translation teams working together on manuscripts; the resulting translations will become part of a growing collection that in turn can be used for language and cultural study. In the first phase of the project, we are pre-populating this archive with lexical information drawn from established online lexicons and reference materials. In the next phase, we will explore translation activities that draw upon the collective efforts of language learners, teachers, and translators; native community members; archivists and librarians; and transdisciplinary scholars with interests in indigenous peoples, cultures, histories, and languages. These translations will help make the original document collection more accessible to readers and language learners, while also further expanding the lexical dataset undergirding the site.

Archivists, librarians, scholars, and indigenous peoples might find such a process useful when building digital archives that facilitate the language perseverance efforts of nations like the Cherokees. Key to this process working well is an understanding that the goals, audiences, purposes, and uses of these translations should be negotiated together. Online spaces can provide for the development of already existing online lexicons if, for example, teams are built that can pay attention to the computational infrastructure already in place at nations, but that can also understand how it is that translation processes and practices like these unfold in the everyday work of the nation's citizens. While it may be tempting to create digital archives that sustain scholarly purposes or preservation efforts above any other concerns, digital archives that are to be useful to indigenous peoples will only be as useful as they are built upon current practices in languaging efforts.

Decolonial translation works from a fundamental hope that through this work, we can imagine ways of being and being together on this earth with a foundational understanding of how deeply and fundamentally interconnected all life is.

Through everyday acts of translation in digital archives using collaboratives built to sustain such efforts, we can encourage the recuperation and perseverance of many knowledges, concepts, and discourses in and on their terms. And we can help to sustain the important recuperative and restorative analyses of indigenous people's languages, particularly at risk in this context of the increasing globalization of English as the lingua franca. Archives and libraries can be the vanguard against indigenous language erosion. These efforts can flourish by developing and practicing decolonial translation processes with teams of tribal representatives, language learners, language teachers, scholars, and archivists for the manuscripts in collections. Indigenous archives become living archives, in other words, when peoples, languages, and knowledges come to be appreciated in and on their terms and when archival materials can be meaningfully integrated into ongoing practices. Decolonial translation methodologies help to ensure the ongoing creation of native knowledges, interpretations, and representations of the past.

Note

1. See, for example, Powell's "Proceedings" and "Digital Knowledge Sharing: Forging Partnerships between Scholars, Archives, and Indigenous Communities;" Atalay's *Community-Based Archaeology: Research with, by, and for Indigenous and Local Communities*, Leopold's "Articulating culturally sensitive knowledge online: A Cherokee case study," and both of Jennifer O'Neal's "Respect, Recognition, and Reciprocity: The Protocols for Native American Archival Materials" and "'The Right to Know': Decolonizing Native American Archives."

Bibliography

Atalay, Sonya. 2012. *Community-Based Archaeology: Research with, By, and for Indigenous and Local Communities*. Berkeley: University of California Press.

Bender, Margaret. 2002. *Signs of Cherokee Culture: Sequoyah's Syllabary in Eastern Cherokee Life*. Chapel Hill: University of North Carolina Press.

Cushman, Ellen. 2012. *The Cherokee Syllabary: Writing the People's Perseverance*. Norman: University of OK Press.

———. 2013. Wampum, Sequoyan, and Story: Decolonizing the Digital Archive. *College English* 76 (2): 115–135. Retrieved from http://www.jstor.org/stable/24238145

Feeling, Durbin, William John Pulte, and Gregory Pulte. 2018. *Cherokee Narratives: A Linguistic Study*. Norman: University of Oklahoma Press.

Jenni, Barbara, Adar Anisman, Onowa McIvor, and Peter Jacobs. 2017. An Exploration of the Effects of Mentor-Apprentice Programs on Mentors' and Apprentices' Wellbeing. *International Journal of Indigenous Health* 12 (2): 25–42. https://doi.org/10.18357/ijih122201717783

King, Kendall. 2016. Who and What Is the Field of Applied Linguistics Overlooking?: Why This Matters and How Educational Linguistics Can Help. *Working Papers in Educational Linguistics* 31 (2). Retrieved from https://repository.upenn.edu/wpel/vol31/iss2/1

King, Kendall A., and Mary Hermes. 2014. Why Is This So Hard?: Ideologies of Endangerment, Passive Language Learning Approaches, and Ojibwe in the United States. *Journal of Language, Identity & Education* 13 (4): 268–282.

Leopold, Robert. 2013. Articulating Culturally Sensitive Knowledge Online: A Cherokee Case Study. *Museum Anthropology Review* 7 (1–2): 85–104.

Lonetree, Amy. 2012. *Decolonizing Museums: Representing Native America in National and Tribal Museums*. Raleigh: University of North Carolina Press.

Mignolo, Walter. 2011. *The Darker Side of Western Modernity: Global Futures, Decolonial Options*. Durham: Duke University Press.

Montgomery-Anderson, B. 2015. *Cherokee Reference Grammar*. Norman: University of Oklahoma Press.

Mooney, James, and George Ellison. 1992. *James Mooney's History, Myths, and Sacred Formulas of the Cherokees*. Asheville: Bright Mountain Books.

Nelson, Joshua. 2014. *Progressive Traditions: Identity in Cherokee Literature and Culture*. Norman: University of Oklahoma Press.

Niranjana, Tejaswini. 1992. *Siting Translation: History, Post-Structuralism, and the Colonial Context*. Berkeley: University of California Press.

O'Neal, Jennifer R. 2014. Respect, Recognition, and Reciprocity: The Protocols for Native American Archival Materials. In *Identity Palimpsests: Archiving Ethnicity in the US and Canada*, ed. Dominique Daniel and Amalia Levi, 125–142. Sacramento: Litwin Press.

———. 2015. 'The Right to Know': Decolonizing Native American Archives. *Journal of Western Archives* 6 (1): 1–17.

Parins, J.W. 2013. *Literacy and Intellectual Life in the Cherokee Nation, 1820–1906*. Vol. 58. Norman: University of Oklahoma Press.

Powell, Timothy B. 2014. The American Philosophical Society: Protocols for the Treatment of Indigenous Materials. *Proceedings of the American Philosophical Society* 158 (4): 411–420.

———. 2016. Digital Knowledge Sharing: Forging Partnerships between Scholars, Archives, and Indigenous Communities. *Museum Anthropology Review* 10 (2): 66–90.

Schweitzer, Ivy, and Gordon Henry. 2019. *Digital Afterlives: Futures of Indigenous Archives Essays in Honor of the Occom Circle*. Hanover: The University Press of New England.

Tlostanova, Madina V., and Walter Mignolo. 2012. *Learning to Unlearn: Decolonial Reflections from Eurasia and the Americas*. Columbus: The Ohio State University Press.

Vázquez, Rolando. 2011. Translation as Erasure: Thoughts on Modernity's Epistemic Violence. *Journal of Historical Sociology* 24 (1): 27–44.

7

Radical Recordkeeping: How Community Archives Are Changing How We Think About Records

Jeannette A. Bastian

> *The activity of 'archiving' is … always a critical one, always a historically located one, always a contestatory one.*
> —Stuart Hall ("Constituting an Archive," *Third Text*, 15 (July 2008):89)

Introduction

Since their formal emergence in the nineteenth century, archives in Western society have generally been associated with governments and large institutions such as universities, state historical societies, and major corporations. Archives and records theory and practice was developed primarily to support the maintenance of these entities and their national and institutional narratives. But today, these traditional archival spaces as well as their theories and practices are being both augmented and challenged by community archives, a grassroots movement that, beginning in the late twentieth century, has become a champion of the narratives of the marginalized, the forgotten, the undocumented, and the ignored. "Community archives grow out of the desire to collect documentary heritage that reflects our common identities, experiences and interests,"[1] writes one archival scholar on the phenomena of the community archives movement.

But along with this desire to reflect and celebrate all segments of the society also comes a questioning of time-honored archival environments and values.

J. A. Bastian (✉)
School of Library and Information Science, Simmons University, Boston, MA, USA

As the quote by Stuart Hall suggests, a salient feature of archives and the archiving process has always been fluidity and the recognition that archives are dynamic reflections of the society that creates them. Does the emerging community archives movement represent a counter-narrative to traditional archival practice? No better examples of competing archival values can be seen than in comments from students in my own classroom, where, in a recent exercise on community archives, graduate students studying to become archivists quickly focused on the heart of the debate:

> What struck me about the readings in particular was this conflict between the authenticity of community archives and the distrust of big institutions to preserve that narrative.

> The emergence of independent community archives serves to challenge the professional or traditional conceptions of what constitutes an archive; more importantly, however, these independent archives seek to have a stake in the historical and political making processes of society.[2]

But while students and others may see a conflict between community and institutional archives, this is not necessarily a binary or adversarial relationship, rather the relationship should be seen as an evolutionary one. Community archives offer some potent and radical ways forward for archival development particularly in this age of the digital. At the same time, long established and tested archival theory and practice provide powerful underpinnings, a base from which to imagine the emergence of new theory and practice that reflect social change. Such an evolving process was envisioned by the late Canadian archival theorist, Terry Cook, who outlined four phases or paradigms of archival practice through the twentieth century and into the twenty-first. He described the still nascent fourth paradigm:

> Community-based archiving involves . . . a shift in core principles, from exclusive custodianship and ownership of archives to shared stewardship and collaboration; from dominant-culture language, terminology, and definitions to sensitivity to the "other" and as keen an awareness of the emotional, religious, symbolic, and cultural values that records have to their communities as of their administrative and juridical significance.[3]

As diverse groups of people in a wide variety of locations—both analog and virtual—recognize the need to document themselves outside of traditional archival venues, community archives, as the sites of this documentation, are proliferating as a global movement, as a civic movement, but particularly as a volunteer bottom-up social movement—a movement of the people rather than of the archivists. Community archives are often seen as being in the vanguard of social concerns and social justice, as markers of community-based activism, as offering a participatory approach in a collaboration between archivists and non-archivists, as exemplifying the ongoing development of 'professional' archival (and heritage) practice, and as integral to the ability of people to articulate and assert their identity.

This chapter explores the social phenomenon of community archives, its activist role, and its potential impact on traditional archives. Offering definitions and examples of community archives worldwide, I discuss how this seemingly radical approach to records and recordkeeping can augment and enhance the archival mission while fulfilling society's documentation imperatives.

A Sense of Communities

Whether virtual or physical, understanding a community archive requires a working definition of community. Defining a community may be the first, and perhaps, most complex step in thinking about community archives. Archivist Andrew Flinn, a pioneer of the community archives movement, notes that

> [d]efinitions of what a 'community' might be are of course particularly complex and fluid and capable of multiple interpretations. Some definitions focus on locality, others on notions of shared beliefs or shared values producing a common purpose. Other discussions examine problems with who it is that seeks to define community and community membership, who determines who is included and who is excluded and whether it should be seen as an inclusive or as an exclusive and divisive concept.[4]

Whether in physical or virtual environments, we tend to think of communities as groups of individuals united around a set of commonalities. These commonalities may be varied and complex but generally coalesce around

- a common place or locality—shared geography;
- a common interest, belief, or lifestyle—shared characteristics other than place that could fit into a variety of categories such as religious beliefs, gender orientation, occupation, ethnicity, origins, activities such as sports, and civic organizations;
- a common purpose—shared events or missions or attachment to a common idea or calling.

These commonalities inevitably overlap, and each of us may belong to many different communities that may fit into one or all of the categories above. Interacting with a community requires understanding its distinctive features, its reason for being, its identity, and its place within the larger society, and all these may be many and diverse.

Importantly, Flinn suggests that the essential feature of any community is that the community defines itself rather than being defined externally by others. This self-identification is also a critical aspect of a community archive.

In addition to the commonalities that draw them together, communities also have other elements that may characterize them. They may be seen as

- relational and longitudinal—a community may consist of a group of individuals who form relationships over time by interacting regularly around shared experiences, which are of interest to all of them for varying individual reasons.
- sites of communion—shared sense of attachment to a place, a group, or an idea. In its strongest form 'communion' entails a profound meeting or encounter (i.e. a natural disaster such as a hurricane).
- often virtual—'imagined' and online but similarly of place, interest, communion, relationships.
- bounded—shared commonality also distinguishes members of one group in a significant way from the members of other groups.

Community is often thought of as a network or local social system. But just because people live in the same location does not necessarily mean that they interact with one another. It is the relationships between people and their networks that are often seen as the most significant aspect of 'community.'[5] Ever since Howard Rheingold first introduced the term 'virtual communities,' in 1993 through the WELL (Whole Earth 'Lectronic Link), a pioneering web-based online community,[6] digital technologies have significantly expanded both the concept of 'community' and the ability of people to interact within these networks. Online communities play out in virtual environments every day through social media networks such as Facebook, LinkedIn, Twitter, Instagram, and a myriad of other forums, networks designed specifically to foster community.

We also associate communities with distinct types of values and actions, and these values are particularly significant in understanding the rationales behind community archives. Communities may create identity and a sense of self for members of the group, and, of particular importance to communities of place, they may foster and promote a sense of collective memory and heritage. In terms of social justice, especially for marginalized populations, communities may act as vehicles of communication and advocacy for the group. Communities may offer social structure, and they often imply deeply held values such as fellowship, trust, and commitment.

At the same time, communities also define their boundaries: shared commonality distinguishes members of a group in a significant way from members of other groups. Community implies both similarities and differences. If some people are inside, then others are outside, and so to some extent, community also involves exclusion.

Defining Community Archives

Although the term 'community archives' entered the archival vocabulary several decades ago, its definition remains ambiguous. A 'community archive' generally refers to the materials generated by not-for-profit and non-governmental entities, by a particular group or community sharing common interests, whether origins, geography, ethnicities, or lifestyles. Community archives are often independent grassroots organizations primarily run by volunteers. Flinn notes that "[t]he defining characteristic of a community archives is the active participation of the community in documenting and making accessible the history of their particular group and/or locality **on their own terms**."[7]

From exploratory beginnings in the twentieth century, community archives as discrete and identifiable entities began to significantly impact the archival world in the early decades of the twenty-first. While community-based informal archives had long existed, the concept of community archives was largely unexplored and unfamiliar to archivists. Their ad hoc and highly diversified natures often went unrecognized as archival, and their content, from small marginal segments of the population and often missing from standard records formats, did not initially capture the imaginations of archivists who historically have focused on institutional records and the acquisition of manuscript collections. In addition, community archives often ignored standard archival practice, not only in their acquisitions but in their views of records themselves, and in their nonconformity to accepted notions of provenance, a fundamental organizing archival principle.[8]

The digital turn, beginning in the last decades of the twentieth century, forced archivists to focus their energies on re-evaluating and reconceptualizing their practices to meet new demands. With archivists increasingly absorbed by the challenges posed by digital environments, community archives did not initially take priority. This has changed in the past decade; with a shift in social perceptions, marginalized communities, used to being overlooked by formal institutions, have focused increasingly on documenting themselves both as a way of asserting their own identity and seeking social justice. Archival educator Michelle Caswell uses the anthropological term 'symbolic annihilation' to describe "the ways in which mainstream media [and by implication, archives] ignore, misrepresent, or malign minoritized groups." Her research finds that "community archives can have important epistemological, ontological, and social impacts on members of marginalized communities."[9] Archivists, in turn, are becoming increasingly attuned to the documentation imperatives of marginalized groups and their responsibilities to those needs. Community archives offer a way to reach beyond traditional archival institutions that are often viewed as exclusive and exclusionary.

Origins

The origins of community archives are obscure, but it does seem clear that in a wide variety of guises, community archives have existed ever since groups of people have felt the need to affirm their own identities within or apart from the wider society. Historical societies, municipal centers, local history rooms, and religious organizations are only a few of the different settings that serve to establish and express group identity whether that of a town, a region, an ethnicity, or even that founded upon an affinity or a belief. Since records, in all their many modalities and forms, follow from the articulations and actions of people, they become the organic expressions of any group of people wishing to proclaim itself both for its own sake and to the larger world.

Over time, community archives have responded to and fulfilled a spectrum of community needs. From roles as chroniclers and documenters of community engagement in war in the 1940s, as archives existing outside institutional spaces such as the Lesbian Herstory Archives founded in 1975,[10] as counter-narratives to "official history books and institutions of public culture" in the South Africa of the 1990s[11] to social justice advocacy today, community archives have reacted to the imperatives of their time.

By 2001, the growing community archives movement had caught the attention of the British *Public Library Journal*, which declared that

> Community Archives have become a grass roots movement – there is no funded coordination (though undoubtedly there should be). It is not something that is being organised from the top down, it is simply seeding all over the country as people hear of the idea and want to do it in their own locality.[12]

The term 'community archives' itself as a specific designation came into general use in the twentieth century to characterize a nontraditional archival collection tied to a specific group, one that may be undocumented or underdocumented by traditional archival institutions and generally initiated and organized by volunteers. A search through the professional literature identifies usage of the phrase as early as 1942 when an article in *Library Journal* places 'community archives' within the sphere of the public library. "Libraries as Community Archives in Wartime" emphasizes the archival obligations of libraries in documenting the wartime activities of particular towns, encouraging those involved in World War II to create archives of their war experiences at the public library. The author writes that "every type of library has its archival function in wartime. The public library can keep the record of the activities of the community and of the war's impact on it. The college and university library can keep similar records of the wartime history of the institution, its faculty, students and alumni."[13]

'Community archives,' however, is not a universally recognized or acknowledged term. As Flinn and Gilland point out,

> Despite the perhaps near universal practice of individuals and communities collecting materials which they deem to be significant in ways that are not necessarily subject to professional oversight or located in formal institutional settings, in some countries this practice has been recognized and described by those in the archival field as 'community archiving', in other countries different terms are used and in others still such activities have received little or no recognition.[14]

In addition, those regions using the term 'community archives' may assign it slightly different meanings. In the United Kingdom, for example, community archives have been generally defined as a grassroots, bottom-up movement where the community creates its own, very local, archives. Supported by government grants, the Community Archives and Heritage Group, a website developed in the United Kingdom, hosts and advocates for community archives.[15] In New Zealand and in Canada, community archives are advised and supported by the national archives—the government helps to create or foster these community-based archives with and for the community. In Canada, Libraries and Archives Canada offers funding to community archives through its Documentary Heritage Communities program that aims to ensure that "Canada's continuing memory is documented and accessible to current and future generations by adopting a more collaborative approach with local documentary heritage communities."[16] Similarly, in New Zealand, The Community Archive is "a hub for New Zealand's archival organisations to showcase their collections. It is a free, easy to use mini archive management system supported by Archives New Zealand."[17] As in the Community Archives and Heritage Group, this is a hosting site, inviting various groups, including community archives, to upload their materials. Archives New Zealand offers this site as a digital and more inclusive continuation of its National Register of Archives and Manuscripts. As in the UK site, the Community Archive also offers tools and instructions for all aspects of archival preservation and organization. In Australia, the national archives offer grants to community heritage groups to preserve 'locally owned' objects. They identify the groups eligible to apply for these grants as "local historical societies, regional museums, public libraries, and Indigenous and migrant community groups."[18]

Elsewhere, community archives have assumed a more adversarial role in relationship to their national archives. In South Africa, for example, both SAHA, the South African History Archive, and GALA, the Gay and Lesbian Archive, exist as counter-narratives to official archives, giving voice to those excluded. SAHA, established in the 1980s by anti-apartheid activists, is an independent human rights archive that is "dedicated to documenting, supporting and promoting greater awareness of past and contemporary struggles for justice through archival practices and outreach, and the utilisation of access to information laws."[19] GALA "was formed … to address the erasure and omission of LGBTIQ stories and experiences from public institutions such as official archives in (South) Africa."[20]

If, as it appears, definitions of community archives may be region specific, then what constitutes a community archive in an American context? Several years ago, in a seminar on community archives, students were asked to identify a community archive that they wished to become involved with. The experiences of my students, though limited both by geography and numbers, suggest that in the United States the term 'community archives,' while leaning heavily toward the independent social justice model of South Africa, also embraces a vision that could include a range of community heritage sites that might include small town historical societies preserving an elitist history, statewide initiatives documenting its diverse populations, or subcultures coalescing around alternative documentation.[21]

A community archive in the United States may be grassroots as well as elitist, historical as well as contemporary, topical as well as general, public as well as private and nonprofit, and as much concerned with historical values, personal and group identity, and collective memories as with social issues. Community archives are found in many different kinds of community groups—civic organizations, local historical societies, cultural heritage centers, and even municipal offices; all might play roles in a community that meet the definition of community archives.

Characteristics of Community Archives

Community archives are often distinguished by their radical departure from standard archival institutions, and many of them share certain core characteristics. South African archivist Kathy Eales notes that "[a] key premise of community archiving is to give substance to a community's right to own its own memories."[22] A deep belief in archives and history for and about the community, a broad and inclusive definition of what should be in a community archive, community-led mechanisms for reporting and establishing authority, and a strong belief in autonomy and partnership, are a few of the essential features. As independent grassroots organizations are primarily run by volunteers and are often sites of resistance and social justice, community involvement in the development and management of the collection is critical. And community archives are often resistant to professional intervention.

A strong digital presence, but often a reliance on limited community resources and scarce external funding to maintain that presence, creates an often precarious existence. But the challenges of digital sustainability are mediated by the deeply held belief in a community archive as a community-owned accessible space that, for the community, is also a place of safety and protections, often a place of resistance and as a testament to a marginalized, often forgotten presence.

What's in a Community Archive

A significant difference between community archives and more traditional archives is their content, informed by their perspective on archives or archival records. Archives, either in paper or in digital format, are defined in the Society of American Archivists as

> materials created or received by a person, family, or organization, public or private, in the conduct of their affairs and preserved because of the enduring value contained in the information they contain or as evidence of the functions and responsibilities of their creator … permanent records.[23]

A record is defined more narrowly as

> data or information that has been fixed on some medium; that has content, context, and structure; and that is used as an extension of human memory or to demonstrate accountability.[24]

However, community archives may not adhere to these definitions but require a broader interpretation. While artifacts are traditionally the purview of museums, books of libraries, and papers—whether digital or analog—of archives, in a community archive, all formats belong equally and often belong together. An archival record may be whatever the community values as such, in part because the context of creation or the provenance of the item or object may be thought of as the community itself. The Community Archive, therefore, may include a range of materials, from traditional manuscripts and organizational records to interviews, newspapers, artwork, objects, and ephemera of community events, in short, anything the group considers essential to its identity.

The archival principle of provenance dictates that records be organized by the person, family, or organization that created or compiled them. The person, family, or organization then becomes the context for understanding the records. To preserve this context, records from different creators or compilers cannot be mingled. In this way, records stand as credible evidence of actions, interactions, and historical data. Cook suggests that community archives confer an added dimension to the idea of provenance noting, "the records in community archives are not just archival resources, but part of the identity of those communities—there is an 'identity provenance' that gives them significant meaning as autonomous archives."[25] In Cook's reading, the community itself is the wider context of the records within its archives.

This view of the community as the creator of the collection leads to the embrace of an array of formats and types of materials. The Lesbian Herstory Archives, for example, describes itself as "a magical place—part library, part museum, a community gathering space" housing "the world's largest collection of materials by and about lesbians and their communities." Its collections include a wide variety of objects, items, books, and—yes—archival papers as well.

The materials in a community archive may be organized in ways that make them more accessible to users who may not be familiar with the complexities of finding aids and standard archival arrangements. SAADA, the South East Asian American Digital Archive, for example, arranges its collections in multiple ways for more transparent access. Users can browse the site by themes, by time period, by type of material, as well as by the more archivally standard 'creator' or 'source.' Project Save, a digital photo archive based in Watertown, Massachusetts, that is committed to preserving Armenian history through photographs, organizes its 45,000 photographs by changing exhibits and by themes.[26]

Digital Spaces

Both SAADA and Project Save are digitally based. One of the most significant and transformative features of community archives is their strong digital presence, and many community archives live only on the web. Because accessibility for their communities is prime, because participation, interaction and continuing dialogue are all essential characteristics of community archives, and because the visual is favored over the textual, the web and its many digital affordances has significantly impacted the growth and proliferation of this community phenomenon.

The development of inexpensive scanning and other software supports relatively easy engagement with heritage materials in an open access online context and encourages the creation and sharing of complex individual and collective narratives. The distributed networks of the web also redefine geographical spaces, extending and creating community by disrupting and destroying traditional barriers.

The same technology, however, presents problems of its own, furthering the still-existing digital divide and raising questions about sustainability, proprietary platforms, and the ownership of digital heritage. These issues are being addressed in various ways. Murkutu, for example, an open access platform, was developed as a " grassroots project aiming to empower communities to manage, share, narrate, and exchange their digital heritage in culturally relevant and ethically-minded ways … an open source platform flexible enough to meet the needs of diverse communities who want to manage and share their digital cultural heritage in their own way, on their own terms."[27] National and regional websites, such as the UK's Community Archives and Heritage Group, provide new platforms while facilitating accessibility through their tools in more precise terms.[28]

Conclusion: The Radical Impact of Community Archives

In a wide-ranging analysis in *Archival Science*, Caswell identifies five areas in which community archives could (and should) impact traditional practice. These areas, which Caswell sees as core principles, include participation (community involvement), shared stewardship (partnering with other institutions), multiplicity (diversity of materials), activism (community empowerment), and reflexivity (self-reflection and dialogue). She writes,

Although community-based memory work is as diverse as the organizations that practice it, and not all such organizations mirror all of these principles, the principles do reflect shared commonalities that emerge across many such organizations. In outlining these principles, I am advocating that community-centric values trickle up to mainstream archival practice in relation to records documenting human rights abuse.[29]

With these principles in mind, how might community archives change archivists' approach to their own standard theory and practice as well as influence the public's understanding of archives? Here are a few areas to consider:

- Archives as sites of social justice where the act of keeping archives becomes a form of political activity through collecting records that promote the values and identities of marginalized groups
- Archives as sites of empowerment and advocacy through the ability of communities to document themselves
- Archives as key advocates of identity and collective memory
- Revising the official master narratives of traditional archives with the counter-narratives of under-documented parts of society
- Positioning archives as welcoming and accessible spaces by opening archives to all perspectives
- Re-examining traditional archival principles such as provenance, custody and organization, making them responsive to the access needs of multiple communities

That traditional archives are absorbing some of the lessons of community archives is clear in the efforts, particularly by academic archives, to create focused community collections featuring community voices. At the University of North Carolina's Southern History Collection, for example, their recently funded initiative, "Building A Model For All Users: Transforming Archive Collections Through Community-Driven Archives," proposes to form "meaningful, mutually supportive partnerships [with community archives] that provide communities with the tools and resources to safeguard and represent their own histories."[30] The University of Massachusetts Boston, Archives and Special Collections supports the Mass Memories Road Show, an "event-based public history project that digitizes family photos and memories shared by the people of Massachusetts."[31] Increasingly, as archives and special collections focus on the underdocumented communities in their midst, they are also learning that they need the agreement, cooperation, and active participation of these groups in order to build authentic collections.

The ever-modulating roles of community archives suggest close and enduring affinities between communities and the records they create, an affinity and informal relationship that archivists in the past have often set aside, preferring to put archives into neat and manageable boxes rather than deal with that often sprawling messy relationship on its own terms. But it is through this relationship between people and their records that community archives—by becoming spaces that accommodate multiple voices in multiple modalities and visions—represent a further step in the evolution of archival thinking, one that moves away from, repudiates, and disrupts formalized hierarchical structures toward a recognition that archives, no matter where they are kept, are the records of society as a whole.

Notes

1. Rebecka Sheffield, "Community Archives," in *Currents of Archival Thinking*, 2d. ed. 351–372.
2. Anonymous comments by the author's students at the Simmons University School of Library and Information Science.
3. Terry Cook, "Evidence, memory, identity, and community: four shifting archival paradigms," *Archival Science*, 13 (June 2013), 118.
4. Andrew Flinn, "Community Histories, Community Archives: Some Opportunities and Challenges," *Journal of the Society of Archivists*, 28 (October 2007), 153.
5. Many of these values have been adapted from "What is Community," http://infed.org/mobi/community/
6. Howard Rheingold, *The Virtual Community, Homesteading on the Electronic Frontier* (Basic Books, 1993).
7. Andrew Flinn, Mary Stevens, and Elizabeth Shepherd, 'Whose Memories, Whose Archives? Independent Community Archives, Autonomy and the Mainstream', *Archival Science*, 9 (2009), 71–86.
8. Provenance refers to the creators of records be it a person, a family, or an organization. The principle of provenance dictates that collections of records be organized within the context of those creators and that furthermore they be maintained [if possible] in the order in which they were created.
9. Michelle Caswell, Marika Cifor, and Mario H. Ramirez, "To Suddenly Discover Yourself Existing": Uncovering the Impact of Community Archives, *American Archivist*, 79 (Spring/Summer 2016): 57.
10. The Lesbian Herstory Archives was founded in 1975 in a private residence. It is still maintained in a private residence today. For more information, see http://www.lesbianherstoryarchives.org/
11. Kathy Eales, "Community archives: Introduction," *South African Archives Journal*, 40 1998, Vol. 40.

12. Chris Pearson, "A Community Captured," *Public Library Journal*, Summer 2001, Vol. 16 Issue 2, p39–39, 1p.
13. Pelham Barr, "Libraries as Community Archives in Wartime," *Library Journal* 67 (1942): 588.
14. Anne Gilliland and Andrew Flinn, "Community Archives, What are we really talking about," CIRN Prato Community Informatics Conference 2013, Prato, Italy, Centre for Community Networking Research, Centre for Social Informatics, Monash University, 2013.
15. https://www.communityarchives.org.uk/
16. Libraries and Archives Canada, Documentary Heritage Communities Program, https://www.bac-lac.gc.ca/eng/services/documentary-heritage-communities-program/Pages/dhcp-portal.aspx
17. "The Community Archive, National Register of Archives and Manuscripts," http://thecommunityarchive.org.nz/
18. NAA, "Community Heritage Grants," http://www.naa.gov.au/about-us/partnerships/chg/index.aspx
19. SAHA, Archive for Justice, http://www.saha.org.za/about_saha.htm
20. GALA, "History of GALA," https://gala.co.za/about/history/
21. Student projects included embedding themselves into a small historical society near Boston, participating in a statewide documentation project spearheaded by a Boston-based university, and volunteering at a zine library operating out of a storefront.
22. Kathy Eales, "Community archives: introduction," *South African Archives Journal* (1998) 40.
23. Richard Pearce-Moses, *A Glossary of Archival and Records Terminology* (Chicago: Society of American Archivists, 2005). https://www2.archivists.org/glossary/terms/a
24. Ibid., https://www2.archivists.org/glossary/terms/r/record
25. Terry Cook, Evidence, Memory, Identity, and Community: Four shifting archival paradigms, *Archival Science*, 13 (June 2013): 95–120.
26. https://www.projectsave.org/
27. http://mukurtu.org/about/
28. Community Archives and Heritage Group, "CAHG Vision Statement," https://www.communityarchives.org.uk/content/about/history-and-purpose
29. Michele Caswell, "Toward a Survivor-Centered Approach to Human Rights Archives: Lessons from Community-Based Archives." *Archival Science* 14: 3–4 (2014): 310–311.
30. The Lewis Round Wilson Special Collection, "Community-Driven Archives Overview," https://library.unc.edu/wilson/shc/community-driven-archives/about/
31. Joseph P. Healey Library, "Mass Memories Road Show," http://openarchives.umb.edu/digital/collection/p15774coll6

8

Digital Archives for African Studies: Making Africa's Written Heritage Visible

Fallou Ngom

Misrepresentations of Literacy in Africa

For centuries, many Western-trained scholars (including Africans) have considered sub-Saharan Africa to be a region with no written tradition, partly because they are unaware of the long history of writing in the region. Many assume that writing emerged in sub-Saharan Africa as a result of the European colonization in the nineteenth century. In reality, sub-Saharan Africans had been reading and writing in multiple languages and writing systems long before the colonial encounter. Many in the region had begun authoring important documents in Arabic, their native tongues using Ajami scripts (enriched forms of the classical Arabic script), and other locally invented writing systems long before Europeans set foot on the continent.[1]

Many early visitors in sub-Saharan Africa and colonial administrators were aware of the literacies that had existed in the region prior to European colonization and endure to this day. For example, Baron Roger (1787–1849), who served as French Governor of Senegal from 1822 to 1820, reported that there were "more negroes who could read and write in Arabic in 1828 than French peasants who could read and write in French." Francis Moore (death date, 1756) of the Royal African Company of England, Ibn Battuta (1304–1369), Leo Africanus (1494–1554), Mongo Park (1771–1806), and other travelers reported the significance of Islamic education and literacy in many places they

F. Ngom (✉)
Boston University, Boston, MA, USA
e-mail: fngom@bu.edu

visited in sub-Saharan Africa.[2] In 1882, over 1000 inhabitants of four Senegalese cities (Dakar, Rufisque, Saint-Louis, and Gorée) petitioned against the compulsory military service to the colonial French government. Those with traditional local names signed the petition using their Wolof Ajami script, and those with names of Islamic origin signed in Arabic. Arabic and Ajami had been used in correspondences and diplomatic relations between sub-Saharan African and Europeans in their initial encounters, including in treaties and signatures of official documents (Fig. 8.1).[3]

The current misrepresentation of the forms of literacies and literacy rates in sub-Saharan Africa in academia and the media is due to several factors. These include (1) prejudice and ignorance, (2) the Eurocentric definition of literacy and the resulting overemphasis on African oral traditions that began as the balance of power shifted in favor of European imperial powers in Africa, and (3) the usual separation of North Africa from sub-Saharan Africa in academia and the media. As Kane (2012) notes, the works of many *non-Europhone intellectuals of Africa* have been dismissed partly because many European Orientalists and Arab scholars consider their insights to be of little or no scholarly benefit, and many are unaware of their rich archives of written materials in Arabic and Ajami scripts. One of the consequences of ignoring their works, Kane notes, is reflected in the historiography of Africa; there are few historians interested in Arabic or Ajami sources of Africa because many assume that most of the sources on Africa's past are either oral or written in European languages.[4]

The narrow definition of literacy as the ability to read and write only in European languages or the ability to use the Roman script, which has been imposed on most of sub-Saharan Africa since the colonial era and inherited by postcolonial African elites, governments, and international organizations, continues to treat as illiterate millions of non-Europhone Africans who had been reading and writing all sorts of documents in both Arabic and Ajami scripts before and after European colonization. Because Ajami writings have been generally excluded in official literacy statistics, there is no comprehensive census of literacy rates in Ajami scripts in Africa. However, a limited census in Labé, Guinea Conakry, shows that over 70% of the population are literate in the local Fula Ajami writing system (including 20–25% of women); in Diourbel, Matam, and Podor in Senegal, about 70% are literate in Wolof Ajami (called *Wolofal*), and in Hausa-speaking areas of Niger and Nigeria, over 80% of the population are Hausa Ajami literates.[5] Another limited census conducted in 1999 revealed that in Guinea Conakry, 93% of a sample of 77 male Quranic school graduates claimed competence in their Fula Ajami writing system. In Senegal, between 25% and 75% of male adults in villages

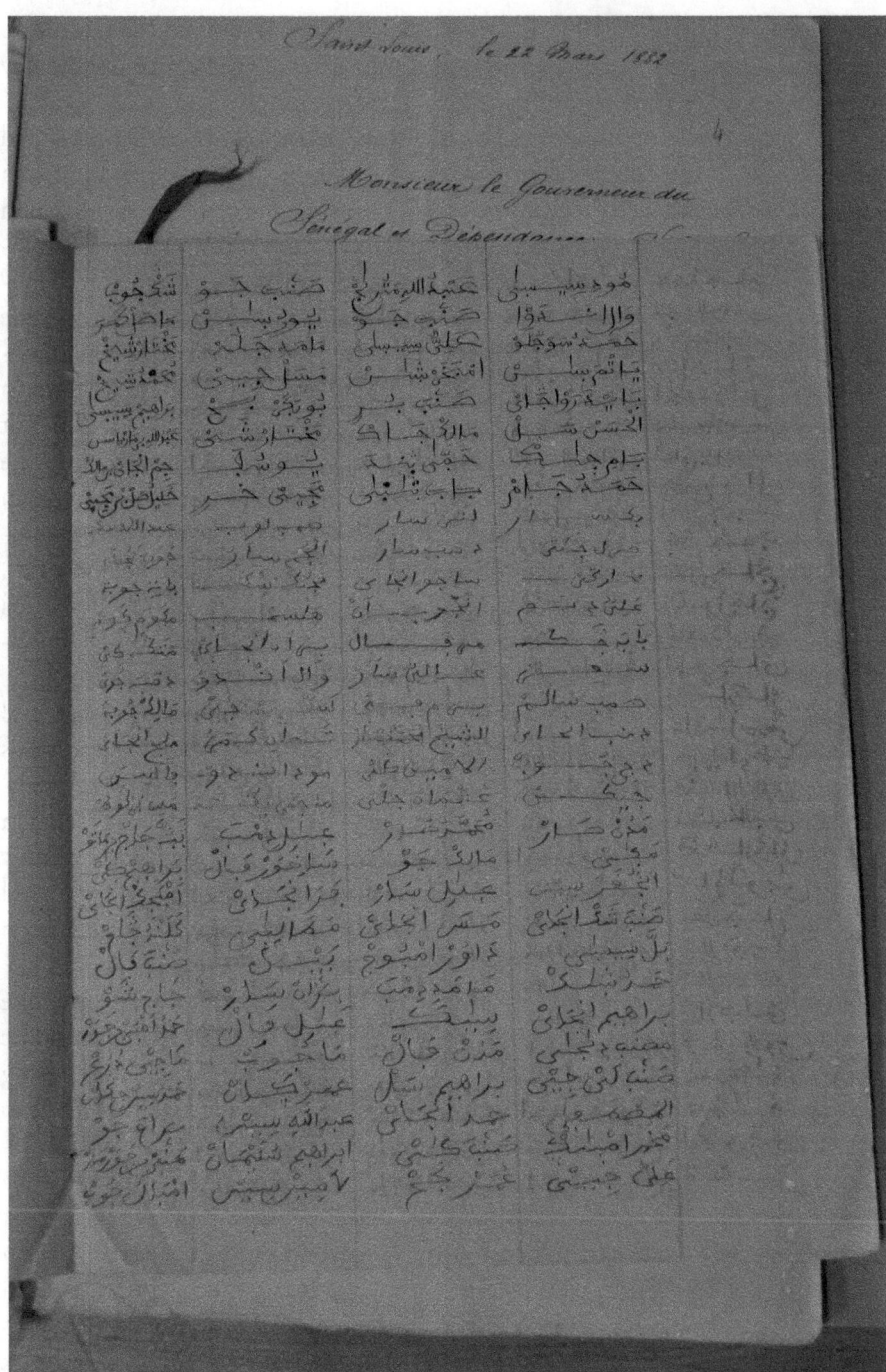

Fig. 8.1 Excerpt from the petition of the inhabitants of Rufisque, Senegal, sent to the colonial Governor of French West Africa in 1882 with signatures in Arabic and Wolof Ajami script. (Source: Lettre des habitants de Rufisque, 6 avril 1882, Sénégal, XVI, 1a, Archives Nationales d'Outre Mer, Aix-en-Provence, France)

contacted, and between 10% and 25% of women, also claimed the same level of literacy in Ajami. In all cases, the proportions were well above the literacy rate in French for the predominantly rural communities.[6]

The Eurocentric definition of literacy, which disregards local literacies and important written sources of knowledge, was one of the tools that European colonial powers used to legitimize their "civilizing mission" in sub-Saharan Africa. Although many of the first European travelers acknowledged the significance of literacy in sub-Saharan Africa, the region had to be reframed as illiterate and uneducated to justify the European imperial colonial project and the imposition of Europe's models of literacy and education. Postcolonial sub-Saharan African states, which largely emerged between the 1950s and 1960s in the spaces European colonial powers charted during the Scramble for Africa at the 1884 Berlin Conference, never succeeded in reversing or correcting the Eurocentric definition of literacy and its enduring legacies in Africa. Instead, postcolonial African states have perpetuated the Eurocentric definition of literacy through the educational systems they inherited from the colonial apparatus.

As a result, many Africanists today (including those trained in postcolonial African institutions) do not take seriously or are unaware of the non-Europhone written archives in their own countries due to the Eurocentric education system they received that has shaped their thinking, teaching, and research frameworks. Using the popular West African storytelling traditions of the *griot caste* (caste of bards), they often overemphasize African oral traditions as the most important and sole legitimate source of "authentic" African knowledge. Thus, they only engage oral and European sources that they know in their works. In so doing, they have inadvertently replicated and expanded the flawed colonial definition of literacy and the perception of sub-Saharan Africa as the exceptional land of exclusive orality.

The usual treatment of North Africa and the Middle East as forming one Islamic ethnolinguistic and historical zone, which is reflected in academic programs such as MENA (Middle East and North Africa), and the resulting distancing of North Africa from sub-Saharan Africa have also contributed to the widespread misrepresentations of sub-Saharan Africa's written and intellectual heritage. The usual separation of North Africa from sub-Saharan Africa ignores the long historical, ethnolinguistic, religious, and intellectual ties that have connected these two parts of Africa's natural landmass. North African and sub-Saharan African peoples have been in contact in multiple ways and for different reasons for millennia. Sometimes their interactions were mutually beneficial, and other times they were bigoted and oppressive to the Black population, as reflected in the Moroccan conquest of Timbuktu in 1591 and the long trans-Saharan Islamic slave trade and its lasting legacy of racism toward Black people in North Africa and the Middle East.[7]

The existing evidence indicates that sub-Saharan and North Africans did not treat the great Sahara Desert, an insurmountable barrier. Instead, they construed it as a sea and saw their caravans as ships to transport people and goods northwards and southwards, including pilgrims, merchants, scholars, teachers, clerics, gold, and books.[8] The trade, religious, and intellectual ties between sub-Saharan Africa and North Africa resulted in the development of important cities, towns, and learning centers that brought together scholars, teachers, students, and merchants from various parts of Africa. The once wealthy cosmopolitan fabled city of Timbuktu in present-day Mali (also known as the City of the 333 Saints) had a vibrant multiracial, multiethnic, and multilingual intellectual community that rivaled any medieval European city.[9]

The Berber Andalusian author and diplomat, Hasan b. Muhammad al-Wazzan al-Zayyati better known as Leo Africanus (c.1494–c.1554), reported that the sale of books was the most lucrative business endeavor when he visited the thriving city of Timbuktu.[10] Though Timbuktu has become popular due to its numerous manuscript archives that have been the recent focus of scholars and the media, it was not unique. There have been other important learning centers with renowned scholars, poets, jurists, teachers, students, calligraphers, leather bookcase makers, book sellers, scribes, and copyists in many sub-Saharan societies for centuries.[11]

In sub-Saharan Africa, written archives in Arabic are as important as written sources in Ajami scripts because many local scholars are multilingual and multiliterate. Multilingualism and multiliteracy are often the norm in the region as many people live in multilingual communities and interact regularly with people (including colleagues and students) who speak, read, and write in Arabic as well as in their local Ajami scripts developed for their languages. Thus, many sub-Saharan African scholars have produced documents in both Arabic and Ajami scripts. These scholars include women such as Nana Asma'u (1793–1864) of Northern Nigeria, and Soxna May Mbàkke Sr. (1908–1964) of Senegal and her sister, Soxna May Mbàkke Jr. (1925–1999).[12]

Some of these scholars write in Arabic when addressing the Muslim intelligentsia within and beyond their communities, and produce poems and prose texts in their local languages using Ajami scripts when communicating with their local audiences, including when teaching their students new concepts.[13] The tradition of polyglottic competence (oral fluency and literacy in multiple languages and writing systems) that characterizes many non-Europhone scholars of Africa is reflected in a poem by Moor Kayre (1869–1951), one of the most famous Wolof Ajami poets of Senegal, West Africa. Kayre celebrates the stellar training he received from his teacher, Ahmadu Bamba (1853–1927), with the following words: "[Oh Bamba] you made us [so] erudite till we rival Arabs [in their own Arabic poetry] and can compose poems both in Arabic and Ajami."[14] African scholars like Kayre are proud of their polyglottic competence and education, which they celebrate as a badge of honor and marks of their intellectual sophistication. Paradoxically, they remain excluded from official literacy statistics, and their extensive written archives are omitted in the story of sub-Saharan Africa.

Arabic and Ajami Writing Traditions of Africa

Thanks to the pioneering works of late John Hunwick, O'Fahey, and their colleagues, and the growing popularity of the Timbuktu manuscripts, an important part of sub-Saharan Africa's rich written heritage in Arabic has been uncovered.[15] Hunwick and his colleagues focused primarily on Arabic literatures of Africa, leaving African Ajami literatures as secondary. Their works show how Arabic had served as *the Latin of Africa* for over 800 years before European colonization and how the documents uncovered to date demonstrate a vibrant intellectual life and important debates on society in sub-Saharan Africa that have been ignored by the overwhelming majority of Europhone intellectuals.[16] Over the last two decades scholars have begun to turn their attention to Ajami sources, which complement oral, Arabic, and Europhone sources of Africa.

The development of Ajami writing traditions in Africa is not different from those found in other communities around the world where the Arabic script was brought through Islam. Just as the Latin script spread around the world through Christianity and was enriched to write many languages, the Arabic script also spread around the world through Islam and was enriched to write many languages in predominately Muslim societies.[17] As Lüpke and Bao-Diop note, African Ajami literacies are primarily acquired as a by-product of acquiring literacy in Arabic in traditional Quranic schools in Africa.[18] For centuries local traditional Quranic schools (which are different from modern Arabic and Islamic schools largely funded by Arab states in the Persian Gulf) have produced what I have called *Quran-derived dual literacies* in sub-Saharan Africa: literacy in classical Arabic and Ajami scripts.[19] These dual literacy skills are typically acquired at the elementary levels of traditional Quranic education when students are taught the classical Arabic script of the Quran, how to put them together, vocalization diacritics, and are tasked to memorize the entire Quran using reed pens, black ink, and wooden boards like those in Fig. 8.2.

Fig. 8.2 Wooden boards used in traditional Quranic schools in Senegambia. (Picture taken in Ziguinchor, Senegal, by Fallou Ngom in January 2018)

The primary goal of the elementary phase of traditional Quranic education in sub-Saharan Africa is to ingest the word of God (the Quran) in the heart and the body of students through memorization so that each of them becomes what Ware calls a *Walking Quran*, that is, a moral and spiritual exemplar as taught by the Quran and epitomized by Prophet Muhammad.[20] While classical Arabic literacy is taught in traditional Quranic schools using wooden boards, teaching Ajami literacy is not generally part of the Quranic school curriculum. Ajami literacy is a grassroots form of literacy that is acquired through regular exposure to the materials that circulate in local learning centers and communities, including educational texts in the local Ajami scripts; comments and translations in Ajami; exegesis of Islamic texts in Ajami; popular poems of great local Ajami poets habitually read, recited, and chanted in local communities; family records; and personal correspondences, to name only these.

Since the elementary Quranic education phase focuses on memorization and learning the classical Arabic script, students can generally read and write classical Arabic without speaking or understanding Arabic, and they can also generally read and write in their own language using the local Ajami script by the time they complete their elementary studies. Thus, those who stop at this elementary level to learn other skills and crafts and become farmers, shopkeepers, tailors, carpenters, and the like use their Ajami literacy skills to document their lives and activities in local languages. They produce all sorts of documents dealing with their religious and non-religious preoccupations, including financial records, letters and notes, and medicinal recipes, among other documents.

After the elementary phase of traditional Quranic studies in sub-Saharan Africa, some students pursue advanced studies in different domains, including astrology, exegesis of liturgical texts, law, Sufism, grammar, logic, poetry, medicine, numerology, and calligraphy. Some conduct additional peripatetic learning to study other specialized knowledge with renowned experts in the region. The peripatetic learning tradition has brought many African scholars and families from different countries and ethnolinguistic groups together. After completing their studies, they usually hold important positions in society. They become respected scholars, teachers, healers, diviners, advisors, scribes, religious leaders, and judges, among other notable professions. In contrast to those whose education ended at the elementary level of Quranic education, these people are competent in Arabic, and they communicate in writing in both Arabic and Ajami depending on their audiences and objectives.[21]

The 136-page bilingual text in Arabic-Hausa Ajami from which the excerpt below is taken is a sample of what Hunwick has called "market editions" because they are readily available in local markets.[22] Kurfi digitized this particular text that belongs to the genre called *Asirai* (Hausa: Secrets) from Sayyida Raliya Muhammad, the daughter of a famous local Hausa healer and diviner in Northern Nigeria. The document contains talismanic resources, techniques for diagnosing and treating various kinds of illnesses, and divination methods which are widely practiced by both men and women in Northern Nigeria.[23]

The complementarity between Arabic and Ajami literacy in this genre is reflected in Fig. 8.3. The title of the document is written in Arabic, and the information about the author at the bottom is written in Hausa Ajami. The image also captures important aspects of Hausa society. The bearded man seated represents a local healer and diviner (Hausa: Malam) who serves much like a physician and therapist in America where one goes for consultation, diagnosis, treatment of various ailments, or counsel for real and imagined concerns. The users of such texts are diverse. They include males and females as well as children and adults as reflected in the image of the woman with her

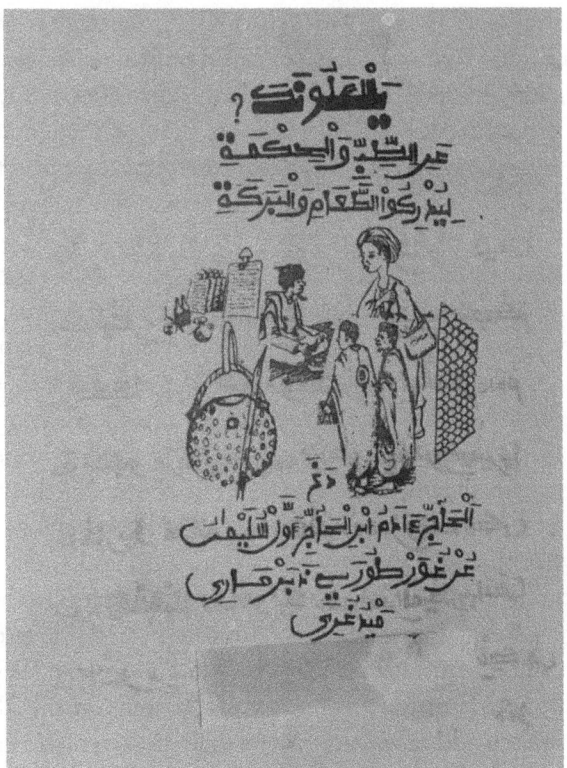

Fig. 8.3 A sample bilingual Arabic-Hausa Ajami document from Mustapha Kurfi's collection illustrating dual literacies in Northern Nigeria. (Source: https://open.bu.edu/handle/2144/11722)

two sons visiting the seated man. The image also reflects aspects of the material culture of dual literacy (Arabic and Ajami) in Hausa society as the inkwells, reed pen, and wooden tablets indicate.

Languages that have been written with the enriched forms of the Arabic script commonly called Ajami abound in Africa, Asia, and Europe. They include Spanish, Portuguese, Afrikaans, Fula, Hausa, Kurdish, Malay, Mande languages, Osmanli (Ottoman Turkish), Pashto, Persian, Sindhi, Swahili, Urdu, Uyghur, and Wolof, to name only a few. In Africa, there are over 80 languages with Ajami records.[24] Brigaglia and Nobili show that the culture of writing in the Arabic alphabet has existed in West Africa since the early eleventh century.[25] The earliest document showing African Ajami writing featuring Songhai, dates from the thirteenth century, and testifies that a conventionalized Ajami writing system was present from the sixteenth century onward.[26] African Ajami documents dating back to the sixteenth century were uncovered in 2000 in Niger.[27] Many West African slaves brought the dual literacies they acquired in Africa prior to their enslavement to the Americas. Arabic and Ajami materials produced by African slaves have been uncovered in the Americas.[28] In South Africa, Afrikaans was first written in the Jawi Ajami script by Muslim Malay slaves.[29] However, many of the earliest Ajami manuscripts in Africa are lost due to enduring preservation challenges. Many manuscript owners I met in Africa between 2014 and 2018 reported that local climatic conditions and hazards such as fire, rain, mice, and termites had destroyed some of their oldest and most precious manuscripts.

Historically, Ajami writing systems developed from the Arabic script in the same way the Arabic script itself developed from the Aramaic script. Using a corpus of pre-Islamic Arabic-language inscriptions dated from 328 C.E. and 568 C.E., Daniels shows how Nabataean Arabs once modified the ancient Aramaic script with diacritics to represent the sounds of their language that did not exist in Aramaic. The original Aramaic letters largely retained their shapes, but what changed was that Nabatean Arabs added diacritics to represent Arabic sounds that did not exist in Aramaic.[30] Ajami traditions in Africa and elsewhere around the world have followed the same process that had produced the Arabic script itself. From the Wolof people in West Africa to the Uyghur in China, Ajami practitioners typically rely on the 28 basic Arabic letters to which they add new diacritics (usually dots, which I call "the powerful dots") to represent the sounds in their languages that do not exist in Arabic. The following table shows an example of how the Arabic script has been enriched in Wolof society to produce an extensive body of Wolof Ajami literature in prose and poetry.

The two letters in the second column of Fig. 8.4 reflect the lack of standardization of Ajami writing systems in Africa. Thus, some writers alternate between two letters to represent one sound of their language. Professional scribes and scholars, however, tend to have their own conventions, and their texts contain few variations between letter and sound. While the lack of standardization of Ajami writing systems in Africa has made deciphering Ajami texts difficult for outsiders, it has not impeded the flourishing of Ajami writing traditions. This is because local Ajami users are familiar with the variations in their writing systems, local conventions, and the styles in the texts that circulate in their communities. Market editions of Ajami books are produced, copied, and sold in market places and specialized bookstores.[31]

In order to read African Ajami texts, outsiders need several skills. These include (1) knowledge of the African language in the document, (2) knowledge of the classical Arabic letters that have been enriched with diacritics to write specific vowels, consonants, and tones (for tonal languages such as

Wolof Phonemes with no Arabic counterparts	Wolofal letters used for these phonemes
1. p	ݒ
2. g	ݘ, ک
3. ñ	ݘج
4. ŋ	غ, ݘ
5. č	ݘج
6. mp	ب, ݒ
7. nt	ن, ت
8. nj	ݘج
9. nk	ن, ک
10. mb	ݒب
11. nd	ݘ, د
12. nč	ݘج
13. ng	غ, ݘ
14. nq	ف, ق

Fig. 8.4 Most common Wolofal (Wolof Ajami) letters used to write Wolof consonants that do not exist in Arabic. (Source: Fallou Ngom (2010, 14–15))

Yoruba), (3) knowledge of the segmentation conventions used in the text as an entire phrase can be written as one word in Ajami texts, (4) knowledge of the society, culture, and history (including worldview, metaphors, maxims, riddles, and heroes and heroines), and (5) differentiating language from script. Ajami texts are easily confused with Arabic texts because they look alike, and writers often begin and end with Islamic doxologies in good Arabic as customary in Muslim writings, whether dealing with religious or non-religious subjects. Thus, uninformed readers may not know that the body of the text is actually an African language written with an enriched form of the Arabic script.

The confusion of Ajami with Arabic texts has led to mischaracterizations of Ajami texts as "bad Arabic" because of the assumption that the authors attempted to write Arabic but failed. Such misunderstandings are reflected in some libraries. Some of the oldest African Ajami texts held in Europhone libraries are mislabeled as *arabe indéchiffrable* ("undecipherable Arabic").[32] Just because the Arabic script is used to write a language does not mean that the language has changed. To use metaphor, "script serves as clothing for a language." It does not change the fundamental nature of the language. History tells us that a language may put on the Arabic, Roman, or Cyrillic script or other scripts as clothing for a period of time, which may change depending on political, ideological, or economic factors. Turkish, for example, was once written in Ajami script before the Roman alphabet was adopted for the language.[33] Sometimes, a language may wear several types of clothing simultaneously. For example, Wolof, Fula, Yoruba, and many African languages are now written in the Roman script in government-supported programs, while their centuries-old grassroots Ajami writing traditions continue to flourish despite official backing.

Besides the flawed definition of literacy that treats Ajami users as illiterate, African Ajami literacies have been nearly invisible to many Western scholars due to lack of trust and the *observer's paradox*.[34] Owners of precious Ajami manuscripts are not always willing to share their materials with outsiders they do not trust, partly because they do not understand why the sudden interest in their written traditions and archives that have been dismissed for centuries by Western-trained scholars, local elites, or NGOs. Lüpke and Bao-Diop report that the presence of a European female researcher with a young female Cameroonian Christian assistant in 2004 triggered negative local responses regarding the use of Ajami and the reach of Quranic schools. But when they emphasized their interest in Ajami literacy, assured interviewees that they were not sent by the government or an NGO, and hired a male Muslim guide who made contact in the absence of the European female researcher, the *observer's paradox* was overcome. By making these methodological changes, they were able to gain the trust of a number of stakeholders of Ajami writing and have access to documents in Fulfulde and Hausa Ajami.[35]

Making Visible Non-Europhone Archives of Africa

Digital technology is helping to make visible Africa's abundant written heritage that has previously been overlooked by scholars in the humanities and social sciences in ways unanticipated a few decades ago. Today, Africa's written archives in Arabic, Ajami, and other indigenous scripts such as Ge'ez and Bamum are being preserved and made freely available to scholars, students, and the public worldwide through digital technology thanks to the Endangered Archives Programme (EAP) at the British Library. The EAP is leading the effort of digitizing and making available important endangered archives scattered in different parts of the world. It has supported over 350 digital projects to preserve endangered documentary heritages around the world.[36]

In the United States, Boston University's African Ajami Library (AAL) is the leader in the digital preservation and dissemination of Africa's written archives in Ajami scripts. Founded in 2011 with support from the EAP, AAL is a collaborative initiative between Boston University and the West African Research Center (WARC) in Senegal, West Africa. The AAL is envisioned as a continental open access public repository of Africa's Ajami archives for teaching and research about Africa.[37] While it focuses on Africa's Ajami archives, the repository also includes a substantial number of important Arabic manuscripts authored in sub-Saharan Africa. This is because, as noted earlier, many African writers are polyglots who have produced documents of equal importance in Arabic and their local languages using Ajami scripts. Thus, Arabic and Ajami texts are often mixed in their archives, which are generally kept in their private home libraries. The oldest ones are transmitted from generation to generation through inheritance, which causes some archives to be split between heirs who live in different places.

From 2011 to now, over 30,000 pages of African texts in Arabic and Ajami scripts have been digitized and preserved by the AAL team, making Boston University the home of the largest and most varied digital collections of Africa's written heritage in Arabic-based scripts in North America. The archives in the AAL include four major types of documents: (1) Arabic texts without glosses; (2) Arabic texts with explicatory glosses in Arabic; (3) Arabic texts with bilingual explicatory glosses in Arabic and Ajami scripts; and (4) extensive Ajami texts in seven major African languages. The current collections include 1000 pages of Fuuta Jalon Ajami texts; 1000 pages of Hausa Ajami texts; over 5400 pages of Wolof Ajami texts; over 6000 Malagasy Sorabe Ajami texts; 1000 pages of Fulfulde and Kanuri Ajami texts; and over 18,000 pages of mixed Mandinka Ajami and Arabic texts. Most of these manuscripts were in danger of being lost due to nonoptimal preservation conditions and the death of authors and owners (Fig. 8.5).

The watermarks on some pages of Cissé's manuscript indicate that a British company made the paper in 1822.[38] The manuscript is a poem written in Arabic with extensive interlinear and marginal glosses. Some glosses are vocalized and written in Mandinka Ajami. Red ink is used to highlight key words and letters. There are also small decorative illustrations in red and black ink with Arabic words written inside them. The small designs include the following shapes: square, rectangle, and circle.[39] Keba Dabo Cissé died shortly after my first visit in 2010. His son, Abdou Khadre Cissé, allowed our team to digitize the manuscript in 2018. Several scholars whose archives we have digitized between 2010 and now have died, which highlights the urgency of preserving these written legacies before they are lost.

Ajami archives complement Arabic manuscripts and offer local perspectives that are not often represented in Arabic and Europhone sources as reflected in the popular poem *Taxmiis bub Wolof*, which is widely recited and chanted among the Wolof people of Senegal. The poem was written by one of the most famous Wolof Ajami poets named Muusaa Ka, who was frustrated with some of his Arabophone colleagues who disparage Ajami scholars and poets like

Fig. 8.5 Mixed Arabic and Mandinka Ajami manuscripts from Casamance, Senegal. According to the current owner (Abdou Karin Thiam), some of the manuscripts in this archive are over 200 years old as he is the sixth-generation heir. He inherited them from his father, Nimbaly Thiam, who died in the Mina stampede that occurred in the 2015 pilgrimage in Mecca, Saudi Arabia. (Source: Picture taken by Fallou Ngom in January 2018)

him. He decided to challenge their claims of the superiority of Arabs and Arabic and to enjoin them to construe and embrace ethnolinguistic diversity as a form of divine mercy.[40]

Far from being an outdated tradition, Ajami literacy continues to expand in many parts of sub-Saharan Africa, primarily through Quranic education and secondarily through a process I have called *music-derived literacy* in which people are first mesmerized by the beauty of Ajami poems of great masters they regularly hear recited and chanted in their communities, which leads some to memorize the poems and subsequently learn the Ajami scripts in which the poems were written.[41] Digital technology is now expanding the phenomenon of music-derived literacy as the figure below illustrates (Fig. 8.6).

8 Digital Archives for African Studies: Making Africa's Written...

Romanized transcription	
Sa daara yi di lopitaan	ku ràgg war na lay dagaan
ku ñów nga jox ko garab mu naan	doktoor bi yaa faj xarnu bi
Ràggi xol ak ràggi yaram	yaa koy ràggal ñu xéy gërëm
Ñu ràgg war nañu lay gërëm	ngir yaa wéral seen xarnu bi
Fekkoon nga réew mi defi ndóol	fekkoon nga ñépp defi gool
Yaa tax banuy niinal i bool	yafal nga mbooleem xarnu bi
Fekkoon nga ñii defi lafañ	ñii daanu far ba ne fëlëñ
Ñoo ku ñu ñaan jabar ñu bañ	ñii mel ni man ci xarnu bi
Yaa dikk jag ña fi dàmmoon	jénganti mbir ya fi dëngoon
Yékkati néeg ya suufe woon	bañ man a ànd ak xarnu bi
Amal nga gaa yu amuloon	xamal nga gaa yu xamuloon
Feeñal nga mbir yu nëbbuwoon	dekkal nga ruuhi xarnu bi.

English translation	
Your schools are hospitals	where all the sick people must go
You treat anyone who comes	you are the physician of the century
Sicknesses of the heart and of the body	you cure them all till people are thankful
The sick must be grateful to you	for you have cured their century
You found the country impoverished	and found everybody miserable
You fed us with luxurious food	and nourished everybody in the century
You found some crippled	and some completely depressed
Others were refused wives	and some were [unimportant] like me
You mended those who were broken	straightened what was not straight
Elevated homes that were modest	till they could cope with the century
You gave the have-nots	educated the uneducated
You revealed concealed treasures	you have revived the soul of the century.

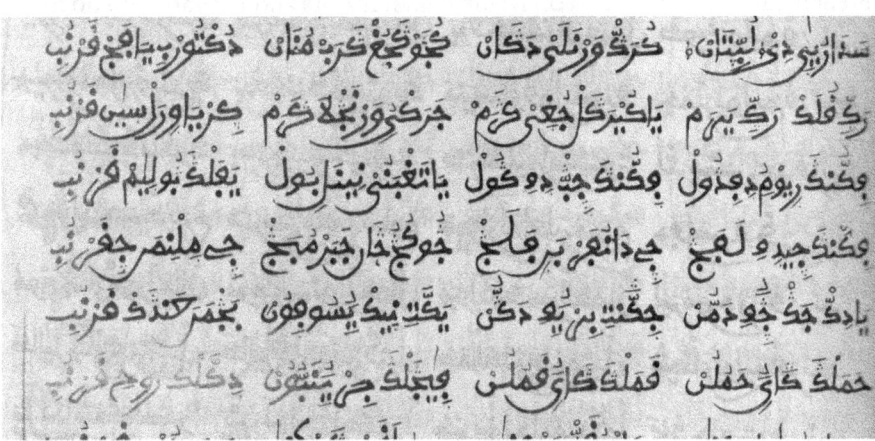

Fig. 8.6 Excerpt from Muusaa Ka's popular Wolof Ajami poem called *Xarnu bi* (The Century) written in 1929 during the Great Depression

The excerpt comes from a 271-verse poem written in Wolof Ajami script.[42] As common in Muslim writings, such poems begin and end with Islamic doxologies in classical Arabic. The beauty of the poem is difficult to render appropriately in English. However, Wolof native speakers who read or listen to its recitation or chanting by a local professional singer of Ajami poetry (Wolof: jàngkat) would be moved by its rich contents and beauty, especially its rhymes (noticeable in the screenshot and the Romanized transcription) and its insightful metaphors that resonate with local audiences. The poet uses popular metaphors throughout the poem to communicate effectively his message to local Wolof speakers, including treating Bamba, his deceased teacher and spiritual guide, as the greatest physician for the physical and spiritual ailments of the century. Written poems like this one are meant to be recited and chanted. They can deal simultaneously with religious and nonreligious subjects, thus challenging the boundaries between orality and written literature and between religious and secular spheres. These domains are entwined and complementary rather than separate and mutually exclusive in the worldview of non-Europhone African writers and their audiences.

The poet documents in great detail local experiences and his interpretations of the impacts of the 1929 Great Depression, which coincided with a period of serious drought in his society.[43] He captures the challenges of the era, including the suffering of farmers, the generalized poverty and hunger and the resulting shamelessness, and lack of moral values and faith he observed in his society. He also offers his perception of the impact of the crisis on the colonial French administration and on Mauritanian Moors and beggars who no longer received their usual gifts from the once generous, wealthy folk in the community. He ties the challenging social conditions of the era to the death in 1927 of their venerated teacher and spiritual guide, Ahmadu Bamba. He describes the magnitude of the crisis, recalls Bamba's teachings and positive impact, and prays in his name for a swift resolution of their predicaments.

The new generations of Bamba's followers are now time-aligning recitations and songs of such Ajami poems with their written versions online to allow listeners both in Africa and the diaspora to hear the message, see the Ajami texts, and learn the letters and verses in the texts. They also time-align Bamba's classical Arabic poems with their recited and chanted versions, thus showing that multimedia digital technology is now expanding both Ajami and Arabic literacy in physical and virtual spaces in Africa and the diaspora. The thousands of individuals who regularly view and listen to time-aligned Arabic and Ajami poems online illustrate both the popularity of such Ajami poems and the significance of music-derived literacy as one of the new areas of research and teaching that these non-Europhone sources of Africa are opening up.

Scholars, students, and the public stand to gain a lot of insights by engaging Ajami sources of Africa. Ajami sources of Africa can enrich the works of many people in multiple ways. Their forms and contents are varied and rich. They include poetry and prose dealing with an array of issues. They document old and new local preoccupations, including religious, intellectual, social, and political issues as well as local mundane day-to-day experiences of both the elites and masses. The recently uncovered records of African Ajami manuscripts include discussions on the meaning of life on earth and the destiny of the soul after death; astrology, numerology, and jurisprudence; metaphysics and ethics; war and peace; European in Africa and local responses; local perspectives on major world events in which Africans were involved (including World War I and II); the value of education and knowledge and social responsibility; satirical, polemical, and protest poetry; talismanic techniques for protection against real or imagined foes; medicinal recipes; road signs and advertisements; historical records and speeches; bureaucratic, diplomatic texts, and treaties with Europeans; texts on grammar and foreign language teaching; biographies, eulogies of iconic leaders; genealogies; correspondences, family journals, and business transactions; and visual arts (including calligraphy).

Some of the recently digitized materials hosted in the AAL digital repository include translations of the Quran in Wolof and the Bible in Hausa Ajami, Muammar Gaddafi's *Green Book*, which conveys his political philosophy in Hausa Ajami script, and documents that are similar in form and content to those produced by enslaved Africans in the Americas. There is substantial evidence that there were educated African Muslim slaves in Rio de Janeiro and Bahia in Brazil, Jamaica, Peru, Belize, Guyana, Bahamas, Trinidad, Haiti, and Maryland in the Americas. When the existing non-Europhone texts from Africa are studied along with those produced by literate African slaves such as Abu Bakr al–Siddiq who kept the records of the plantation of his master in Jamaica in English-Ajami (English written with the Arabic script), Omar Ibn Said of North Carolina, Ayub Suleiman Diallo of Maryland, Lamin Kaba of Georgia, and others, their insights will enhance contemporary research and teaching on transatlantic slavery and African traditions that have endured in the Americas.[44]

Conclusion

The significance of digital technology in enhancing teaching and research on Africa in the twenty-first century cannot be overstated. Digital technology has made possible the preservation, study, and dissemination of previously overlooked sources of knowledge that force revisions of various aspects of academic discourses on precolonial, colonial, and postcolonial Africa. The materials discussed in the chapter represent only a drop in the ocean of written archives in sub-Saharan Africa that remain unknown outside local communities. Thanks to digital technology, these written archives can no longer be dismissed easily. As of the completion of this chapter on January 9, 2020, over 408,000 people around the world have visited and downloaded materials from the African Ajami Library (AAL) digital repository.[45]

The downloads are instructive. They suggest that the downloaders are most interested in health-related and everyday social issues. The top items downloaded in the last six months are the bilingual Arabic-Hausa Ajami texts titled *Kundin Malam Musa Mai Almajirai* (Hausa: The Diary of Malam Musa Mai Almajirai), which deal with traditional Hausa Islamic medicine. The documents include techniques to diagnose and treat ailments and cover issues ranging from love and relationships, winning court cases to recipes for bravery and popularity. Some information, which only the authors and trained practitioners know, is omitted purposefully from the documents to deny unauthorized access to inexperienced individuals. As Mustapha Kurfi, who digitized the texts, notes, omission of information in this genre of African texts serves the same purpose as a modern-day password.[46]

Given the wealth of knowledge in these non-Europhone African sources, the major goals of the AAL team include (1) digitizing at least 100,000 pages of Arabic and Ajami texts by 2030 from all regions of Africa where such records exist and making them available to scholars and students worldwide; (2) training new generations of students and scholars who can decipher Ajami texts in major African languages and have full access to Africa's non-Europhone sources; (3) translating Africa's Ajami chefs-d'oeuvres into major European languages and Arabic; and (4) making Africa's non-Europhone written archives readily available worldwide so that they become part of the discourses on the continent in the same way European medieval and contemporary texts inform studies on Europe and its populations, cultures, and epistemological traditions.[47]

Notes

1. Helma Pasch, "Competing Scripts: The Introduction of the Roman Alphabet in Africa," *International Journal of the Sociology of Language* 191 (2008): 65–109; David Dalby, "Further Indigenous Scripts of West Africa: Manding, Wolof, and Fula Alphabets and Yoruba Holy-Writing," *African Language Studies* 10 (1969): 161–191; and Fallou Ngom, "West African Manuscripts in Arabic and African Languages and Digital Preservation," *Oxford Research Encyclopedia of African History*," edited by Thomas Spear, 1–28 (New York: Oxford University Press, 2017).

2. For more on this, see Ousmane Oumar Kane, *Beyond Timbuktu: An Intellectual history of Muslim West Africa* (Cambridge: Harvard University Press, 2016), 1–20.
3. See Archives Nationales d'Outre Mer, Aix-en-Provence, France: Annex to the convention between the Emperor of France and the King of Malagea, May 5, 1854, Sénégal, IV, 28a; Convention entre l'Empereur des Français et le Roi de Malaguia, 5 août 1854, Sénégal, IV, 28a; Lettre de Diaorine Boul Madeguène Samba, Chef des notables et des hommes libres, SG, SN, IV, 98b; Lettre des habitants de Gorée-Dakar, 22 mars 1882, Sénégal, XVI, 1a; Lettre des habitants de Rufisque, 6 avril 1882, Sénégal, XVI, 1a; Lettre des habitants de Saint-Louis, 22 mars 1882, Sénégal, XVI, 1a; and Palabre de traité entre le Roi de France et le Roi de Bar, 13 mai 1817, Sen/ IV/ 1.
4. Ousmane Oumar Kane, *Non-Europhone Intellectuals* (Dakar: CODESRIA, 2012), 8–9.
5. Mamadou Cissé, "Écrits et Écriture en Afrique de l'Ouest," *Revue Electronique Internationale des Sciences du Language* 6 (2007): 77–78.
6. Peter Easton, "Education and Koranic Literacy in West Africa," *IK Notes* 11 (August 1999), 1–4, http://documents.worldbank.org/curated/en/581121468329358898/pdf/23424-Replacement-file-IKNT11.pdf
7. Kane, *Beyond Timbuktu*, 6–7; Graziano Krätli and Ghislaine Lydon, eds, *The Trans-Saharan Book Trade: Manuscript Culture, Arabic Literacy and Intellectual History in Muslim Africa* (Leiden: The Netherlands: Brill, 2011); David Robinson, *Muslim Societies in African History* (New York: Cambridge University Press, 2004); Bruce S. Hall, *A History of Race in Muslim West Africa, 1600–1960* (New York: Cambridge University Press, 2011); and Chouki El Hamel, *Black Morocco: A History of Slavery, Race, and Islam* (New York: Cambridge University Press, 2013). For the trans-Saharan slave trade, see John Wright, *The Trans-Saharan Trade* (New York: Routledge, 2007).
8. Robinson, *Muslim Societies*, 27–41.
9. Kane, *Beyond Timbuktu*, 6–10; and Shamil Jeppie and Souleymane Bachir Diagne, eds, *The Meaning of Timbuktu* (Cape Town: HSRC Press, 2008).
10. Kane, *Beyond Timbuktu*, 50; and Amin Maalouf, *Leo Africanus*, translated by Peter Sluglett (Chicago: New Amsterdam Books, 1986).
11. Kane, *Beyond Timbuktu*; 41–74; Lamin Sanneh, *Beyond Jihad: The Pacifist Tradition in West African Islam* (New York: Oxford University Press, 2016); Rudolph T. Ware, *The Walking Qur'an: Islamic Education, Embodied Knowledge, and History in West Africa* (Chapel Hill: University of North Carolina Press, 2014); and Fallou Ngom, *Muslims Beyond the Arab World: The Odyssey of Ajami and the Muridiyya* (New York: Oxford University Press, 2016).
12. Jean Boyd and Beverly B. Mack, eds, *Collected Works of Nana Asma'u, Daughter of Usman 'dan Fodiyo (1793–1864)* (East Lansing: Michigan State University Press, 1997); Beverly B. Mack and Jean Boyd, *One Woman's Jihad: Nana*

Asma'u- Scholar and Scribe (Bloomington: Indiana University Press, 2000); Ngom, *Muslims beyond the Arab World*, 201–215; and Soxna Maymuna Jr. Mbàkke, *Wolofalu Soxna May* (Dakar: Imprimerie Serigne Saliou Mbacké, 2007).

13. Dmitry Bondarev, "Multiglossia in West African Manuscripts: A Case of Borno, Nigeria," in *Manuscript Cultures: Mapping the Field*, edited by J. B. Quenzer, D. Bondarev and J.-U. Sobisch (Berlin: De Gruyter, 2014), 113–155; Louis Brenner and Murray Last, "The Role of Language in West African Islam," *Africa: Journal of the International African Institute* 55, 04 (1985): 432–446; Fallou Ngom, "Ajami Literacies of West Africa," in *Tracing Language Movement in Africa*, edited by Ericka A. Albaugh and Kathryn M. de Luna (New York: Oxford University Press, 2018), 143–164; and Fallou Ngom and Mustapha H. Kurfi, eds., 'Ajamization of Islam in Africa: Special Issue of *Islamic Africa* 8, 1–2 (Leiden: Brill, 2017).
14. Ngom, *Muslims beyond the Arab World*, 219.
15. John O. Hunwick, "Catalog of Arabic Script Manuscripts at Northwestern University," *Sudanic Africa* 4 (1993): 210–211; For references of other volumes and archives on Arabic sources of Africa, see Ngom, "West African Manuscripts in Arabic and African Languages and Digital Preservation," 2017.
16. John O. Hunwick, *West Africa, Islam, and the Arab World: Studies in Honor of Basil Davidson* (Princeton, NJ: Markus Wiener Publishers, 2006), 53–62; and Kane, *Non-Europhone Intellectuals*, and Kane, *Beyond Timbuktu*.
17. Meikal Mumin and Kees Versteegh, eds., *The Arabic Script in Africa: Studies in the Use of a Writing System* (Leiden: Brill, 2014); Tal Tamari and Dmitry Bondarev, eds., "Qur'anic Exegesis in African Languages," *Journal of Qur'anic Studies* 15, 3 (2013); and Ngom, *Muslims beyond the Arab World*.
18. Lüpke and Bao-Diop, "Beneath the Surface," 20–21.
19. Ngom, "Ajami Literacies of West Africa," 144–152.
20. Ware, *The Walking Qur'an*, 1–39.
21. Kane, *Beyond Timbuktu*, 74–95; and Ngom, "Ajami Literacies of West Africa," 144–152.
22. John O. Hunwick and R. S. O'Fahey, *Arabic Literature of Africa, Volume 2: Writings of Central Sudanic Africa* (Leiden: Brill, 1995), 7–8.
23. Mustapha H. Kurfi and Fallou Ngom, *African Ajami Library: Digital Preservation of Hausa Ajami Manuscripts of Nigeria* (Boston: Boston University Library, 2015): http://hdl.handle.net/2144/11722
24. Meikal, Mumin, "The Arabic Script in Africa: Understudied Literacy," in *The Arabic Script in Africa: Studies in the Use of a Writing System*, edited by Meikal Mumin and Kees Versteegh (Leiden: Brill, 2014), 41–78.
25. Andrea Brigaglia and Mauro Nobili, "Central Sudanic Arabic Scripts (Part 2): Barnāwī," *Islamic Africa* 4, 2 (2013): 201.

26. Friederike Lüpke and Sokhna Bao-Diop, "Beneath the surface-Contemporary Ajami Writing in West Africa Exemplified through Wolofal,' in *African Literacies: Ideologies, Scripts, Education*, edited by Kasper Juffermans, Yonas Mesfun Asfaha, and Ashraf Abdelhay (Newcastle upon Tyne: Cambridge Scholars Publishing, 2014), 3; and Paulo Fernando de Moraes Farias, *Arabic Medieval Inscriptions from the Republic of Mali: Epigraphy, Chronicles and Songhay-Tuāreg History* (Oxford: Oxford University Press, 2003).
27. David Gutelius, "Newly Discovered 10th/16th c. Ajami Manuscript in Niger Kel Tamagheq History," *Saharan Studies Association Newsletter* 8, no. 1–2 (2000): 6.
28. Nikolay Debronravin, "Literacy among Muslims in Nineteenth-Century Trinidad and Brazil," in *Slavery, Islam and Diaspora*, edited by Behnaz A. Mirzai, Ishmael Musah Montana, and Paul E. Lovejoy (Trenton, NJ: Africa World Press, 2009), 217–236; Ivor Wiks, "Abu Bakr al–Siddiq of Timbuktu," in *Africa Remembered: Narratives by West Africans from the Era of the Slave Trade*, edited by Philip. D. Curtin (Madison: University of Wisconsin Press, 1967), 152–169; and Allen, Austin, *African Muslims in Antebellum America: Transatlantic Stories and Spiritual Struggles*. New York: Routledge, 1997).
29. Muhammed Haron, "The Making, Preservation and Study of South African Ajami Manuscripts and Texts." *Sudanic Africa* 12 (2001):1–14; and Kees Versteegh, "A Remarkable Document in Arabic- Afrikaans: The Election Pamphlet of 1884," in *The Arabic Script in Africa: Studies in the Use of a Writing System*, edited by Meikal Mumin and Kees Versteegh (Leiden: Brill, 2014), 365–380.
30. Peter T. Daniels, "The Type and Spread of Arabic Script," in *The Arabic Script in Africa: Studies in the Use of a Writing System*, edited by Meikal Mumin and Kees Versteegh (Leiden: Brill, 2014), 25–39.
31. Ngom, "Ajami Literacies of West Africa," 159; and Fallou Ngom, "Murid Ajami Sources of Knowledge: The Myth and the Reality," in *From Dust to Digital: Ten Years of the Endangered Archives Programme*, edited by Maja Kominko (Open Book Publishers, 2015), 119–164.
32. Mamadou Cissé, "Écrits et Écriture en Afrique de l'Ouest," *Revue Electronique Internationale des Sciences du Language* 6 (2007): 84.
33. Geoffrey Lewis, *The Turkish Language Reform: A Catastrophic Success* (New York: Oxford University Press, 2002).
34. Lüpke and Bao-Diop, "Beneath the Surface," 11–12.
35. Ibid.
36. British Library's Endangered Archives Programme: https://eap.bl.uk/
37. Boston University's African Ajami Library: https://open.bu.edu/handle/2144/1896

38. Eleni Castro, "Mandinka and Arabic Manuscripts of Casamance, Senegal," November 14, 2018, https://blogs.bl.uk/endangeredarchives/2018/11/mandinka-ajami-arabic-manuscripts-casamance-senegal.html
39. To visualize the entire manuscript, see Abdou Khadre Cissé's Collection at the Boston University's African Ajami Library: https://open.bu.edu/handle/2144/28415
40. Ngom, *Muslims beyond the Arab World*, 59–66.
41. Ngom, *Muslims beyond the Arab World*, 32–34.
42. See the Romanized transcript of the entire text: http://www.daaraykamil.com/XARNU-BI.pdf. For the Ajami text, see Muusaa KA, *Xarnu bi*, Mustafaa Gey, editor (Touba: Imprimerie Librairie Cheikh Ahmadou Bamba, n.d.).
43. For more on the poet, see Sana Camara, "Ajami Literature in Senegal: The Example of Sëriñ Muusaa Ka, Poet and Biographer," *Research in African Literatures* 28, 3 (1997), 163–182.
44. For useful references on literate African slaves in the Americas, see Sylviane A. Diouf, *Servants of Allah: African Muslims Enslaved in the Americas* (New York: New York University Press, 1988); Grace Turner, "In His Own Words: Abdul Keli, a Liberated African Apprentice," *Journal of the Bahamas Historical Society* 29 (2007): 27–31; Rolf Reichert, *Os Documentos Árabes do Archivo Público de Estato da Bahia*, no. 9, *Série Documentos* (Universidade Federal da Bahia: Centro de Estudos Afro-Orientais, 1970); Mahir Şaul, "Islam and West African Anthropology," *Anthropology Today* 53, 1 (2006): 3–33; William Brown Hodgson, *The Gospels, Written in the Negro Patois of English, with Arabic Characters by a Mandingo Slave in Georgia* (New York: Ethnological Society of New York, 1857); Michael A. Gomez, "Muslims in Early America," *Journal of Southern History* 60, 4 (1994): 671–710; and Martin, B.G., "Sapelo Island's Arabic Document: The 'Bilali Diary' in Context," *Georgia Historical Quarterly* 78, 3 (1994): 589–601.
45. The statistics are updated every six months. Click on "Show Statistical Information" at the bottom of the webpage for updated statistics: https://open.bu.edu/handle/2144/1896
46. Kurfi and Ngom, *African Ajami Library:* http://hdl.handle.net/2144/11722
47. For more on the research agenda on Africa's Ajami archives at Boston University, see the nascent field called *Ajami Studies* in Ngom, *Muslims beyond the Arab World*, 247–25. For materials to teach Ajami literacy to new generations of students and scholars in the humanities, social sciences, and professional fields working in African communities with Ajami traditions, see Alex M. Zito, *Diving into the Ocean of Wolofal: First Workbook in Wolofal/Wolof Ajami* (Boston University: African Studies Center, 2010); and Mustapha H. Kurfi, *Jorgan Koyan Hausa Ajami a Aiwace: A Practical Guide to Learning Hausa Ajami* (Boston University: African Studies Center, 2017). The development of new Ajami teaching resources (including for public health professionals) is underway.

Bibliography

Austin, Austin. 1997. *African Muslims in Antebellum America: Transatlantic Stories and Spiritual Struggles.* New York: Routledge.

Bondarev, Dmitry. 2014. Multiglossia in West African Manuscripts: A Case of Borno, Nigeria. In *Manuscript Cultures: Mapping the Field*, ed. J.B. Quenzer, D. Bondarev, and J.-U. Sobisch, 113–155. Berlin: De Gruyter.

Boyd, Jean, and Beverly B. Mack, eds. 1997. *Collected Works of Nana Asma'u, Daughter of Usman 'dan Fodiyo (1793–1864).* East Lansing: Michigan State University Press.

Brenner, Louis, and Murray Last. 1985. The Role of Language in West African Islam. *Africa: Journal of the International African Institute* 55 (04): 432–446.

Brigaglia, Andrea, and Mauro Nobili. 2013. Central Sudanic Arabic Scripts (Part 2): Barnāwī. *Islamic Africa* 4 (2): 195–223.

Camara, Sana. 1997. Ajami Literature in Senegal: The Example of Sëriñ Muusaa Ka, Poet and Biographer. *Research in African Literatures* 28 (3): 163–182.

Castro, Eleni. 2018. Mandinka and Arabic Manuscripts of Casamance, Senegal, November 14. https://blogs.bl.uk/endangeredarchives/2018/11/mandinka-ajami-arabic-manuscripts-casamance-senegal.html

Cissé, Mamadou. 2007. Écrits et Écriture en Afrique de l'Ouest. *Revue Electronique Internationale des Sciences du Language* 6: 63–88.

Dalby, David. 1969. Further Indigenous Scripts of West Africa: Manding, Wolof, and Fula Alphabets and Yoruba Holy-Writing. *African Language Studies* 10: 161–191.

Daniels, Peter T. 2014. The Type and Spread of Arabic Script. In *The Arabic Script in Africa: Studies in the Use of a Writing System*, ed. Meikal Mumin and Kees Versteegh, 25–39. Leiden: Brill.

Diouf, Sylviane A. 1988. *Servants of Allah: African Muslims Enslaved in the Americas.* New York: New York University Press.

Dobronravin, Nikolay. 2009. Literacy among Muslims in Nineteenth-Century Trinidad and Brazil. In *Slavery, Islam and Diaspora*, ed. Behnaz A. Mirzai, Ishmael Musah Montana, and Paul E. Lovejoy, 217–236. Trenton: Africa World Press.

Easton, Peter. 1999. Education and Koranic Literacy in West Africa. *IK Notes* 11 (August): 1–4. http://documents.worldbank.org/curated/en/581121468329358898/pdf/23424-Replacement-file-IKNT11.pdf. Accessed 12 May 2019.

El Hamel, Chouki. 2013. *Black Morocco: A History of Slavery, Race, and Islam.* New York: Cambridge University Press.

Farias, Paulo Fernando de Moraes. 2003. *Arabic Medieval Inscriptions from the Republic of Mali: Epigraphy, Chronicles, and Songhay-Tuareg History.* Oxford: Oxford University Press.

Gomez, Michael A. 1994. Muslims in Early America. *Journal of Southern History* 60 (4): 671–710.

Gutelius, David. 2000. Newly Discovered 10th/16th c. Ajami Manuscript in Niger Kel Tamagheq History. *Saharan Studies Association Newsletter* 8 (1–2): 6.

Hall, Bruce S. 2011. *A History of Race in Muslim West Africa, 1600–1960.* New York: Cambridge University Press.

Haron, Muhammed. 2001. The Making, Preservation and Study of South African Ajami Manuscripts and Texts. *Sudanic Africa* 12: 1–14.

Hodgson, William Brown. 1857. *The Gospels, Written in the Negro Patois of English, with Arabic Characters by a Mandingo Slave in Georgia.* New York: Ethnological Society of New York.

Hunwick, John O. 1993. Catalog of Arabic Script Manuscripts at Northwestern University. *Sudanic Africa* 4: 210–211.

Hunwick, John O., and R.S. O'Fahey. 1995. *Arabic Literature of Africa, Volume 2: Writings of Central Sudanic Africa.* Leiden: Brill.

Jeppie, Shamil, and Souleymane Bachir Diagne, eds. 2008. *The Meaning of Timbuktu.* Cape Town: HSRC Press.

Ka, Muusaa. n.d. *Xarnu bi.* Ed. Mustafaa Gey. Touba: Imprimerie Librairie Cheikh Ahmadou Bamba.

Kane, Ousmane Oumar. 2012. *Non-Europhone Intellectuals.* Dakar: CODESRIA.

———. 2016. *Beyond Timbuktu: An Intellectual History of Muslim West Africa.* Cambridge, MA: Harvard University Press.

Krätli, Graziano, and Ghislaine Lydon, eds. 2011. *The Trans-Saharan Book Trade: Manuscript Culture, Arabic Literacy and Intellectual History in Muslim Africa.* Leiden: Brill.

Kurfi, Mustapha H. 2017. *Jorgan Koyan Hausa Ajami a Aiwace: A Practical Guide to Learning Hausa Ajami.* Boston: Boston University/African Studies Center.

Kurfi, Mustapha H., and Fallou Ngom. 2015. *African Ajami Library: Digital Preservation of Hausa Ajami Manuscripts of Nigeria.* Boston: Boston University Library.

Lewis, Geoffrey. 2002. *The Turkish Language Reform: A Catastrophic Success.* New York: Oxford University Press.

Lüpke, Friederike, and Sokhna Bao-Diop. 2014. Beneath the Surface? Contemporary Ajami Writing in West Africa, Exemplified through Wolofal. In *African Literacies: Ideologies, Scripts, Education,* ed. Kasper Juffermans, Yonas Mesfun Asfaha, and Ashraf Abdelhay, 88–114. Newcastle upon Tyne: Cambridge Scholars.

Maalouf, Amin. 1986. *Leo Africanus.* Trans. P. Sluglett. Chicago: New Amsterdam Books.

Mack, Beverly B., and Jean Boyd. 2000. *One Woman's Jihad: Nana Asma'u- Scholar and Scribe.* Bloomington: Indiana University Press.

Martin, B.G. 1994. Sapelo Island's Arabic Document: The 'Bilali Diary' in Context. *Georgia Historical Quarterly* 78 (3): 589–601.

Mbàkke, Soxna Maymuna, Jr. 2007. *Wolofalu Soxna Maymunatu Jr.* Dakar: Imprimerie Serigne Saliou Mbacké.

Mumin, Meikal. 2014. The Arabic Script in Africa: Understudied Literacy. In *The Arabic Script in Africa: Studies in the Use of a Writing System,* ed. Meikal Mumin and Kees Versteegh, 41–62. Leiden: Brill.

Mumin, Meikal, and Kees Versteegh, eds. 2014. *The Arabic Script in Africa: Studies in the Use of a Writing System*. Leiden: Brill.

Ngom, Fallou. 2010. Ajami Scripts in the Senegalese Speech Community. *Journal of Arabic & Islamic Studies* 10 (1): 14–15.

———. 2016. *Muslims Beyond the Arab World: The Odyssey of Ajami and the Muridiyya*. New York: Oxford University Press.

———. 2017. West African Manuscripts in Arabic and African Languages and Digital Preservation. In *Oxford Research Encyclopedia of African History*, ed. Thomas Spear, 1–28. New York: Oxford University Press.

———. 2018. Ajami Literacies of West Africa. In *Tracing Language Movement in Africa*, ed. Ericka A. Albaugh and Kathryn M. de Luna, 143–164. New York: Oxford University Press.

Ngom, Fallou, and Mustapha H. Kurfi, eds. 2017. ʿAjamization of Islam in Africa: Special Issue of Islamic Africa 8, Volume 1–2. Leiden: Brill.

Pasch, Helma. 2008. Competing Scripts: The Introduction of the Roman Alphabet in Africa. *International Journal of the Sociology of Language* 191: 65–109.

Reichert, Rolf. 1970. *Os Documentos Árabes do Archivo Público de Estado da Bahia, no. 9, Série Documentos*. Salvador: Universidade Federal da Bahia/Centro de Estudos Afro-Orientais.

Robinson, David. 2004. *Muslim Societies in African History*. New York: Cambridge University Press.

Sanneh, Lamin. 2016. *Beyond Jihad: The Pacifist Tradition in West African Islam*. New York: Oxford University Press.

Şaul, Mahir. 2006. Islam and West African Anthropology. *Anthropology Today* 53 (1): 3–33.

Tamari, Tal, and Dmitry Bondarev, eds. 2013. Qurʾanic Exegesis in African Languages. *Journal of Qurʾanic Studies* 15 (3): 1–297.

Turner, Grace. 2007. In His Own Words: Abdul Keli, a Liberated African Apprentice. *Journal of the Bahamas Historical Society* 29: 27–31.

Versteegh, Kees. 2014. A Remarkable Document in Arabic-Afrikaans: The Election Pamphlet of 1884. In *The Arabic Script in Africa: Studies in the Use of a Writing System*, ed. Meikal Mumin and Kees Versteegh, 365–380. Leiden: Brill.

Ware, Rudolph T. 2014. *The Walking Qurʾan: Islamic Education, Embodied Knowledge, and History in West Africa*. Chapel Hill: University of North Carolina Press.

Wiks, Ivor. 1967. Abu Bakr al–Siddiq of Timbuktu. In *Africa Remembered: Narratives by West Africans from the Era of the Slave Trade*, ed. Philip D. Curtin, 152–169. Madison: University of Wisconsin Press.

Wright, John. 2007. *The Trans-Saharan Trade*. New York: Routledge.

Zito, Alex M. 2010. *Diving into the Ocean of Wolofal: First Workbook in Wolofal/Wolof Ajami*. Boston: Boston University/African Studies Center.

Part III

Archival Politics

9

Nambiquaras in Paris: Archival Images, Appearances, and Disappearances

Beatriz Jaguaribe

Paris, 2016

In January of 2016, I was following the trail of my grandfather's undertaking in the 1920s when he went to Paris in order to perfect the map of Mato Grosso at the premises of the Sérvice Géographic de l'Armée.[1] My grandfather, Francisco Jaguaribe Gomes de Mattos (1881–1974), was a geographer and cartographer. He was also a military man and the head of the Cartography Section of the Rondon Commission. In the first three decades of the twentieth century (1907–1930), Candido Rondon (1865–1958), an advocate of positivism and military officer, ventured into the vast hinterlands of Brazil into what are now the states of Mato Grosso, Mato Grosso do Sul, Rondônia, and parts of Amazon.[2] From 1907 to 1915, Rondon was in charge of stringing telegraph lines from Mato Grosso and the Amazon. By the time he had finished this daunting enterprise, telegraph communication had become dated due to the advent of radio transmissions.

Nevertheless, the expeditions into Mato Grosso and adjacent areas continued because the telegraphic enterprise was part of a larger project that comprised the mapping of Mato Grosso, the reinforcement of the state's presence in the backlands of Brazil, the survey of the region's topography, the inspection of frontiers, and the classification of flora and fauna for scientific knowledge and economic gain. Above all, the Rondon Commission had

---

B. Jaguaribe (✉)
School of Communication, The Federal University of Rio de Janeiro, Rio de Janeiro, Brazil

succeeded in making contact with the numerous indigenous tribes of those regions. Rondon, who was himself a descendent of Bororo, Terena and Guará Indians, and Brazilian settlers, thus became legendary not only for his extensive penetration into uncharted territory but mostly for his nonviolent approach to the indigenous tribes. The motto "To die if necessary, to kill never" became a pledge, a mission, and a signature of his commitment to human dignity and national unity. The recognition of the indigenous population's right to the land and the acknowledgment of their endangered position did not alter their ranking in the positivist chart of cultural evolution. According to this criterion, the indigenous tribes of Brazil's hinterlands were deemed to be congealed at the primitive fetishistic stage. Incorporation into the national imagined community necessarily meant acculturation, although Rondon acknowledged indigenous peoples as being part of distinct nations within the territory of Brazil.[3] The members of the Rondon Commission were fully aware of the atrocities constantly perpetrated against the indigenous peoples of Brazil. They did not ignore the brutality of the rubber tappers, the domesticating strategies of both Protestant and Catholic clergies, in addition to the sheer violence of the state itself. Given his historical moment and circumstances, Rondon's approach was innovative and humanitarian as he adamantly rejected retaliation against indigenous attacks and favored persuasion, exchange of gifts, and the overall protection of the indigenous populations.[4]

Yet as Souza Lima (1995, 2015) and others have argued in numerous studies, Rondon's policies toward the indigenous populations were conditioned by the tutelary regime that inhibited any effort of self-governance on the part of the indigenous nations. As Bigio and other scholars have emphasized, aside from his personal empathy, convictions, and humanitarian beliefs, Rondon also pragmatically needed the work force of the indigenous population for the construction of the telegraph lines. Indeed, the cooperation of the Terenas and Bororos in the construction of the telegraph line in the south zone of Mato Grosso had been decisive. Aside from actually building the line, indigenous guides and indigenous men working as telegraph operators were essential to the success of the entire enterprise (Bigio 2000). During my research, I found microfilmed images of 120 photographs of the expeditions of the Rondon Commission anonymously donated to the Société de Géographie in 1925. The photographs were taken from several different expeditions; some were prior to the formation of the Rondon Commission itself and formed part of the early exploits of Candido Rondon at the beginning of the century when he was stringing telegraph poles throughout the state of Mato Grosso. The most iconic photographs were authored by the most prominent photographer of the Rondon Commission, Luiz Thomaz Reis, and some especially remarkable images are still photographs from the film footage of the famous Rondon-Roosevelt expedition of 1913–1914.[5]

In the French library, these images were accessible through microfilm. They have captions but there are no dates, nor is there any mention of the names of the photographers who took these pictures. In Brazil, the bulk of these images belong to the archives of the Museum of the Indian in Rio de Janeiro. Similar to other images included in the microfilm roll that depicted panoramas and inhabitants of Latin America, the images of the Rondon Commission are part of a collection that is languishing from lack of contextualization and meaning. Although these images have not been censored, although they lack the startling component of the unexpected, and although they are not aesthetically extraordinary, the dispersed images of the Rondon Commission donated to the Société de Géograhie are quite potent because they are emblematic photographs of a conflicted past. The workers, soldiers, officers, students, and indigenous peoples portrayed in these photographs constitute the visual memory of the Rondon Commission that so dramatically altered the ecological, social, and political landscapes of Mato Grosso and the Brazilian West. Above all, the disputes surrounding this memory still have a strong resonance for the ongoing struggle to recognize and honor indigenous identities and land demarcations.

My intention in this chapter is not to engage in an evaluation of the legacies of the Rondon Commission, nor do I intend to deconstruct the figure of Rondon himself. Such efforts of evaluation whether in the form of critical revisions or laudatory appraisals have been done by scholars, activists, indigenous representatives, government officials, and anonymous users of social media. Likewise, there has been a rich and varied anthropological critique of the social and cultural implications of the Rondon Commission and their relation to the indigenous populations. As a literary critic and as a scholar of media studies, my analysis focuses on narrative discourses and on the aesthetic production of images. My inquiry offers a critical reading of the relation between selective narratives/images and aesthetic codes, and it also envisions these pictures as registers of memory that bespeak the legacy of a politics of recognition. The title of this chapter that transposes the Nambiquaras of Mato Grosso to Paris suggests how disparate contexts enable a montage reading of these images.

The photographs and mostly the films made by the Rondon Commission catered to national audiences. The collection of photographs donated to the Sóciete de Géographie was meant to advertise the civilizing mission of the Brazilian state while offering enticing pictures of unknown indigenous populations. In search of the possible meanings of these images, I explore three interconnected themes: the *photographic pact*, the *aesthetic and documentary registers* of the photographic portrait and the narratives of the Rondon Commission, and, finally, the way these images and narratives are invested with different meanings by *archives and museums* during emblematic moments of Brazilian history.

The symbolic life of images does not depend just on differing contexts of creation, circulation, and reception, but it is also linked to the material substance that makes these images tangible. The images of the Rondon Commission made in fragile glass plates and in film attest not only to the progressive technological adaption of the photographers engaged in the Commission, but also such material changes express the human effort of producing these photographs in arduous circumstances. The extraordinary material difficulties of the photographic and filmic endeavors were emphasized in the reports produced by Thomaz Reis and in the prefaces of the illustrated books of the Commission. Alongside the narratives of how glass plates were shattered during the crossing of rivers and jungle treks and of how film was devoured by insects, the reports of the Commission also mention the deaths of expedition members who were measuring rivers for the making of the map of Mato Grosso, a cartographical effort that took decades to be completed. Yet, if the images persist and the maps endure, the façades of both pictures and maps do not reveal the multiple histories and the experiences that were lived in order to make these representations. Rondon himself stresses in the preface of the first tome of the book *Indians of Brazil* that the photographic efforts of the Rondon Commission were patriotic acts (Rondon 1946: 4, 5). Thus Rondon states:

> There is no exaggeration, therefore, to affirm in this colorless but truthful sketch that many of these photographs that are now being browsed inside civilized ambiances and that are being offered to scholars of Science and to fellow citizens interested in things that are essentially Brazilian and that gaze with sympathy at the "Problem of the Indian" demanded much abnegation, much patriotic effort, much sweat, much fatigue and also, at times, the blood and life of our compatriots in order for us to be able to contemplate and comment on them seated in the comfort of our surroundings. (Rondon 1946: 4, 5, my translation)

Documentary realist photographs such as those produced by the Rondon Commission elicit an interpretative effort of the relations between the past and the present. On the one hand, there is a demand for a contextualized reading of a past accessed through its vestiges. On the other, there is an anachronistic reading of these vestiges because the images of the past that emerge are read through the eyes and the contexts of the present. Although Denise Portugal Lasmar (2011) examined, classified, and thoroughly inspected the archives of the Museu do Índio and produced the most minute research available, information about the photographers of the Rondon Commission is still quite scarce. My intent is not to reconstruct historically who these photographers were and how they specifically took their pictures. Rather I seek to emphasize the regimes of visibility that produced the photographic pact and conditioned the reading of these images. I explore them as archives of an embattled social memory.

The images donated to the Société de Géographie arrived in Paris during the heady cultural atmosphere of the 1920s when artistic modernism and avant-garde movements enhanced the aesthetic potentialities of "primitive" art as a source of artistic renewal. Yet if the non-European was celebrated and appropriated by the avant-garde, the exoticization of Africans, Asians, and the indigenous populations of the Americas not only fomented sensationalist images in posters, propaganda, and forms of popular entertainment but also figured in the famous international expositions that exhibited human zoos for European audiences (Blanchard et al. 2012). Alongside the popular entertainment afforded by the exoticization of non-Europeans, the 1920s were a remarkable moment of ethnographic display as the artifacts and materials gathered in colonial expeditions were integrated into the collections of the new museums of ethnology (Conklin 2013).

In the year 2016, the 120 images of the Rondon Commission pertaining to the photographic archives of the Société de Géographie were housed in the National Library of France in the Cartography Section. Most of these images are quite well known. What remains unknown is the name of the donor. In the office of the Société de Géographie at Boulevard Saint Germain, the registration file reveals only the date of the donation. A bigger mystery is how they ended up in Paris. Aside from their dislocation and the symbolic meandering that such a cultural shift entailed, the other factor that claims attention relates to the haunting quality of these images. It is this quality that Roland Barthes evokes in his understanding of the indexical nature of the photographic image by stressing that photographs represent the "return of the dead".

As is well known, Barthes' interpretation of the analogical photographic image suggests that it contains a residue of a presence captured in a past time. The camera lens makes an image of the present, and that image will become a past for future eyes to see. The axiom "this was" gives the photographic act the capacity to reproduce a semblance of what had been. As photographic images are reproducible, their "aura", to use Benjamin's term, resides in the fossilized representation of a past temporality that will never return. In his deconstruction of Barthes' notion of indexicality, John Tagg comments:

> [W]hat Barthes calls 'evidential force' is a complex historical outcome and is exercised by photographs only within certain institutional practices and within particular historical relations, the investigation of which will take us far from an aesthetic or phenomenological context. (Tagg 1988: 4)

Tagg insists on the material production of the image as a technical process. The apprehension and understanding of the chemically made image as being "real" is shaped by a regime of power, symbolization, and contextualized rhetoric that conditions readings, selections and interpretations.

Nevertheless, the novelty of the photochemical process modifies regimes of visibility, and it conditions readings and responses to the image. I am not suggesting a causal connection wrought by technological determinism. As many scholars have suggested, prior to the advent of photography, there had emerged a predisposition and a social demand that anticipated the technical invention itself (Crary 1990). Yet the emergence of technical inventions and their popularization create new orders of reception and sensibility. A photographic image can be manipulated, recontextualized, and appropriated by a regime of visibility entirely disparate from the one in which it was initially made. Despite these considerations, the photographic images that respond to documentary criteria based on realist verisimilitude produce not the past itself but selected and framed images of the past. I evoke the frayed debate concerning photographic realism because the images of the past, especially the images of an annihilated, traumatic, or conflictive past compel us to position ourselves in relation to the archives of memory and the writings of history. Images matter because they activate repertoires, imaginaries, emotions, and agency. They can be potentialized or discarded by distinct regimes of circulation that condition visibility and reception. The forgotten images of the Rondon Commission stocked in the Parisian archives were made in order to enhance the notions of a nation ruled by the belief in progress, evolution, the veracity of scientific fact, and the hierarchy of authority and Eurocentric civilization. The indigenous bodies captured by the camera lens were discordant with this model, and an important component of this pedagogy of the gaze was to register the mimetic transformation of the "primitive" into the acculturated worker.

Sent to the Société de Géographie in the 1920s, this selection of images of the Rondon Commission was not included in the handsome volume, *Tresors Photographiques de la société de géographie*, published in 2006. The only

Brazilian images included in this publication comprise a portrait of the Brazilian emperor, Dom Pedro II, who had become a member of the Société in 1864, and a landscape with a viaduct by the famous Brazilian photographer Marc Ferrez.

Founded in 1821, the Société de Géographie is reputedly one of the oldest geographical societies in the world. It counted among its founding members notable men such as Humboldt, Champollion, and Chateaubriand. In 1922, Rondon was nominated a *membre correspondent*, the highest distinction the Société conferred to its foreign members. In issues of the review published by the Société such as *La Géographie* and also in the *Annales de la Géographie*, Rondon is mentioned in articles and laudatory essays.[6] Yet in my research of these publications during the decade of the 1920s, I did not find the donated photographs of the Rondon expeditions among the published pictures.

Aside from his renown as an explorer, Rondon also gained prominence through his pacification policies toward the Indians. In the French context of the 1920s, he was mostly seen as a geographic explorer, and his recognition grew from his affiliation with geographic societies and with the military. Indeed, the task of one of his main collaborators, Francisco Jaguaribe, was to perfect the map of Mato Grosso for the French Sérvice Géographic de L'ármee. General Gamelin, who was the head of the French military mission in Brazil in the 1920s, viewed Rondon as a "friend of France", a military officer who could utilize French methods to reform the Brazilian army.[7] From the perspective of the French military and the geographical society, Rondon's strategies of acculturation and pacification toward the Indian tribes of Mato Grosso were rather minor issues. But from the perspective of the ethnographic eye of precursors such as Paul Rivet (1876–1959) who was to become such an outstanding figure in the creation of the Museé de L'homme in 1937, the cultural diversity of South American Indians, their origins, and linguistic variety were major concerns.[8] Rivet, a professor at the Institut d'ethnologie created in 1925, would become, in 1928, director of the Museum of the Trocadero.

In an article published in 1913 in the *Journal des Société des Americanistes*, Rivet mentions the undertaking of the Rondon Commission by emphasizing how a member of the French diplomatic service had informed him of the merits of the Brazilian integrationist policy. Based on the declarations of the French Vice-Consul, Paul Serre, in Bahia, Rivet highlights the difference between the pacifications of Rondon and the extreme exploitation of the indigenous populations by the Peruvian rubber entrepreneurs of Putumayo. Rivet emphasizes Rondon's "Indigenous origin and his knowledge of a great number of Amazonian languages" and commends the relevance of the Indian Protection Service (Serviço de proteção ao índio) (Rivet 1913: 688, my translation).

Despite the lively debates in the Société des Americanistes, the study of the Native populations in the American continent was largely related to linguistic and archeological discussions (Cavignac 2012: 32).

Even if the photographs of the Rondon Commission had chanced to be viewed by prominent ethnographers such as Paul Rivet who would later have such a decisive role in promoting Lévi-Strauss' expeditions in Mato Grosso, they did not form part of a broader *ethnographic display*. By *ethnographic display* I am designating not only the objects exhibited in the glass cases of museums but also the objects and pictures seen at World Fairs, printed in the press, and appropriated by avant-garde artists such as the surrealists. Whereas African art, namely the often-mentioned encounter of Picasso with African masks in the dusty domains of the Museum of the Trocadero, has been crucially signaled as an inspiration for the reinvention of modernist art, the varied manifestations of indigenous culture in the Americas had a more complex trajectory of appropriations.

As Elizabeth Williams has suggested, the aesthetic viewing of pre-Columbian art was considerably advanced by the 1928 exhibit at the Louvre curated by Alfred Métraux and Georges-Henri Rivière (Williams 1985: 146). At the level of reception there was a marked distinction made between the cultural artifacts of the former vanquished Aztec and Inca Empires and the images of actual indigenous tribes of the central plateaus of Brazil with their rudimentary agriculture and their hunting and gathering practices. Despite their excellent quality most clearly detected in the pictures produced by Thomaz Reis' notable talent, the photographs of the Commission were not as aesthetically evocative as those produced by Edward Curtis in his monumental depiction of the Native Americans of the United States. They did not rely on the pictorialist tradition and did not offer the dramatic pathos wrought by the atmospheric landscapes in evocative tones of sepia, black, and white. Reis' images reveal his eye for composition, just as José Louro's photographs offer compelling individual portraits that go beyond mere typology.

The Rondon Commission images failed to provide the arousing spectacle and exotic entertainment capable of enticing a general public. The indigenous tribes of Mato Grosso did not correspond to the *physique du role* of the glamorous or threatening savage, and only a few landscape images had the aesthetic impact of the dense tropical vistas of the Amazonian forest. Furthermore, the pictures of the very modest telegraph installations were far from arresting, and even less appealing were the several images of the ragged workers struggling through the thicket with their machetes. These images in particular were not made to elicit feelings of social outrage at the deplorable work conditions these men faced. Rather, they were produced as testimonial proof of work being done under adverse circumstances. Ethnographically, the photographs failed to offer an extensive typology because they were too concerned with reinforcing the saga of the Brazilian national construction—a subject that was of minimal interest to French geographers, ethnographers, and anthropologists who were either bent on producing their own national and imperial narratives and images or were seeking ways to criticize them.

Thus, the very crucial and foundational purpose of the Rondon Commission, namely the venturing into the Brazilian hinterland by Brazilians exclusively—not by foreign explorers nor by Portuguese colonizers—was relevant mostly to Brazilians themselves as they played out the disputes over the national imagined community and the implementation of a modernizing project. By contrast, Curtis' photographs published in monumental tomes reveal the photographer's personal stamp and his view of the beauty of Native American Indians, the grandiosity of the American landscape, and the pathos of a tribal form of life on the brink of extinction by the modernization of the American West. Common to both endeavors is the belief (in the case of the photographers of the Rondon Commission) and the romantic lament (in the case of Curtis) that these indigenous tribes would no longer endure as they had in the past (Fig. 9.1).

Fig. 9.1 The second photograph is a portrait of the guide Matias Toloiri, Expedition of 1907. Photograph by Luiz Leduc. (Source: This image is part of the collection of the Société de Géographie)

As the product of the nineteenth-century romantic imagination, Indianism in Brazil cast the encounters between Portuguese conquerors and exotic Indians as the inaugural founding moment of the nation.[9] By doing so, these monumental paintings and novels erased the overwhelming presence of the enormous enslaved African diaspora in Brazil. When the Indian motif was reinvented by the Brazilian modernist artists, mainly the writer Oswald de Andrade (1890–1954)—author of the *Manifesto Antropófago* (*Cannibal Manifesto*, 1928)—and the painter Tarsila do Amaral (1886–1973), they opposed previous appropriations of the romantic imaginary that sought to enhance mythical nation-building. Influenced by the international avant-garde— both artists circulated widely in Paris in the 1920s—Andrade's cannibal satire premised on the creative need to devour cultural otherness was a literary construct, an inspired recasting of the stereotypical man-eating Indian that was created as an omnipresent image during the Portuguese conquest of Brazil. By embracing cannibalism, Andrade sought to overturn a subaltern status by strategies of cultural appropriation and recreation.[10]

Cannibalism was an ultimate bricolage, a novel form of empowerment and authorship. As a creative anarchic invention, it challenged hierarchies by conceptualizing cultural belonging through absorption and metamorphosis, rather than through orderly emulation and progress. Nothing could be further from Andrade's carnivalesque irreverence than Rondon's positivist mission. While the comparison seems arbitrary given Andrade's artistic ambitions and Rondon's military ones, in addition to their generational separation, still, modernist Brazilian artists did appropriate ethnographic material not only for art but also to enhance national multiculturalism. The famous modernist composer Villa-Lobos (1887–1959), who also spent formative years in Paris in the 1920s, featured in his musical scores the chant of the Paresi Indians of Mato Grosso recorded by the ethnographer Roquette Pinto (1884–1954), who had worked closely with Rondon in an expedition in 1912. Mario de Andrade (1893–1945), for his famous fictional book, *Macunaíma* (1928), drew upon T. Koch Grünberg's research into Amazonian myths and in his travel narrative the *Turista Aprendiz* (1976) used the photographic camera as an interpretative ethnographic tool. Raul Bopp (1898–1984), another modernist writer, recasts Amazonian myths in his poem, *Cobra Norato* (1931). Whether in Oswald de Andrade's irreverent spoof on cannibal appropriation as a cultural strategy, or in Mario de Andrade's attempt to build a new national consciousness based on a pluralistic awareness, the modernist gesture required a rejection of a positivist hierarchical authority. Whereas the modernist invention was cultural and based on an experimental attitude largely devoid of direct contact with indigenous groups, the exploratory ventures of the Rondon

Commission confronted tangible peoples, physical obstacles, and material deprivation.

The images donated to the Société de Géographie are part of the commemorative album of 1922 dedicated to his Excellency General Fernando Setembrino De Carvalho, Minister of State and War. The pictures come from several different expeditions, beginning with the excursions into the southern part of Mato Grosso from 1905 to the 1920s. The majority of the donated images emphasize the achievements of the Commission, in particular communication, pacification, and education. They also stress the agricultural richness of the land and the diversity of the indigenous tribes. Last but not least, many pictures were devoted to the civic emblems of the nation. Indeed, Rondon was purportedly so bent on promoting civic consciousness through ritual indoctrination that he carried a gramophone into the depths of the forest in order to play the national anthem even in the most untimely occasions (Diacon 2004: 23). It was as if he insisted on imprinting the positivist motto "Order and Progress" emblazoned on the Brazilian flag onto the very Mato Grosso wilderness itself. These ritualistic acts—the pledge of allegiance to the flag, the honoring of the national pantheon, and the singing of the anthem—so dear to nationalism, became a petrified code, a military coercion quite divorced from the impulses of the common soldiers, many of whom had been forcefully recruited for the Rondon Commission as punishment for rebelliousness (Maciel 1998: 131).

The photographic act entailed two simultaneous functions: testimony and classification. Documentation was at the service of empirical data gathering in order to produce general laws. The indexical effect of the images captured by the analogical camera preserved the live bodies of those that would cease to exist not only as human beings but as Paresis, Terenas, Bororos, and Nambiquaras. Yet the point to be made is that the individual portraits of the Nambiquaras, Bororos, and Parecis, among other groups, reveal to our contemporary eyes the singularity of presences that became relevant as vestiges of memory defying historical interpretations. As Eduardo Kingman comments in his evocative essay on the uses of archives as history and forms of preserving memory:

> It is as if nations in order to construct themselves and constitute hegemony needed a great dose of collective amnesia, not only in relation to remote facts—related to their origins such as the making of the Heroes of the Nation in their actions of extermination against native populations—but also in relation to recent processes, as with the maintenance of security in dictatorial and constitu-

tional governments, including those that call themselves progressive. (Kingman 2012: 131, my translation)

When images escape from the ordering of archives or when they stray from the logic of official history, they compel us to denaturalize our categories. Unlike the neighboring nations of Hispanic America whose violent wars of Independence allowed for the construction of national pantheons of patriotic liberators, in Brazil, the process of independence was negotiated with the Portuguese crown and failed to produce compelling heroes. During the period of the Old Republic (1889–1930), the national pantheon of heroes was often evoked, but it held very little popular appeal. In this scenario of feeble civic patriotism, the figure of Rondon and his exploratory feats gained heroic prestige. But what do these images reveal of the tattered and barefoot anonymous workers of the telegraph line? What do they suggest of the common soldiers and their officers? How were the various indigenous groups remembered? Aside from aesthetic considerations concerning the positioning of the camera and the effect of the light on the expression of those depicted, these images reawaken social and cultural conflicts, and they also, paradoxically, ascertain the disappearance and the continuity of lives. Contrary to the prevailing mentality at the time of their making, not all the indigenous populations of Brazil were acculturated in conformity with the rulings of the Old Republic (1889–1930). Above all, in contemporary Brazil, the ongoing disputes concerning indigenous rights and land ownership have been further intensified by debates relative to what it means to be indigenous or to be considered indigenous (Pacheco de Oliveira 2010, 2013). Seen through contemporary eyes that emphasize the political right to be indigenous, these images no longer refer simply to indigenous peoples on the verge of extinction as was the premise of their original making. In the contemporary moment, such images can be reclaimed as a testament of an ongoing ancestry.

Few subjects of indigenous portraits were given names. Those that were had either rendered some service to the Commission or were eminent chieftains or the spouses of chieftains. Yet these portraits fail to comply with the codes of bourgeois portraiture in identifications and poses, neither can they be reduced to mere typology as pictures of token natives. Nuances of expression affirm singular presences. In the captions of the portraits donated to the Société de Géographie, indigenous individuals were identified by their specific tribes. Thus, the references to "… the wife of the chief of the Barbados uses, as is expected, more ornaments than other women". The caption to the portrait of a young woman reads "Pareci Indian in her hut", another image bears the caption, "a robust Nambiquara Indian", and yet another, "Nambiquara Indian in his usual pose". When indigenous groups are pictured collectively, the captions highlight general characteristics such as "The timid Urumis were prevailed upon and let themselves be photographed" and "Previously wild and suspicious the Barbados now arrive at the service station in a friendly manner". Although the captions of the photographs donated to the Sérvice de Géograhie are similar to those of the Album of 1922, they are not identical.

The photographic pacts between the indigenous peoples portrayed and their photographers of the Rondon Commission avoided aggression or condescension toward the subjects, but asymmetry inhered in unequal access to power. Forging a civil pact between photographer and subject, to use Ariella Azoulay's term, was impossible since the photographic act could not ensure any agency for those depicted. Such a civil pact was impossible because the regime of tutelage denied indigenous subjects the status of autonomous and free individuals. Furthermore, the notion of an individual portrait premised on Western ideas of individuality did not immediately resonate with indigenous peoples embedded in collective and metamorphic notions of being in the making.[11] In the more prosaic terms of profiting, the depicted indigenous subjects were in no position to negotiate a photographic pact, given their lack of access to the reception, interpretation, and circulation of their images. In his reports, Thomaz Reis details how trinkets and gifts were used as payment to subjects for their photographs.[12]

Although crucially committed to the idea of progress, Comte also prophesized that, "The living will necessarily and increasingly be governed by the dead". Comte's dictum was premised on the notion of the persistence of human improvement expressed by the works of great men. Rondon, who was a fervent positivist all his life and married his wife for a second time in order to observe a proper ritual at the Positivist Temple of Rio de Janeiro in 1903, surrounded himself with positivist officers and was a believer not only in the scientific and philosophical writings of Comte but also in his teachings on the religion of humanity. Rondon's model of self-fashioning owed much to the heroic canon of great men whose great deeds perpetuated their names in posthumous glory. Yet the emblematic photographs taken by Luiz Thomaz Reis where he is offering gifts to the Paresi Indians and also in the images where he is positioned next to the Paresis at the waterfall of Utiarity give rise to different allegorical overtones. It is as if once again the conquest of the New World was being waged. But the time warp presented by the "as if" reveals the fraught contact zones between indigenous tribes and Western colonizer (Pratt 1992) (Figs. 9.2 and 9.3).

Fig. 9.2 Photograph by Thomaz Reis, Album of 1922. Rondon distributing gifts to the Paresis. (Source: Museu do Índio)

The crucial difference revealed in these pictures is that the "zone of contact" was negotiated within the narrative of the nation itself and it was not premised on the model of an external colonizer confronting "natives". As a mestizo man, Rondon becomes a colonizer, pacifier, and also kin to the indigenous peoples he encounters. Once again, the shiny beads of conquest become a symbolic and material trading tool. As part of the modernizing strategies of the Republic, beads of barter were given together with machetes and telegraph messages. Rondon was a Brazilian of Indian descent attempting to incorporate indigenous populations that had been previously slaughtered by rubber tappers, farmers, or representatives of the state. Despite the pacification policy and the status of respect owed to the indigenous peoples, the silencing of the indigenous subject is still at stake.

It is in light of this silencing that the anthropologist Souza Lima has emphasized that the representational endeavors of the Rondon Commission

> actualize the ideas that are present in our colonial archive of representations and practices where the Indigenous peoples are treated as a transitory category because once they had been exposed to "civilization", they would adhere to it by

Fig. 9.3 Photograph by Tomaz Reis, Album of 1922. Rondon with Paresis at the waterfall of Utiariti. (Source: Museu do Índio)

pure mimetic effect and due to the obvious advantages in being "civilized". (Souza Lima 2015: 433–435, my translation)

According to Souza Lima, the photographs of the Rondon Commission

compose a collection that depicts a generic Indian where the heterogeneous is unified by an exogenous gaze and by the action of the powers of tutelage that assemble them together. Although different peoples are acclaimed by an abundance of specific portraits (as if the intuition had been to somatically distinguish human types) the photographs demonstrate most of all the actions of the Commission, they contribute to its extolment just as they can serve to study it. (Souza Lima 1992: 133, my translation)

In a similar fashion, Fernando de Tacca suggests that the photographs and films of the Rondon Commission reinforce a preordained typology based on the portrayal of the indigenous subjects as noble savages, pacified individuals, or civilized subjects (Tacca 2001).

Tacca suggests that:

> [i]n a signifying perspective, the idea of the construction of an image of the Indian that exists simultaneously as a kind of "myth of origin" capable of integrating civilization recurs throughout all of the images of the Rondon Commission. (Tacca 2017: 164, my translation)

The "myth of origin" that Tacca mentions is engrained in the Indianist reading of Brazil's foundation as a nation where the indigenous element becomes part of the hegemonic construction inaugurated by the contact between indigenous and non-indigenous peoples. Images of "savage", "pacified", and "acculturated" indigenous peoples repeat typologies, and they constitute acts of symbolic naming. Although there is a timeline that suggests the gradual transformation of indigenous peoples into "acculturated citizens", the existence of non-acculturated indigenous peoples makes the imagined community of the national project into a continuous enactment of its beginnings. The nation is constantly being founded with a repetitive assemblage of typologies. If the evolutionist time line is linear and progressive according to the positivist chart, the repetitive inauguration of the nation through contact with the "primitives" suggests that "progress" is elusive. Furthermore, certain images offer ambiguous readings even though they were made to extol the feats of the Commission.

In the specific case of Luiz Thomaz Reis (1870–1940) recognized mainly as a filmmaker, his images reveal an acute aesthetic sense and a pioneering ethnographic effort. Indeed, the film *Rituals and Feasts of the Bororo* (1917), currently recognized as the first ethnographic film of the twentieth century, captures realistically the social interactions of the Bororo as an expressive culture, and the sequences of the camera filming bodies, landscapes, and rituals reveal a range of emotions. In his reports addressed to Amilcar Botelho, the head of the central office of the Rondon Commission in charge of propaganda efforts and press releases, Reis details his search for an image of the non-acculturated Indian. Reis understood his task as one of arousing emotional and aesthetic responses from the audience. In the same report to Amilcar Botelho, Reis stresses:

> There is among them practices that are innocent and others that are truly horrible; now in cinematography, an art like any other, it changes its registers as it has to follow the inclinations and the taste of the public; what is horrible, pleases; the more barbarous the scene, all the better to improve the frayed nerves of our audiences who are avid for sensationalism. (Magalhães 1942: 325, my translation)

Reis links the exoticization of the Indian to new forms of sensationalist entertainment that provide shock and awe to urban audiences.

As the head of the cinematography section of the Rondon Commission and as its main photographer, Reis was intensely engaged in his filmic and photographic activities. Through the relentless efforts of Amilcar Botelho Magalhães, the head of the Central Office of the Rondon Commission, the photographic and filmic production of the Rondon Commission was widely advertised. Due to lack of documentation, it is impossible to gauge if photographers such as José Louro who took such compelling portraits of the Nambiquaras and the Paresis were also attuned to the repercussions of his photographic activity. Veering away from the epic overtones of Reis' most renowned pictures and also from the flatness of photographic images that merely detail the construction work and various rituals of the Rondon Commission, Louro's pictures capture facial expressions and bodily postures—nuances that suggest the specificity of the persons being portrayed and the circumstances of their portraiture. In a picture from the 1920s, three young Paresi pupils flank their teacher, Olga Higgins. Their restrained bodily postures and the discrete sadness of their facial expressions reveal a pathos that goes beyond photographic depictions of the "civilized Indian". The modest ribbons, bows, and flowers on the frocks of the Paresi pupils convey the plights of indigenous girls mimetically transformed into suitable youngsters with the expected trappings of femininity and dutifulness. The respectable shabbiness of their adornments and the contrast between their physiques and the Western figure of the schoolteacher reinforce their subordination. Olga Higgins' expression of sad resigned determination does not convey the joys of teaching but rather suggests the starkness of duty (Fig. 9.4).

The portraits of the Nambiquara chief, Nuchilaitê, and his wife are quite different from the portraits of "civilized Indians" and from each other. Nuchilaitê's nonchalance contrasts with the staunch intensity of his unnamed wife (Fig. 9.5).

The civilizing process suggests an erasure of identity as can be gleaned in the portraits of the Nambiquara named Cavaignac, thus designated because of his unusual facial hair. Photographed as an "Indian" armed with his arrows, Cavaignac stares directly at the camera. Transformed into an employee of the state in uniform, Cavaignac looks incongruous beside the officers of the Commission (Fig. 9.6).

In his vast assortment of writings that include speeches, a three-volume book, *Índios do Brasil*, and reports spanning decades, Rondon devotes particular attention to the Nambiquaras: "Among the savage populations of Brazil none has currently awakened such attention as the Nhambiquara or

Fig. 9.4 Photograph by José Louro. Olga Higgins with two of her Paresi students. (Source: *Índios do Brasil*, vol 1, p. 107. Museu do Índio)

Fig. 9.5 Photographs by José Louro, Album of 1922. Chief Nuchilaitê and his wife. (Source: Museu do Índio)

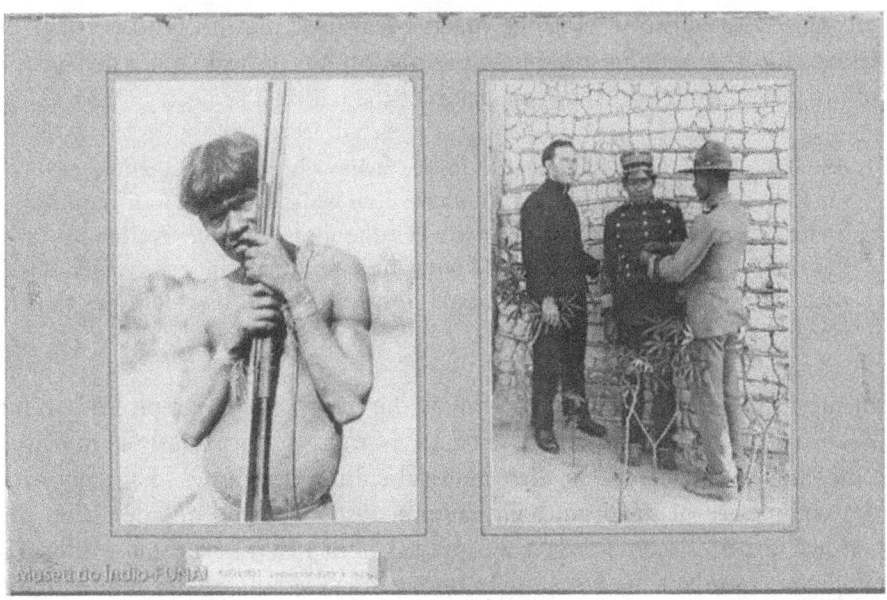

Fig. 9.6 Photographs by José Louro, Album of 1922. Portrait of Cavaignac posing as a Nambiquara and dressed in uniform. Only the photograph of Cavaignac as a Nambiquara was donated to the Société de Géographie.
In the collection given to the Société de Géographie, the portrait of Cavaignac dressed in uniform is absent. There is only his image with his arrows and posing as a Nambiquara. (Source: Museu do Índio)

Nambiquara that live in the extreme north of the state of Mato Grosso" (Rondon 1910: 48, my translation). He continues: "When my expedition began to enter the territory of these Indians they made several warnings that they did not desire us to traverse these lands" (Rondon 1910: 48, my translation). The Nambiquaras actively resisted the encroachment of their land by settlers, rubber tappers, and members of the Rondon Commission. In the expedition of 1907, Rondon and his men were attacked at the margins of the river Juruena in late October. One of the Nambiquara arrows became embedded in the leather pouch of his rifle. In his report, Rondon writes of this expedition: "The Nambiquara are in the proximity of the Juruena, we presume on the left margin of the river and in the valleys of its tributaries. They are warrior Indians, enemies of the Paresis and of the civilized men with whom they do not want any kind of relation, maybe because these, always when they encounter them, pursue them with rifle shots with the intention of expelling them from the regions they conquer for rubber exploitation" (Rondon 1910: 68, my translation). As mentioned previously, Rondon recognized the historic violence practiced against the indigenous tribes of Brazil, but he also understood how negotiation was imperative for the success of the telegraph line and the expansion of the national project:

> Above all, I placed the sentiment of justice facing with meditated reflection on the Saintly Cause of the Indians who have been besieged during four centuries by the most avid greed of our ancestors. Furthermore, the conservation of the line that we proposed to build could not withstand the continuous menace of a tribe with which we had scarcely begun to have relations. (Rondon, Relatório Geral, 1910: 61, my translation)

In the 1930s, Lévi-Strauss would follow the trail of the telegraph lines in his fieldwork. The Nambiquaras offered Lévi-Strauss a particularly compelling case study as the scarcity of their material culture contrasted so sharply with the complexity of their symbolic cultural system. When decades later, the seminal text of *Tristes Tropiques* was published in 1955, Lévi-Strauss offered a poignant, mordant, and obliquely humoristic account of the modernizing venture of Rondon's telegraph line:

> Living on the Rondon Line was much like living on the moon. Imagine a territory the size of France, three-quarters of it unexplored; inhabited only by little bands of nomads, who are among the most genuinely primitive of the world's peoples; and traversed from one end to another by a telegraph line. The picada, or summary track which runs alongside it, is for nearly five hundred miles the region's only landmark. The Rondon Commission undertook a reconnaissance or two to the north and the south, but except for these the traveler may be said to step into the unknown the moment he leaves the picada and even the picada itself is sometimes not easily distinguished. There remains, you may say, the wire itself: but the wire, obsolete from the day of its completion, hung down from poles never replaced when they go to rot and tumble to the ground. (Lévi-Strauss 1996: 262)

The ruinous and outmoded aspect of Rondon's enterprise envisaged by Lévi-Strauss also encompassed the demise of the indigenous tribes that Rondon met. In regard to photographic efforts, Lévi-Strauss also made portraits of the Nambiquara but only included them in later editions of *Tristes Tropiques*. It is as if the photographic record distracted readers from the authority of the written word and ethnographic research. The photographic image, in this case, was illustrative, but it had less authority than the travel narrative and the ethnographic analysis.

Lévi-Strauss comments that for the Nambiquaras the publicly revealed names are shadow names, names given for external use because the real name of a person is shielded from the public eye.[13] Yet, even if true names were publicly revealed, the relation between name and self was not structured according to Western ideas of individual autonomy or social role-playing. In an insightful essay on the contemporary Mamaindê, a Nambiquara group from the northeastern part of Mato Grosso, anthropologist Joanna Miller (2015) comments that they regard the Brazilian national identity card bearing an individual's photograph as the equivalent to the symbolic necklaces that they carry inside their bodies. Bearing their internal and external adornments, the Mamaindê traverse the forest unmolested by the spirits of the wilderness. In a similar fashion, Brazilian citizens are allowed to cross territorial boundaries when they show the police their photo identification cards. According to Miller, for the Nambiquara, the equivalence between ornament and photo is not grounded on representational meaning, nor is it premised on the notion that the photo stands for the person's face. Rather, the equivalency is symbolic and place oriented. The photo as document ensures a right of way.

In contemporary Mato Grosso, the Nambiquaras are composed of distinct groups occupying a diversity of regions in the state of Mato Grosso and also in the south of the state of Roraima. The three distinct languages spoken comply with different geographical locations that include the Nambiquara of the South constituted by groups of the Vale do Guapore and the Chapada dos Parecis, the Sabanê, and the Nambiquara of the North formed by the groups that live in the Serra do Norte of Mato Grosso. Despite the violence they've endured, unlike several other indigenous peoples that have been completely exterminated, the Nambiquara survived although their numbers have been drastically reduced to fewer than 2000 (http://pib.socioambiental.org/pt/Povo Nambiquara).

In 1953, the anthropologist Darcy Ribeiro who had been an active interlocutor of Rondon created the Museu do Índio and the Museum stored documentation that used to belong to the Indian Protection Service and Rondon's archives. In dialogue with Paul Rivet from the Musée de l'homme, who came to Rio in 1954, Darcy Ribeiro attempted to create the Museu do Índio as a cultural and scientific haven against racial prejudice. He emphasized that

> the traditional museums of ethnology were expositions of what those peoples presented as being exotic, different from us: the visitor sought to appreciate headshrinkers, cannibals or self-mutilators, something that offered emotions of amazement or perplexity or even of disgust and rejection, never of solidarity with their dramatic destiny. (Ribeiro 1962: 169–170, my translation)

In accordance with Rivet's universal principles, Ribeiro's ambition was to create an anthropological forum combating racism by emphasizing the diversity of cultures and the equality of all human beings. In the 1950s, Ribeiro and Rondon would promote the creation of the national reservation park of Xingu in Mato Grosso that was finally founded in 1961.

Initially located in the North Zone of Rio de Janeiro in an old nineteenth-century mansion that had formerly housed the Indian Protection Service created in 1910 by Rondon, the Museum of the Indian was relocated to Botafogo in 1977. The former mansion, now designated as the Aldeia Maracanã, was left to crumble, and eventually, it was occupied by distinct groups in 2006. Although the occupants of the Aldeia Maracanã all proclaim themselves to be of indigenous decent, considerable disagreements arose among the dwellers as to who had the right to be considered indigenous. As Daniele Rebuzzi noted in her ethnographic research, some individuals residing in the Aldeia Maracanã were deemed to be

> "fake Indians" (opportunists, people who were trying to gain advantage of the free housing). Neighbors were accused of "not even knowing a song of their ethnic group" or it was said that the new inhabitant was not an Indian but was at that moment "being Indian". (Rebuzzi 2014: 82, my translation)

In 2013, as part of the activities of the World Cup with the final match scheduled in Maracanã, the state authorities decided to remove the occupants of the Aldeia Maracanã. This was actively resisted by the inhabitants of the Aldeia and their political allies, a resistance widely covered in the media. Despite the publicity, a portion of the inhabitants demurred and accepted relocation to public housing. At the end of 2016, after the Olympics, several ethnic groups returned to the Aldeia Maracanã. Among then, indigenous movement leaders with university degrees sought to create an "Indigenous University" in the Aldeia Maracanã (Nitahara 2017, Agência Brasil).

In July of 2016, a group of indigenous people who had been expelled from the Aldeia Maracanã decided to camp out in the current Museum of the Indian after participating in a cultural event. They built a campfire that was extinguished by the employees of the Museum, and eventually, a violent confrontation broke out between police, security guards, indigenous employees of the Museum, and the homeless indigenous group. Because of extensive damages sustained during the clash, the Museum has since been shuttered. Access to the Museum's library can be obtained digitally or by appointment. The confrontation between the homeless indigenous individuals and the Museum of the Indian not only occasioned the shutdown of the Museum, but it also highlighted how the dispute surrounding indigenous identities can become means for obtaining resources and visibility. In the specific case of the Museum of the Indian, an institution belonging to the public patrimony was invaded by a group. The justification for this act was ethnic identity, as if simply belonging to an ethnic group warranted the occupation of public property for their own use. But what is crucial in regard to the questions raised by this chapter is that indigenous identities that were previously adjudicated through a classificatory grid imposed by the non-indigenous are now subject to an intense mutual negotiation between indigenous peoples.

Above all, the concept of acculturation that served to disqualify indigenous subjects that were engaged in hybrid cultural appropriations and modernizing strategies is no longer valid as urban indigenous peoples also claim their indigenous status and as distinct ethnic groups located in remote parts of Brazil also partake of active economic exchanges with society at large. According to the renowned anthropologist Viveiros de Castro, to be indigenous is to consider oneself indigenous and to be recognized as such by fellow indigenous peoples (Viveiros de Castro 2006). Definitions of the indigenous are conditioned by a plethora of political and cultural factors. The scope of the criteria is wide, and it includes the self-definitions of distinct ethnic groups, interpretations forged by a variety of non-governmental organizations (NGOs) and financial institutions, changing policies of the federal government that fluctuate according to distinct agendas, and the input of the consumer market that sells the "authenticity" of indigenous culture through tourist packages.

In the 1950s, the Museum of the Indian created by Darcy Ribeiro sought to overcome an evolutionist positivist agenda by inserting a cultural perspective inspired by Boas and Rivet and also by the work of Brazilian anthropologists. Although the national agenda at that moment was being extensively reworked in favor of the praise of the mestizo culture and ethnic mixing, the attempt of the Museum was to extol the indigenous contribution to Brazilian culture emphasizing the aesthetic beauty of indigenous artifacts and the relevance of indigenous cultures as manifestations of human diversity. The universalizing ambitions of the Museé de l'homme and also the Museum of the Indian at the moment of its creation sought to stress the kinship between diverse peoples. While the Museum of the Indian emphasized the Indian artifacts as objects that had expository value, the photographs of the Rondon Commission were no longer testament to the disappearance of indigenous peoples. In this new context, the images addressed human diversity and signaled the universal validity of all cultures.

In the contemporary moment, agendas of national belonging have become frayed not only because former repertoires no longer convey the cultural representations of a nation that has become simultaneously much more fragmented and also globalized but new social agendas have altered the guidelines of representation, empowerment, and agency. Ethnic diversity has activated new forms of community and self-representation, and the empowerment of formerly silenced groups has become a potent political tool.

In her writings on the cultural policies of museums in Brazil, Regina Abreu noted that the Museum Máguta idealized and created by the Ticunas of the Alto Solimões in the frontiers of Brazil, Colombia, and Peru had become quite successful because it relied on strategies and policies of self-representation (Abreu 2007). But identity politics also are absorbed by marketing strategies of consumer niches and forms of spectacularization that undermine political solidarity among groups. Together with the phenomena of new forms of authorship and agency, the creation of indigenous identities is mutable and shifts according to diverse political, social, and economic demands. As Alcida Ramos has suggested in her well-known essay about the "Hyper-Real Indian", bureaucratic agencies create generic indigenous identities in order to comply with criteria that purportedly will give indigenous peoples access to economic gain and sovereignty of their lands (Ramos 1995).

In the contemporary cartography of Mato Grosso and Mato Grosso do Sul, Rondon's former trails now encompass indigenous reservations, vast plantations, and entire cities planned by agribusiness. The strengthening of indigenous leadership and the increasing number of people who in recent years have declared themselves to be indigenous or of Indian descent confirm that the strategies premised on ethnic identities have been fruitful as they can provide access to resources and give symbolic clout to the subjects claiming indigenous status. This is not to say that the rights and lives of indigenous peoples have not been constantly under threat and undermined. In Brazil, the election of ultra-right-wing president, Jair Bolsonaro, has augmented threats to indigenous lives, terrain, and rights. But the point to be made is that the spread of identity politics by NGOs, anthropologists, indigenous communities, and the consumer market have created diverse ways of "being Indigenous".

Rondon's writings offer many insights of the Brazilian western hinterland, and his descriptions of nature, people, places, and the daily doings of the exploratory expeditions are crucial documents that reveal not only the mentality of a certain historical period but also the quality of his own personal perceptions. Nevertheless, his narrative is often burdened by prosaic descriptions, and his views are regimented so as to emphasize patriotic duty, progress, order, and the march of civilization. By contrast, the images of the

Rondon Commission have gained a life of their own beyond the circumstances of their production. In glass plates, film, microfilm, and now in digitalized version, the pictures of the Nambiquaras that gaze at us from computer screens become incorporeal images in the ephemeral arena of the virtual realm. But they can also be claimed and brought forth to testify and rekindle the aspirations of communities. Created by the Rondon Commission as evidentiary emblems of classification, the images became testaments to diversity and humanity in the 1950s and now have entered the legacy of history and memory for the distinct indigenous people who link their ancestry to those depicted. These categories overlap as testament, classification, diversity, humanitarianism, and memory were/are used by distinct groups for different purposes. Thus, the photographic pacts arising from specific circumstances—specific regimes of visibility and relations of power—cease to validate the reading of images over time.

From the innovative atmosphere of Paris in the 1920s with its assortment of colonial exhibits, ethnographic displays, and avant-garde appropriations of "primitive" art, to contemporary Rio de Janeiro beset by economic crisis, social conflicts, and political turbulence, these images evoke a past of scars, legacies, and aspirations. Pried from the dormancy of forgotten archives, they became spectral digital pictures that haunt the present and posit unanswered questions.

Notes

1. This chapter is part of a larger research project that has received funding from the Conselho Nacional de Desenvolvimento Científico e Técnológico (CNPq) and the Capes of the Brazilian Federal Government. I thank both institutions for their support. I also thank the employees of the Museu do Índio and specifically Thaís Tavares Martins from the iconography section. A version of this chapter has been published in portuguese. See Beatriz Jaguaribe, "Nambiquaras em Paris: imagens de arquivo, deslocamentos e aparições. *Revista Famecos*, REVISTA FAMECOS | PORTO ALEGRE | V. 26, N . 2, MAI .-AGO. 2019 | E-2704 http://dx.doi.org/10.15448/1980-3729.2019.2.32704
2. Auguste Comte's writings and his positivist doctrine were highly influential in Latin America. In Brazil, military officers subscribed fervently to Comte's positivist doctrine. Rondon studies at the military academy with acclaimed positivist professor Benjamin Constant (1837–1891).
3. For a positive appraisal of Rondon's policies toward the indigenous peoples inhabiting Brazil, see Mércio Pereira Gomes' article, "Por que sou rondoniano" in *Estudos Avançados* 23 (65), 2009. In this article, Pereira Gomes

contextualizes Rondon's policies and mentions his acknowledgment of the indigenous populations of Brazil as constituting culturally diverse nations.

4. It is beyond the scope of this chapter to debate the model of integration encamped by Rondon. However, it is worth mentioning that during the Campaña del desierto led by General Roca in 1878, the Argentine army practiced the physical extermination of indigenous populations as part of a state policy. Likewise, in the United States, during its expansionist phase in the nineteenth century, the employment of army troops against Native Americans was a generalized practice. By contrast, Rondon's policy of nonviolence preached assimilation, but it was adamantly against physical oppression or violence. Ricardo Cavalcanti-Siedl notes in his article "A política indigenista, para além dos mitos de segurança nacional" (*Estudos Avançados* 23(65), pp. 149–164, 2009) that Rondon's strategy toward the positioning of the indigenous tribes in their territory presented different models. The prevalent model of assimilation and connection with the state through the presence of the telegraph stations was widely used in Mato Grosso. Yet toward the end of his life, Rondon espoused an alternative view an idea of the indigenous reservation where indigenous cultures could thrive without the pressures of assimilation. It was in this spirit of preservation that Rondon envisioned the creation of the National Park of Xingu, now named the indigenous Park of Xingu. The Xingu park, finally created in 1961, is Brazil's largest indigenous park. It has 2,642,003 acres and is located in the state of Mato Grosso, bordering the state of Pará.

5. The Roosevelt-Rondon expedition received extensive media coverage and did much to enhance Rondon's worldwide fame. The expedition began in December of 1913 and ended in April, 1914. As is well known, Roosevelt nearly died on the expedition. Roosevelt's book, *Through the Brazilian Wilderness* (New York: Charles Scribners and Sons, 1914), provides his firsthand account of the formidable expedition. Thomaz Reis compiled footage from several different films and with Roosevelt's aid exhibited the film, *Wilderness*, to a packed Carnegie Hall on June 15, 1918.

6. Pierre Denis writes a laudatory account of Rondon and of the cartographic efforts under the supervision of Francisco Jaguaribe. The article is entitled: "Résultats Géographiques des Explorations du Colonel Rondon au Matto Grosso", *Annales de Géographie*, Paris, 1924, pp. 46–65.

7. The documents referring to Jaguaribe's mission in France at the service of the Rondon Commission are to be found in the archives of the Sérvice historique de la Défense, Château Vincennes, Code 7 N3391, EMA/2, Brésil, 1918–1940, Mission Gamelin, 1914–1925, 13, 391.

8. Rivet writes the text praising Rondon entitled "La protection des indiens au Brésil", *Journal de la Société des américanistes*, 1913, pp. 687–691.

9. See Doris Sommer's well-known book, *Foundational Fictions: The National Romances of Latin America*. Berkeley: University of California Press, 1993. The best known Brazilian Indianist writer was José de Alencar (1857–1865),

whose romantic novels such as *Iracema* (1865), *O Guarani* (1865), and others became assigned reading in Brazilian schools throughout the twentieth century.

10. The Reading of Oswald de Andrade's cannibal metaphor as a strategy of cultural appropriation and anticolonial satire has become somewhat of a platitude. Among the vast bibliography on the subject, there are dissident interpretations such as the one espoused by Carlos Járegui. Járegui contends that the cannibal metaphor is not the central motif of the "Manifesto Antropófago" because textually what is emphasized is the construction of a matriarchal mythic utopia that existed prior to the arrival of the Portuguese colonial patriarchal order (Jáuregui 2008: 394, 421, 425). Yet even if the Manifesto does not highlight cannibalism as a strategy of cultural appropriation and empowerment, this provocative reading is widely present in the subsequent unfolding of the movement.

11. For an inspired reading of the ontology of being in the context of indigenous cultures in Brazil, see Eduardo Viveiros de Castro's book, *Cannibal Metaphysics*. Minneapolis: Univocal Publishing, 2014.

12. See Micheal Aird' chapter, "Growing up with Aborigines" published in *Photography's Other Histories*, edited by Christopher Pinney and Nicolas Peterson, Durham and London, Duke University Press, 2003, pp. 23–40. In this chapter, Aird discusses how the descendants of Aborigines who had been photographed in exotic poses recast the meaning of these pictures as they envision them as modes of retaining memory and of recognizing their ancestors. In a similar vein, Luciana Alves Barbio in her article, "Comissão Rondon e a representação da identidade Paresí: um diálogo através de fotografias", RECIIC, v5, n. 2, pp. 27–43, June, 2011, comments on, during her research with the Paresi of Rio Formoso, the indigenous people she interviewed that all demonstrated great appreciation for the photographs of the Rondon Commission and searched for images of their ancestors in the pictures.

13. For a discussion of the symbolic meaning of the Nambiquara act of naming, see Marcelo Fiorini's Ph.D. dissertation, "The Silencing of the Names: Identity and Alterity in an Amazonian Society". New York University: New York, 2000.

Bibliography

Abreu, Regina. 2007. Mario de Souza Chagas; Myriam Sepúlveda dos Santos. (Org.). Museus, coleções e patrimônios: narrativas polifônicas. Edição: Rio de Janeiro: Garamond Universitária, p. 138–178.

Aird, Micheal. 2003. Growing Up with Aborigines. In *Photography's Other Histories*, ed. Christopher Pinney and Nicolas Peterson, 23–39. Durham e Londres: Duke University Press.

Azoulay, Ariella. 2008. *The Civil Contract of Photography*. Cambridge: The MIT Press.
Barbio, Luciana Alves. 2011. Comissão Rondon e a representação da identidade Paresí: um diálogo aravés da fotografia. *Revista Eletrônica de Comunicação, Informação e Inovação em Saúde* 5 (2): 27–43, Rio de Janeiro.
Barthes, Roland. 1989. *Câmera clara*. São Paulo: Edições, 70.
Bigio, Eliás. 2000. *A integração nacional*. Rio de Janeiro: Contraponto.
———. 2003. *Linhas telegráficas e integração de povos indígenas: as estratégias políticas de Rondon (1889–1930)*. Brasília: Funai.
Blanchard, Pascal, Gilles Boetsch, Nanette Jacomijn Snoep, Lilian Thuram, and Stéphane Martin. 2012. *Exhibition, L'invention du sauvage*. Paris: Actes Sud Editions. ISBN 2330002602.
Bretón, Víctor. 2015. La politización de la etnicidad en la región andina: apuntes sobre un debate inconcluso. *European Review of Latin American and Caribbean Studies* 100: 41–51.
Cavalcanti-Schiel, Ricardo. 2009. A política indigenista, para além dos mitos de segurança nacional. *Estudos Avançados* 23 (65): 149–164.
Cavignac, Julie A. 2012. L'Américanisme français au début du XXème siècle: projets politiques, muséologie et terrains brésiliens. *Vibrant: Virtual Brazilian Anthropology* [online] 9(1): 24–81. ISSN 1809-4341. https://doi.org/10.1590/S1809-43412012000100002.
Conklin, Alice. 2013. *In the Museum of Man: Race, Anthropology, and Empire in France, 1850–1950*. Ithaca e London: Cornell University Press.
Crary, Jonathan. 1990. *Techniques of the Observer*. Cambridge: MIT Press.
Cunha, Euclides da. 2009. *Obra Completa*. Vol. II. Rio de Janeiro: Ediotra Nova Aguilar.
Denis, Pierre. 1924. Résultats Géographiques des Explorations du Colonel Rondon au Matto Grosso. *Annales de Géographie* 33 (181): 46–65.
Diacon, Todd. 2004. *Stringing Together a Nation*. Durham: Duke University Press.
Dodebei, Vera, and Regina Abreu, eds. 2008. *E o patrimônio?* Rio de Janeiro: Contracapa.
Fiorini, Marcelo Oppido. 2000. *The Silencing of the Names: Identity and Alterity in an Amazonian Society*. New York University, Graduate School of Arts and Science, Doctoral Thesis.
Gomes Pereira, Mércio. 2009. Por que sou rondoniano. *Estudos Avançados* 23 (65): 173–191.
Guérios, Paulo Renato. 2003. Heitor Villa-Lobos e o ambiente atístico parisiense: convertendo-se em um músico brasileiro. *Mana* 9 (1): 81–108, Rio de Janeiro.
Jáuregui, Carlos. 2008. *Canibalismo, Calibanismo, Antropofagía Cultural y Consumo em América Latina*. Madrid: Iberoamericana.
Kingman, Eduardo. 2012. Los usos ambíguos del archivo, la Historia y la memoria. *Íconos, Revista de Ciencias Sociales* 42: 123–133, Quito.
Lasmar, Denise Portugal. 2011. *O acervo imagético da Comissão Rondon no Museu do Índio (1890–1938)*. Rio de Janeiro: Museu do Índio-Funai.

Lévi-Strauss, Claude. 1996. *Tristes trópicos*. São Paulo: Companhia das Letras.
Loiseaux, Olivier. 2006. *Tresors photographiques de la Sociéte de Géographie*. Paris: Bibliothéque national de France/Glénant.
Maciel, Laura. 1998. *A nação por um fio: caminhos, práticas e imagens da Comissão Rondon*. São Paulo: Educ, Fapesp.
Magalhães, Amilcar Botelho. 1942. *Impressões da Comissão Rondon*. Rio de Janeiro: Companhia Editora Nacional.
Miller, Joana. 2015. Carteira de Alteridade: transformações Mamaindê (Nambiquara). *Mana* 21 (3): 553–585.
Nitahara, Akemi. 2017. *Aldeia Maracanã mantém tradições indígenas e cobra reconhecimento*. http://agenciabrasil.ebc.com.br/direitos-humanos/noticia/2017-04/aldeia-maracana-mantem-tradicoes-indigenas-e-cobrareconhecimento.
Pacheco de Oliveira, João. 2006. *Hacia una antropología del indigenismo: estudios críticos sobre los procesos de dominación y las perspectivas actuales de los indígenas en Brasil*. Rio de Janeiro/Lima: Contra Capa/Centro Amazónico de Antropología y Aplicación Práctica.
———. 2010. ¿Una etnología de los indios misturados? Identidades étnicas y territorialización en el Nordeste del Brasil. Desacatos, n. 33, mayoagosto 2010. p. 13–32.
———. 2013. El nacimiento del Brasil: Revisión de un paradigma historiográfico. *Corpus, archivos virtuales de la alteridad americana* 3 (1). https://doi.org/10.4000/corpusarchivos.192.
———. 2016. *O nascimento do Brasil e outros ensaios*. Rio de Janeiro: Contra Capa.
Pratt, Mary. 1992. *Imperial Eyes: Travel Writing and Transculturation*. New York/London: Routledge.
Ramos, Alcida Rita. 1995. O índio hiper-real. *Revista Brasileira de Ciências Sociais* 28 (10): 5–14, São Paulo.
Ranciére, Jacques. 2013. *O destino das imagens*. Rio de Janeiro: Contraponto.
Rebuzzi, Daniele da Costa. 2014. A aldeia Maracanã: um movimento contra o *índio arquivado*. Revista de @ntropologia da UFSCAR, R@U 6 (2): 71–86.
Ribeiro, Darcy. 1962. *A política indigenista brasileira*. Rio de Janeiro: Ministério da Agricultura.
Rivet, Paul. 1913. La protection des indiens au Brésil. *Journal de la Société des américanistes* 10 (2): 687–691, Tome.
Rondon, Candido Mariano da Silva. 1910. *Relatório Geral, 1907–1910*. Papelaria Luiz Macedo: Rio de Janeiro.
———. 1946. *Índios do Brasil. Volume 1*. Rio de Janeiro: Conselho Nacional de Proteção aos Índios.
———. 1994. *História Natural Etnographia*. Rio de Janeiro: Papelaria Luiz Macedo.
Roosevelt, Theodore. 1914. *Through the Brazilian Wilderness*. New York: Charles Scribners and Sons.
Souza Lima, Antonio Carlos. 1995. *Um grande cerco de paz: poder tutelar e indianidade*. Petrópolis: Vozes. https://doi.org/10.1590/s0104-93131997000100013.

———. 2001. *Um grande cerco de paz: poder tutelar e indianidade*, tese de doutorado, Museu Nacional: UFRJ, 1992, TACCA, Fernando de. *A imagética da Comissão Rondon*. Campinas: Papirus.

———. 2015. Sobre Tutela e Participação: Povos Indígenas e Formas de Governo no Brasil, Séculos XX/XXI. *Mana* 21 (2): 425–457.

Tacca, Fernando. 2001. *A imagética da Comissão Rondon*. Campinas: Papirus.

———. 2017. Major Thomaz Reis-Fotografia e cinematografia da Comissão Rondon. In *Rondon, inventários do Brasil 1900–1930*, ed. Lorelai Kury and Magali Romero Sá, 144–169. Rio de Janeiro: Editora Andrea Jakobssson.

Tagg, John. 1988. *The Burden of Representation: Essays on Photographies and Histories*. Minneapolis: University of Minnesota Press.

Viveiros De Castro, Eduardo. 2006. No Brasil, todo mundo é índio. Exceto quem não é. Interview. Povos indígenas no Brasil. http://pib.socioambiental.org

———. 2015. *Metafísicas canibais*. São Paulo: Cosac & Naify.

Williams, Elizabeth. 1985. Art and Artifact at the Trocadero: Ars Americana and the Primitivst Revolution. In *Essays on Museums and Material Culture*, ed. George W. Stocking Jr. Madison: The University of Wisconsin Press.

Sites

http://agenciabrasil.ebc.com.br/tags/aldeia-maracana
http://www.fronteirasemovimentos.com.br/Rondon/nova_pagina_5.htm
Povos Indígenas do Brasil, http://pib.socioambiental.org/pt/Povo: Nambikwara

Archives

Bibliothéque. Nacional de France.
Château Vincennes, Sérvice de la Defense.
Museu do Índio, Rio de Janeiro.
Société. de Géographie.

10

Future Memory: Preserving Diverse Voices from and About China in a Time of Unification of Thought

Rudolf G. Wagner

China and the Internet

The Internet has become an important medium of communication in the Chinese-speaking and the sinological world. It has empowered many people who hitherto had no public voice to join in public debates, has allowed public voices to venture into domains formerly out of their reach, and has become an important archive for sources of relevance for Chinese Studies now and in the future. Given the communication structure of the People's Republic of China (PRC) with its strong and unified censorial control by the Communist Party of China (CPC)—a control that has kept up with the rapid technological transformation of Internet communication and social media—many public utterances concerned with state and society will only be accessible for a very short time (this is true even for official government statements), and many of the more elaborate statements or even works from within the PRC will only surface and survive in the public Internet domain outside the PRC. Even then, their availability over the long term is precarious.

There had been some optimism that the economic opening of China would lead to a relaxing of the censorial controls. This optimism has not been borne out by actual developments. After a brief "liberal" interlude when Hu Yaobang was in charge of Party Propaganda (1978–1981) and then General Secretary of the Party (1981–1986), things have become increasingly restrictive. This

---

R. G. Wagner (Deceased)

followed the demonstrations and crackdown on Tiananmen Square and other cities in June 1989, with the leadership imposing ever tighter controls culminating in the present regime of Party Chairman Xi Jinping. The Party propaganda authorities have also developed more proactive strategies: no longer limited to blocking unwelcome voices, they now push teachers in the country's schools and universities to actively spread Party doctrine, and have also hired an army of "tencent" bloggers who, for modest fees (they are paid by the statement), go online to defend the leadership and denounce critics.

The propaganda authorities employ a number of techniques to control public exchange. These range from blocking information resources (Google, *New York Times*, *Financial Times*, Bloomberg) and persecuting companies offering VPN detours along with the individuals who make use of them, demanding name registration for e-mail accounts, and storage of e-mails on Chinese servers that provide authorities access to their content, to daily lists of banned terms and topics that are routinely deleted from the web, and the deletion of the online and printed communications of public intellectuals and officials who have run afoul of government policies. Efforts of the Propaganda Department to extend their control beyond the nation's borders involve increasing the number of minders for Chinese students in foreign universities and requesting web providers of scholarly works such as Cambridge University Press, Springer, or Taylor & Francis to delete from their offerings to subscribers in the PRC "unwelcome" articles and books. At the same time, the Party is trying to muffle dissent by filling the Internet (as well as scholarly journal and entertainment media) with content aligned with Party priorities. While this model of controlling the public sphere through preventative and proactive measures might not have pleased allies in places such as the European Union (EU) and the Unites States, it appeals to a growing number of governments in Asia and Africa. They have begun acquiring tools (many of them developed in the United States) and are developing their own criteria for distinguishing acceptable from unacceptable public speech.

Nor should it be forgotten that the sophisticated use of Internet communication by voices such as Islamic State of Iraq and Syria (ISIS), groups promoting racial hatred, or foreign governments trying to influence public media and elections, as we have recently seen in the United States, has led to a lively debate outside of China about the need for a legal framework for Internet exchange that would be enforced by national or international government bodies such as the European Union or even a United Nations body. The Chinese Communist Party and government have dominated this discussion, arguing that many states already have regulatory systems similar to those in China and that they are necessary to state security and protecting the public from foreign propaganda and pornography.

A Memory Preserved

There are many reasons why the preservation of diverse Chinese voices beyond the control of the Chinese government is of paramount general interest. Since 1949 if not longer, China has been experiencing some of the most dramatic and accelerated changes of any national population. These rapid changes experienced by the Chinese people represent a precious and invaluable part of human heritage as well as a source of great importance for students of sociology, political science, law, psychology, and mentalité and transcultural interaction whose approaches are historically inclined. For the pre-Internet age, foreign research institutions have made valiant and to a degree successful efforts to preserve the diversity of exchange by countering consistent Chinese government efforts to block information not pre-digested by Party agents. The Red Guard papers from the Cultural Revolution are the best-known examples, but there are also many studies that avoided reliance on a master narrative streamlined according to the government and Party doctrine of the day by relying, for example, on data gathered from interview partners who had left the country or by making good use of the often serendipitous access to archival records.

Still, Party-line content is unstable, displaying frequent shifts. These shifts are accompanied by rearrangements of the official narrative and accessible sources of the past (from the deep to the recent past). By preserving such sources and developing narratives that have escaped the latest government adjustment, foreign Chinese Studies institutions make major contributions to the preservation of China's history. Everyone who has worked in a China institute in the West, Hong Kong, Taiwan, or Japan knows the intense use made of these preserved resources and the arguments developed on their basis by scholars coming from the PRC. In this manner, these resources and arguments even become part of a store of knowledge available for inner-Chinese discussions. As strange as this may sound, once policy shifts, as it does frequently in this context, these resources and the translated writings based on them by foreign authors become privileged parts of the inner-Chinese debate. A good example is the largest man-made famine of the twentieth century from the Great Leap Forward years (1958–1961). It had no place in official PRC memory since it reflected badly on the "flawless" Party leadership. Dealing with it was further complicated by the return of the leaders who had been in charge during the Great Leap Forward to power after the Cultural Revolution. Deng Xiaoping was General Secretary of the Party during the Great Leap. Foreign scholars reconstructed the volume, duration, and geographic distribution of the famine from later demographic data, other foreigners scoured the copies of the *Neibu cankao* (materials for internal reference among the top leadership) that had somehow ended up in the Chinese University of Hong Kong to see what the leadership knew about the crisis, and still others combed local archives during an opportune interval of regulatory confusion. The result was not just invaluable insight into the political process at a moment of great human disaster that coincided with an ideological purge which closed all avenues of critical opinion but also about the ways in which the resulting trauma was marginalized in one of the great feats in the government administration of memory. These studies also created a record that could serve as a crucial information source during a brief and propitious moment within the PRC when the Great Leap was resurrected from amnesia, soon supplemented by publicly available memoirs of people who had survived the crisis. The health of the Chinese body politic depends on instances like these where independent of the government narrative of the moment ongoing external efforts have preserved the country's national past.

China is just one case among many. Altogether, Asia may be considered the laboratory of the twenty-first century. It offers all the extremes from failed states to highly regulated capitalist enclaves, from theocracies to Communist Party–run economies and inherited dictatorships, from deep illiteracy to the top high school students in the world, from nationalist fury to vast refugee movements, and from regions where the permafrost is thawing to allow for the growing of plants from temperate zones to tropical zones that are being dried up by heat or drowned by rising waters. The voices and memories of Asia as it faces these challenges are a vital part of humanity's experience and of the record required for scholarly analysis, but vast sections of this archive have been lost through the natural process of forgetting, through interventions by the political leadership, through neglect, and through the failure to utilize technologies that could help to preserve some of it at a modest cost. Increasingly, these voices and memories are digital in form and dependent for their preservation on storage facilities that can be supervised and managed by political authorities. This management does not simply come in the form of censorship/deletion, but in the PRC endeavors to crowd out other voices with propaganda. To preserve an accurate reflection of the tensions inherent in this structure, efforts cannot be reduced to preserving "dissident" voices before they are deleted. The government's own pronouncements of guidance are as unstable in their existence. They are part of the record of state-society interaction in this period of transition.

The problem does not end here. In Chinese Studies as well as in other fields of scholarship, references to online resources have been rising steeply. A check of these links in Chinese Studies articles shows a specific loss curve ("link rot") that privileges the official administration of PRC memory. Online references to official sources such as the *People's Daily* or Xinhua releases remain accessible over long stretches of time, while those to unofficial sources have a life span of a few seconds, months, or years. Without a depository outside the PRC administration to preserve the sources for references, the verification of scholarly claims becomes ever more difficult quite apart from the fact that the selection of these sources for reference originally involved much work. As it is often the case, the selection of these on-line sources signals their relevancy to the study. (Studies of online references in various science and legal scholarly journals show that even here the "link rot" is very substantial and starts surprisingly early.)[1]

The Digital Archive of Chinese Studies, Institute of Chinese Studies, Heidelberg University, Germany

The steeply increasing Internet communication in the PRC and the equally steeply increasing government activities to control and exploit this new medium, together with the ensuing loss of many relevant voices, led to the 2001 Heidelberg plan to preserve for public access some of the PRC-internal as well as PRC-relevant public debates inside and outside of China in a repository beyond the purview of the PRC propaganda authorities. With initial funding from the Alfried Krupp von Bohlen und Halbach Foundation, we set up the European Center for Digital Resources in Chinese Studies where Digital Archive of Chinese Studies (DACHS) was housed together with databases we subscribed to or developed. http://www.zo.uni-heidelberg.de/boa/digital_resources/dachs/

Remarkably, the Stiftung Preussischer Kulturbesitz in Berlin with its large and stable resources incorporated and expanded our original plan to increase the number of source databases, scholarly work, and media from China and make them accessible throughout Germany. The CrossAsia platform is now available to all Asian Studies institutions in Germany providing what by any standard is the best or close to the best online resource pool for scholarly research in Chinese Studies. http://staatsbibliothek-berlin.de/die-staatsbibliothek/abteilungen/ostasien-alt/recherche-und-ressourcen/crossasia/ It has contributed hugely to leveling the playing field among German institutions on China research. Meanwhile, Heidelberg has continued to develop further specialized databases. (http://www.zo.uni-heidelberg.de/boa/digital_resources/list_az_de.html)

For DACHS, which because of copyright concerns remains behind a password, but not a paywall, we gradually developed a set of criteria for the selection of data for download and preservation. These are:

From the PRC as well as overseas Chinese-language discussions. Targeted downloads:

Articles/topics that led to broad discussions in the PRC.
Writings by and about individuals who might be considered "public intellectuals."
Debates about the role of Party/government in the public sphere as well as relevant government decrees and speeches by leaders.
Memoirs about the PRC past in the form of texts, interviews, and TV programs from inside and outside China.
Government propaganda of relevance to international relations.

Automatic downloads:

Small numbers of newspapers and online periodicals with often contested content.
About 50 blogs.

From Western-language sources about the PRC

Well-documented articles in out-of-the-way places (wide range of PRC topics from law to the economy, from the military to religious groups).

In terms of finances and personnel, DACHS is a small operation (one to two technical staff, three to four "feeders" with the bulk coming from one). Efforts to secure long-term institutional support were not successful, since this was not recognized as a "project," and resources for library development were only gradually considered usable for the development of digital resources. Since 2005, the German Research Foundation (DFG) has been providing some support in the framework of funding for a "Virtual professional library East and South Asia" in Heidelberg. But the research hours required for targeted searches remain underfunded. A good example of a targeted search: In 2004, the *Nanfang renwu* journal in Canton published a list of what they called the most important "public intellectuals" of the Chinese-speaking world. We concluded that the Party would see this as a competition to its monopoly of an authoritative voice in the public sphere and would soon crack down. We therefore collected all resources and available information and discussion about these 50 people. Shortly thereafter, the issue of the periodical was banned, as was the use of the term public intellectual and the writings of these people disappeared from the Chinese internet. From this example, it is clear that developing such an archive demands a continuous hunt for relevant pieces and then rapid decision-making. DACHS has made efforts to develop cooperation with other scholars and institutions, including Leiden University, where scholars were interested in the budding field of Chinese online poetry and fiction. A second strategy to enhance DACHS was to offer students who had done research about online discussions for their MA or PhD dissertation projects to upload these very targeted harvests into DACHS. A third strategy was to offer *China Studies* journals the option to ask authors who referred to online resources to save the downloads in DACHS in order to keep them accessible, an overture that was mostly unsuccessful. The life of DACHS very much like that of the *China Digital Times* in Berkeley continues to depend largely on a few individuals willing to put in the labor to maintain it.

DACHS, at present, holds about six million files from 13,156 websites, of which about a third are Chinese-language sites. It automatically downloads the communication at 177 websites (newspapers, blogs, discussion forums), the large majority of them Chinese. Most of the work goes into targeted downloads of source documents and scholarly/journalistic articles. DACHS has a modest 150+ users. We have not made great efforts to spread the use because of the ongoing effort to create a framework that would host the entire set of data, which involves transferring the data to WARC format, an ISO standard format for Web archives since 2009. We are also working on a unified search engine for all the data irrespective of their language and format. This is a hugely complex enterprise and will take time. At present, searches operate via keywords in English.

In conclusion, targeted archiving of Chinese public voices outside the control of the PRC government is a paramount enterprise. It cannot be done mechanically, but requires a labor-intensive "hunting" approach very much like the collecting of relevant print books from the PRC (given the vast field of "neibu" books that are not publicly accessible, but of great importance). This approach presupposes "hunters" who are familiar with a wide range of issues discussed in the PRC, the key platforms where these are discussed, the most important actors in the public domain, and a backup staff of technically savvy people who can make momentous and immediate decisions to preserve crucial materials. It would be optimal to proceed in a collaborative fashion with the various hunters joining and feeding a common database. To facilitate multidimensional searches in increased depth, data collected by specialized groups or for particular scholarly research should be collected and integrated. This could and should be supplemented by an agreement with China journals that their authors automatically deposit the online resources they quote for long-term archiving to secure accessibility. The option to offer to authors who have privately accumulated such digital resources and are willing to share them with others to upload them should be pursued because these targeted collections often represent hundreds of hours of highly specialized work. Storage is becoming ever cheaper. Vigilance and precaution, however, remain a necessity because the PRC authorities will undoubtedly seek to plug these holes in their perpetual effort to administrate the collective perception and memory.

Note

1. DPC/PADI "What's new in digital preservation" write: "Following their influential study published in *Science* in 2004 (vol. 302, pp. 787–788), Dellavalle and colleagues have produced more evidence of the volatility of Web references in the medical literature. Their recent studies have included references in oncology journals (Hester, et al., 2004) and the Internet citation policies of high-impact STM journals (Schilling, et al., 2004). These support other recent studies of URL references in the biomedical literature (Crichlow et al. 2004; Wren, 2004); the stability of Web references has also been cited as being a critical issue for the publication of clinical trials (Tumber and Dickersin, 2004, pp. 278–279). Bar-Ilan and Peritz (2004) have provided a similar analysis of Web documents in the informetrics sub-discipline of information science."
http://www.dpconline.org/graphics/whatsnew/issue9.html#2. For a summary of the more recent research on "link rot," see https://journalistsresource.org/studies/society/internet/website-linking-best-practices-media-online-publishers

11

Cold War Archives and Democratic Aspirations in Latin America

Kirsten Weld

The notion of "human rights archives" has gained much currency in recent years, both inside and outside the academy. If in a certain moment it was possible to see records as merely incidental to larger processes of legal and social repair in the aftermath of massive political violence—nearly 20 years ago, the transitional justice scholar Louis Bickford wrote that "an emphasis on archival preservation is often not explicitly highlighted as a key ingredient to deepening democracy and the long-term vibrancy of democratic practices in countries that have experienced traumatic pasts"—that moment has passed.[1] A number of factors have contributed to this shift. First is the rise of human rights, from the 1970s onward, as the dominant paradigm for interpreting political contestation.[2] This has led episodes of social tumult and political atrocity to be viewed, increasingly, as matters of individual victims and perpetrators requiring adjudication in court. The roughly parallel rise of "transitional justice," comprising a set of practices designed to support capitalist democratic governance in the wake of its abrogation, is also related, since many of the core processes of transitional justice—trials, lustrations, and the like—depend heavily on the recuperation of documentary evidence.[3] This growing interest in human rights and transitional justice more generally is reflected in the relevant academic fields: law, history to some extent, and archival science, where, archivist Michelle Caswell reports, the appeal of human rights frameworks has "exploded" in the past decade.[4] It makes sense:

K. Weld (✉)
Department of History, Harvard University, Cambridge, MA, USA
e-mail: weld@fas.harvard.edu

© The Author(s) 2020
S. L. Mizruchi (ed.), *Libraries and Archives in the Digital Age*,
https://doi.org/10.1007/978-3-030-33373-7_11

the logics of human rights and transitional justice presuppose the documentability of truth, as well as a belief in the possible redress of historical wrongs via what in Latin America is commonly referred to as the "recuperation of historical memory."[5] And it turns out that post–Cold War Latin America is particularly fruitful territory for considering the complex relationships between archives, justice, democracy, and the law, because of its many national truth commissions, varied efforts to prosecute dictatorship-era officials, and activist initiatives to rescue and deploy the documents of past repressive regimes in the service of building new political and social orders.[6]

However, if human rights, *pace* Samuel Moyn, are a kind of utopia, then so too are human rights archives. There is no inherent or necessary correlation between the availability of more documents and the existence of more truth, accountability, rights, or justice; however, these concepts might be defined in a particular time and place.[7] The records of past repressive regimes—like all records—are incomplete, flawed, potentially duplicitous, and tremendously challenging to safely rescue, store, and use, for both logistical and political reasons.[8] (Digital preservation techniques circumvent certain of these challenges but give rise to others, as we shall see.) The existence of abundant evidence, documentary or otherwise, does not guarantee the smooth execution of courtroom justice, especially in precarious post-conflict settings in which judicial institutions remain under either the direct control or the indirect sway of ancien régime officials. Nor does the smooth execution of courtroom justice offer forms of repair that correspond to the structural and collective nature of state violence.[9] And because, as anthropologist Carlota McAllister writes, Latin American justice seekers in the neoliberal world order have framed their demands in the terms of "a post-Cold War liberalism for which violence theoretically lay beyond the pale," complex and nuanced possible histories of political struggle, including armed struggle, have been minimized in favor of thin legal narratives of perpetrators and victims.[10] Archivally speaking, this means that the recovery of armed social movements' records, and/or records involving struggles for economic and social equality, has often fallen by the wayside, with implications for future historians' ability to undertake nuanced and politically attuned analyses of past events.

Paradoxically, then, the very human rights framework that has enabled greater citizen access to certain kinds of archives has also served to block or diminish access to others.[11] Archivist Trudy Huskamp Peterson points out that "by making human rights synonymous with crimes by states, we obscure the larger picture of human rights: the diverse civil and political and social and economic and cultural rights that are outlined in the Universal Declaration of Human Rights."[12] Moreover, as liberal campaigns for courtroom justice have replaced the more frontal, status quo–upending battles for socioeconomic redistribution that inspired Cold War elites and their international sponsors to take recourse to military rule and state terror in the first place, adjudicating the past can seem, at times, to have taken precedence over agitating in the present.

Yet while records documenting past human rights violations are no panacea, they remain important to broader processes of social repair, often in ways that transcend the probative value of the words printed on the documents' pages. Archivist Eric Ketelaar highlights an "essential connection between archives and human rights: the violation of these rights has been documented in the archives and citizens who defend themselves appeal to the archives …. If the fact of oppression appears in records originally inscribed for surveillance and tyranny, they can also be used for reclaiming human rights and regaining freedom."[13] Certainly, one important way archives can be deployed in post-violence or post-conflict settings is through trials, and often the value of recovering so-called human rights archives is cast in these terms: *now, with evidence in the state's own hand, we will be able to prosecute*. Felicitously, however, given the difficulties of holding them, trials are not the only way forward, and legal repair is not the only contribution that archives can make. Rather, as the efforts of various Latin American social movements to mobilize around archival access reveal, archives are intimately bound up with broader ecological processes of social repair: the reconstitution of collective and activist communities, increased public ownership over practices of memorialization and commemoration, digitization and open-access initiatives, and the rewriting of contested histories and school curricula, to name only a few. To understand the breadth and impact of the many possible "activations" of so-called human rights archives, we must look beyond the strictly legal or juridical, instead examining the collective and contingent processes by which social actors have worked to literally re-member, or rebuild, the archives from which they derive reparatory value.[14]

Modalities of Injury and Repair

The second half of the twentieth century in Latin America, as Gabriel García Márquez once observed, was a period of turmoil and horror so intense—featuring dictatorships, mass disappearances, political murders, refugee crises, and genocide—that it constituted an "outsized reality."[15] Riven by conflicts over economic redistribution, entrenched power, modernity, and ideology, the countries of the Americas, almost without exception, lived the global Cold

War as a kind of simultaneous dream and nightmare: the heady rush of new ideas and coalitions; the joy of collective politics; the radicalization produced by pushback from elites and a disapproving United States; and then the collapse, the bitter realization that revanchist forces would give no quarter in their determination to extirpate challenges to their power.

The nature of these conflicts varied among countries and, in many cases, among regions within countries. In Guatemala, a long history of profound structural racism against the country's majority indigenous Maya population, coupled with a virulent anticommunism informed by United States' national security doctrine, inspired both the army's genocidal scorched-earth campaign against Maya villages in rural guerrilla-contested areas and the police's surgical assassinations and disappearances of student, religious, and labor leaders in the capital city. In El Salvador, the civil war was shorter and more evenly matched; the Farabundo Martí National Liberation Front came very close to achieving its goal of overthrowing the right-wing government, forcing the state to concede that it could not defeat the guerrillas militarily despite its recourse to massacres of civilians and its extensive assistance from the United States. In Chile, the democratically elected president Salvador Allende pursued a constitutional path toward socialist transformation before his overthrow in a 1973 coup led by General Augusto Pinochet, who relied heavily on the tools of torture and forced exile to dismantle pro-Allende sectors; Pinochet was eventually ousted from power by a citizen plebiscite. In Argentina, the military junta, in its so-called National Reorganization Process (*el Proceso*), threw sedated captives from airplanes; kept pregnant detainees in custody until they gave birth, killing the mothers and giving the babies to conservative families to be raised with new identities; and collaborated with other regional militaries, in an initiative led by Chile, to track and murder political opponents throughout South America. While each country's odyssey was distinct, many of them shared common elements: military rule, the committing of systematic crimes against humanity by states, more sporadic violations of human rights by armed insurgent groups, a deep imbrication in global Cold War geopolitics, and an end to open hostilities roughly by the time of the fall of the Berlin Wall. Archives were a key technology of state terror in all four countries, as intelligence agencies beefed up their record-keeping capacity in order to better track and control enemies of the state; in Guatemala, the elite Estado Mayor Presidencial, a high-level intelligence unit notorious for carrying out executions and abductions of dissidents, was known popularly as "El Archivo": the archive.

Post-dictatorship states seeking to sift through the wreckage turned to a new institution: the truth commission. Major national truth commissions were held in most Latin American countries; since 1982, governments have undertaken them in Argentina, Bolivia, Brazil, Chile (twice), Grenada, Guatemala, Ecuador (also twice), El Salvador, Haiti, Honduras, Panama, Paraguay, Peru, and Uruguay, both requiring and generating massive amounts of documents.[16] At the same time, Latin American social movements made access to the archives of past repressive regimes one of their signal political demands; the region's dictatorships had relied heavily on the crime of forced disappearance to dismantle progressive networks, and survivors hoped that these regimes' documents would help identify the whereabouts and resting places of the disappeared.[17] In 1992, Paraguay's "Terror Archives"—the records of its secret police during the Stroessner dictatorship—were discovered, processed, and used in the country's truth commission.[18] After some 20 years of campaigning for access to state security records, in 2005, Guatemalan activists stumbled upon the voluminous and decaying archives of the country's defunct National Police; they launched a still-ongoing effort to rescue and digitize them, now known around the world as the Historical Archive of the National Police (AHPN), all while lobbying for the declassification of the corresponding military archives.[19] In 2008 in Uruguay, President Tabaré Vázquez created the National Archive of Remembrance to make accessible records from more than a decade of military rule.[20] In Brazil in 2009, President Luiz Inácio Lula da Silva ordered the creation of the website "Memories Revealed," where his administration published declassified army records from the country's 20-year dictatorship.[21] In 2010, Argentina declassified all available military records from its Dirty War and reversed its amnesty law for army officials; in Chile, survivors of torture press on with a campaign to secure the release of any remaining documents of the DINA, or Dirección de Inteligencia Nacional, the intelligence service established by General Augusto Pinochet and run by General Manuel Contreras, and of the CNI, or Central Nacional de Informaciones, its successor outfit.[22] One could even say that during the region's "pink tide" of leftist and left-leaning governments (roughly 1998–2016), the Americas saw an "archival cascade" comparable to what political scientist Kathryn Sikkink terms "the justice cascade," and indeed, the two cascades are related: with more documentation of Cold War dictatorships' war crimes have come more trials of military and police perpetrators, although such trials have generally been difficult to secure, and comparatively few and far between.[23] As leading archivists have noted, "the relationship between human rights work and documentation practices has been intimate, vital and co-constitutive, exemplified by the central figure of documentation within transitional justice movements."[24]

If the juridical impulse of post-1970s human rights discourse and practice has been one factor fueling the archival cascade, another has been a gradual change in ideas about the management and use of state records over the course of the past century or so: the rise of the notion that citizens should enjoy the right to access the documents that their governments keep about them. For the vast majority of the period of human history in which rulers have systematically kept written records about the ruled, dating at least as far back as Ancient Greece, there has been little tradition of public access to state records; it was quite the opposite, with *arcana imperii*, the principle of state secrecy, reigning insofar as official documentary production was concerned. That changed with the French Revolution and the birth of the modern nation-state, inaugurating the concept of the publicly accessible national archives—which both implicitly and explicitly privileged records documenting the exercise of state power.[25] It was not until the 1960s and 1970s that a push for archival access from below took hold, with the world's social justice, civil rights, decolonization, and democratization movements including, if obliquely, the demand that particular communities should be able to write their own histories, and should enjoy access to the raw materials—the documents—needed to do so. This involved both the staking of claims to records produced by powerful institutions (governments, churches, universities) and a commitment to activist practices of self-documentation, as seen, for example, with Chile's Vicaría de la Solidaridad during the Pinochet dictatorship.[26] In the 1980s, the Argentine human rights activist, torture survivor, and Nobel Peace Prize laureate Adolfo Pérez Esquivel played a role in conceptualizing and promoting a new legal concept, the right to habeas data—literally, "you should have the data."[27] An informational analogue to habeas corpus, habeas data holds that an individual has the right to access any information about herself or her family that is held by her government. While in recent years it has taken on connotations related to issues of data privacy in the digital age, it originated as a tool of citizen redress under dictatorships that practiced the signal terror tactic of forced disappearance, aspiring to grant individuals the right to access state security files about their absent family members. Since its genesis as a strategy for attempting to force governments to reveal the whereabouts of the disappeared, habeas data has been adopted as a constitutional recourse in Brazil, Paraguay, Colombia, Peru, Ecuador, and Argentina, where the Argentine Supreme Court, in implementing habeas data protections, argued that these afforded citizens "the rights to identity and to reconstruct one's own history, which are closely aligned with human dignity."[28]

From the ashes of the twentieth century's bloody conflicts emerged a series of initiatives designed to standardize and globalize these evolving understandings of the relationships between archives and the protection of human rights. At a meeting in Mexico in 1993, the non-governmental International Council on Archives, a leading association of archival institutions and practitioners, decided to convene a panel of experts "to discuss problems related to archives of former repressive regimes, and to draw up a series of recommendations on how to handle such archives." The report yielded by their effort, titled "Archives of the Security Services of Former Repressive Regimes" and authored by the Spanish archivist Antonio González Quintana, drew on paradigmatic examples of political transitions from the 1970s and 1980s—Greece, Spain, Chile, Argentina—to argue for the key role of archives in enabling or supporting political change. As one of the first major attempts to articulate a set of best practices where the archives of past repressive regimes were concerned, the 1997 report stressed, above all, the fundamental importance of *not* destroying such records. Quintana cited the Greek case as a cautionary tale: Greece had used the documents from its 1967–1973 dictatorship period to compensate victims and lustrate state institutions, but then it destroyed them, on the logic that it was "undesirable to keep references, in registries and public archives, to people who had been vindicated for activities or attitudes considered illegal in the previous regime." This not only tied the hands of historians to come but foreclosed the possibility that different compensatory uses for the records might be envisioned in future moments. As Quintana put it, "the right of peoples and nations to choose their own path to political transition will be seriously affected by the availability of documents. Without archives their choice may not be properly made."[29]

The Quintana report, therefore, outlined a set of practical recommendations reflecting "the necessity to submit archives of the repression to the law." Records produced or kept by "former repressive bodies," Quintana argued, should be placed under the control of the new democratic authorities, who have a responsibility to assess, protect, and preserve those holdings; the records should be safely transferred to official archival institutions under the purview of the national archival systems or special transitional bodies (e.g., a reparations commission or lustration committee); special legislation must be passed in order to protect the records and enshrine them officially as cultural patrimony; national archival legislation must be developed, and it must establish norms for citizen access as well as protections for citizen privacy; the "new state" should compile a full report on the execution of the above measures, and the archivists managing such records should adopt a code of ethics regulating their conduct, which should include the stipulation that "the individual rights of victims of political repression take precedence over historical investigation."[30]

Also in 1997, the United Nations Commission on Human Rights (UNCHR) adopted the French jurist Louis Joinet's "Principles Against Impunity," a document detailing the rights of victims and the responsibilities of states in contexts of massive human rights violations.[31] Joinet, in his discussion of the "right to know," included six provisions specifically relating to the handling of records, which echoed Quintana's conclusions and recommended further proactive steps: for example, that countries implement protective measures to punish the illicit destruction or trafficking of archives pertaining to human rights violations. Updated in 2005 by the jurist Diane Orentlicher, the revised Joinet-Orentlicher principles establish what today remains the international standard for the treatment of archives in contexts where "barbarous acts…have outraged the conscience of mankind": that democratic states must take the technical, legislative, financial, and political steps necessary for the keeping, protection, use by truth commissions or other legal bodies of inquiry, citizen access to, and management of any documentation pertaining to violations of human rights and humanitarian law. The principles define human rights archives expansively, interpreting the category as covering records "from sources including (a) national governmental agencies, particularly those that played significant roles in relation to human rights violations; (b) local agencies, such as police stations, that were involved in human rights violations; (c) State agencies, including the office of the prosecutor and the judiciary, that are involved in the protection of human rights; and (d) materials collected by truth commissions and other investigative bodies."[32]

While it is true that neither the Quintana report nor the Joinet-Orentlicher principles "constitutes binding law," as John D. Ciorciari points out, the documents have nevertheless been "influential in shaping discourse at the UNCHR and in other international forums on the relationship between archival work and human rights."[33] This evolving notion of the "right to the truth" has been enshrined in a number of important national and international arenas.[34] Dozens of countries have passed versions of the Freedom of Information law; in 2006, the Inter-American Court of Human Rights (IACHR) ruled, in the case of *Reyes v. Chile*, that the American Convention on Human Rights supports "the right of all individuals to request access to State-held information"; both the Organization of American States and the United Nations (UN) have officially declared their support for victims' "right to truth," and the UN has named 24 March, the anniversary of Salvadoran archbishop Oscar Romero's 1980 assassination, the International Day for the Right to the Truth Concerning Gross Human Rights Violations and for the

Dignity of Victims. In 2010, the International Covenant for the Protection of All Persons from Enforced Disappearance came into effect, and the particular nature of forced disappearance—a crime whose very power lies in how it deprives surviving family members of any information about a disappeared loved one—meant that recommendations for its repair would necessarily focus on access to information. Indeed, the Convention affirms "the right of any victim to know the truth about the circumstances of an enforced disappearance and the fate of the disappeared person and the freedom to seek, receive, and impart information to this end."[35] Also in 2010, the IACHR made another significant ruling, this time in the case of *Gomes Lund v. Brazil*, which ended more than two decades of legal battle by ruling against Brazil and its long-standing refusal to turn over documentation pertaining to some 70 guerrilla fighters who disappeared from the country's Araguaia River region during the 1970s. In addition to holding the state liable for the deaths of the guerrillas and mandating broad reparatory measures, the IACHR also ruled that the *secreto de estado*, or the national security argument for preserving state secrets, could not be used to deny access to documentation of crimes against humanity. It also included an extraordinary provision obligating the Brazilian government, if it were to claim that the relevant archives detailing the murders of the guerrillas had been destroyed, to investigate and prosecute those responsible for their unlawful destruction.[36]

In many respects, the evolution of the "right to truth" and the development of norms governing the protection of human rights archives are positive steps. They have contributed to the successful preservation and/or release of important caches of state-level documentation, which in turn have had powerful impacts on those whose lives were chronicled in the files. For all the challenges of prosecuting the past in court and all the ways in which state records can be vexing and problematic sources, justice and access to information remain not only powerful rallying cries for post-conflict social movements but non-negotiable conditions for the establishment of representative forms of governance.

However, they also raise critical questions. What visions or interpretations of history do transitional justice frameworks presuppose—or foreclose? How do the challenges of marshaling records for the purposes of legal and social repair highlight the inadequacy of the language of political "transition"? Does the transitional justice focus on certain kinds of conflicts, dictatorships, and violations unduly shift the attentions of would-be archival democratizers toward the Global South in the same way that international human rights tribunals have, all while eliding the responsibility of the West's former empires to come clean about their own chilling campaigns of ethnic cleansing, state-sponsored killing, forced resettlement, and other modalities of colonial control? Why do the programmatic best-practices documents pertaining to human rights archives focus on the obligations of states, when it is far more likely that such bodies of records will instead be forced open by citizens?

Where Theory Meets Practice

The term "transitional justice" implies two fundamental conditions: transition and justice. Yet in many of the social and political contexts where transitional justice methodologies have been implemented, the "transition" has been partial at best, and the amount and extent of "justice" that can reasonably be achieved without jeopardizing political stability often leaves much to be desired. While the language of transition posits a break, a change from a previous poisoned order to a new and democratic future, examples from Latin America suggest a less linear, more complex trajectory; as Greg Grandin writes, "Latin America's move away from military dictatorships in the 1980s was less a transition than it was a conversion to a particular definition of democracy," one focused on individuals' political and legal rights at the expense of collective social and economic rights.[37] In Guatemala, the civilian leadership that followed military rule remained closely allied with the army and deeply resistant to implementing the terms of the country's UN-brokered peace accords; prosecutions have been few and far between. In El Salvador, the peace agreement ending armed hostilities did little to address the socioeconomic grievances that had given rise to those hostilities in the first place, and the hard-right Nationalist Republican Alliance (ARENA) party's control over the first two decades of peacetime Salvadoran politics portended badly for economic redistribution and judicial reckoning.[38] In Chile, Pinochet stepped down as the head of state but retained his position as commander-in-chief of the army, representing the constant threat of return to military rule if the center-left Concertación coalition confronted the legacies of the dictatorship too directly (as Pinochet reportedly proclaimed, "The day they touch any of my men, the rule of law is over"); only after 1998, when Pinochet was apprehended in London, did space begin to open up domestically for the pursuit of trials against wartime officials, a shift dubbed "the Pinochet effect."[39] Even in Argentina, where the military junta had thoroughly discredited itself with its embarrassing show in the Falklands conflict, the political landscape was so volatile in the years following the junta's fall from power that the transitional Alfonsín government implemented legislative limits to possible prosecutions (the notorious "Full Stop" and "Due Obedience" laws).

As the political transitions were incomplete, so too were the archival transitions, not least because when perpetrators remain powerful, they keep their files close. In Guatemala, the official truth-seeking bodies of the 1990s were stonewalled in their efforts to gain access to state records by conservative, army-allied civilian governments. The most influential releases of records documenting state terror—the "Diario Militar" army file chronicling nearly 200 targeted executions from 1983 to 1985, and the voluminous archives of the defunct National Police—came about not via political consensus or concerted state efforts but rather via an insider leak (the Diario Militar, in 1999) and by serendipitous accidental discovery (the police archives, in 2005).[40] In El Salvador, the results have been even more mixed: military and police records remain closed, and the only substantive state documents that have appeared—for example, the so-called Yellow Book of detainees—were, similarly, stumbled upon in a private home.[41] And even though the Guatemalan and Salvadoran peace processes yielded official, United Nations–backed truth commissions, the on-the-ground risks were so intense in both countries that the UN embargoed both commissions' records for 50 years, sealing them in a storage depot in New Jersey and requiring a head of state's petition and personal approval from the UN Secretary-General to be released. We will never know, therefore, what value these truth commission records might have had for several generations of scholars or activists in either country. (The same is true of the Truth and Reconciliation Commission [TRC] records in South Africa.[42]) In Chile, many of what observers assume to be the most high-impact records—those maintained by the DINA and CNI, as well as regular army files—remain embargoed or disappeared, their whereabouts unknown. While the Bachelet government made important strides where official memory of the dictatorship is concerned, journalists who have probed the issue of the missing files have been the targets of harassment.[43] In Argentina, similarly, it took several decades after the fall of the juntas for progressive new governments, in this case the Nestor Kirchner and Cristina Fernández de Kirchner administrations, to bring state power meaningfully to bear on the question of opening the archives. (The aforementioned advances in democratizing access to the records of Dirty War regimes risk stalling, or being reversed altogether, now that the pink tide governments have largely been voted out of office, replaced with parties representing traditional conservative ruling elites.)

The resistance or inability of Latin American states—even newly democratic states with the best of intentions vis-à-vis reckoning with the past, although historically these have been few and far between—to comply with the stipulations of the Quintana report, or the Joinet-Orentlicher principles, suggests that the theory of how to handle human rights archives aligns imperfectly with the practice of how human rights archives are actually handled. The extant best-case recommendations focus predominantly on the responsibilities of the state—that the state must pass certain kinds of archival legislation, make publicly available certain kinds of records, and so on. What these recommendations ignore, however, is the fact that in the comparatively few cases in which sitting governments have indeed made significant tranches of past regimes' files accessible to citizens or to prosecutors, it has almost never been the result of a democratizing political will from above. Rather, such victories for archival access should instead be attributed to the tenacious advocacy of civil society organizations: human rights groups, families of the killed and disappeared, or other "minority" actors incurring significant political risk by speaking out. This dynamic is not only true for archival matters but for post-conflict or post-dictatorship justice in general—especially in the years following the immediate signing of peace accords, once the white UN vans and international consultants have decamped for more pressing locales. As Cath Collins notes of human rights trials in Argentina and Chile, "justice developments … have been instigated and driven by minority civil actors. State responses … generally have oscillated between indifference and active dissuasion" or have taken decades of waiting.[44] The story is the same when it comes to archives from past repressive regimes: if they have been released at all, it has been only after tremendous amounts of pressure from civil society organizations and their international allies. Even then, usually the files are only opened many years after the fact, when the possibilities for courtroom justice are greatly diminished (perpetrators age and die) and the likelihood increases that high-impact documents might be destroyed, either willfully or through simple neglect.

From the case studies of Guatemala, El Salvador, Chile, and Argentina, it seems, then, that the juridical value of human rights archives is only one of many ways in which records documenting massive state-sponsored violence can contribute to social reconstruction, much like how trials, as Laurel Fletcher and Harvey Weinstein argue, are but one of many elements necessary to a broader ecology of social repair. In the ecological model set out by Fletcher and Weinstein, the individualizing telos of the juridical—whose efficacy at "healing wounds," building consensus about the past, and "bringing closure" in post-conflict settings has, Fletcher and Weinstein point out, little empirical foundation—exists in a larger constellation of reparatory measures. Collective violence demands collective responses, including a wide variety of nonlegal interventions, from community-level interventions (memorials, restitution of property, cultural initiatives, exhumations of mass graves, truth-seeking initiatives led by religious or social organizations) and state-level alternatives to legal intervention (truth commissions), psychosocial interventions, community-generated responses (community mourning rituals, popular education projects), and beyond.[45] In any of these spheres, archives have a major role to play, as specialists in community archiving remind us.[46]

Museums, for example, can and do deploy documents—whether those generated by past regimes or those collected and produced by dissident social movements—as a way not only to provide a window into the past but to leverage what Lisa Gitelman calls the "know-show" function, or the authority, of written documents for maximum persuasive power.[47] The Museo de la Memoria in Santiago, Chile, is a case in point: the museum abounds with documents, both originals and reproductions. These include the following: executive decrees suspending civil liberties and abolishing political parties, signed by junta leaders like Pinochet and Gustavo Leigh; the passports of supposed *revoltosos*, or subversives, bearing the stamps of exile; photographs and film clips; underground pamphlets from resistance organizations; solidarity posters from around the world; excerpts of the reports from Chile's two official truth-seeking initiatives, the Rettig and Valech commissions; letters sent to family members by detainees in prison and concentration camps, penned in tiny scrawls on miniscule scraps of paper to be rolled up in cigarettes or smuggled out in shoes. The museum also manages much of the surviving archival material pertaining to human rights violations from 1973 to 1990, in a publicly accessible facility integrated into the architecture of the museum. In 2014, the museum logged more than 140,000 in-person visits and its online archives and libraries counted nearly 400,000 users; by enshrining documents as part of the public sphere, the museum multiplies and democratizes their potential impact.[48] The same is true of the Museo de la Palabra y la Imagen (MUPI) in San Salvador, El Salvador, which has transformed itself into something of a popular archive, inviting the public to donate or loan documents or objects of significance to the country's history in order that they can be widely shared.

In order for documents to be incorporated into public life, however, they need to be gathered, recuperated, and wrested free; sometimes this is only possible through long processes of contentious struggle between archons and citizens, struggles which, in the Guatemalan context, I have referred to as "archive wars." Yet it is not only the finished result, the transfer or opening of the files and the new knowledge that such transfers and openings afford, that has a meaningful impact. In Guatemala, at least, just as powerful was the *process itself* of fighting for access to army and police files, and of doing the work—in the case of Guatemala's recovered National Police archives, an unprecedented, tremendous amount of work—necessary to turn those decaying, disordered records into tools for the empowerment of citizens and the recuperation of historical memory. Archivists Wendy M. Duff and Verne Harris refer to archival description itself as a way of building power ("the power to describe is the power to make and remake records and to determine how they will be used and remade in the future"). In places and times in which social justice activists have been able to claim physical and intellectual control over documents that had once been used against them, the act of obliterating one archival logic (that of social control and repression) and constructing a second (that of opening, remembering) can be deeply reparative for those individuals involved in the process.[49] The rediscovery of the National Police records and concomitant creation of the AHPN obliged Guatemala's splintered activist community to come together, reunited activists who had not seen each other in decades, helped forge intergenerational bonds between older generations of militants and new generations of postwar progressives, and reactivated old memories and traumas in a way that those working to rescue the archives found challenging to handle, but emotionally productive.[50]

Justice activists have built other kinds of archives in the pursuit of social repair, ones not limited to the written word or the printed page. A paradigmatic example is the effort by Argentina's Grandmothers of the Plaza de Mayo, and later the Guatemalan Forensic Anthropology Foundation (FAFG), to construct libraries of DNA samples collected from thousands of citizen volunteers. Courtroom justice is perhaps one goal of DNA collection, but not the primary one; instead, the main objective is to reunite families torn apart by dictatorship and civil conflict, whether via the chaos of military attacks on rural villages (Guatemala) or via the systematic practice of severing family bonds by having the infant children of detainees rendered for adoption by military families (Argentina). Such reunions ideally take place between a living grandparent and living grandchild, but posthumous reunions, between surviving family members and the remains of loved ones killed by state forces and identified by DNA testing, have also allowed families and communities to accompany processes of exhumation and inhumation, to grieve privately, and to mourn collectively.[51]

The Internet has facilitated the diffusion of archival documents pertaining to state-sponsored violence, resistance, forced disappearance, and social reconstruction. The National Security Archive, a US-based nonprofit that uses the Freedom of Information Act to promote the declassification of government documents related to US foreign policy, has made tens of thousands of US documents available online for Latin American justice movements to read and analyze and use; many such documents have been entered as evidence in trials of military and police officials in countries like Argentina and Guatemala, but so too have they been used as teaching tools, in works of art (e.g., the Chilean artist Voluspa Jarpa's *Tres formas de secretos* sculpture installation at the Museo Fundación Salvador Allende in Santiago), and in myriad other ways. The Internet helps groups like the Grandmothers and the FAFG to recruit donations for the DNA archive; it allows museums like the MUPI to post a "document of the month" (as of this writing, the document was a typed letter from peasant leader Mario Zapata to his father on the eve of his execution by government firing squad in El Salvador's bloody *matanza* of 1932), and it allows survivors of political conflict to reencounter their pasts through the eyes of the Other. "I remember it very well, because when this document appeared, I was about sixteen or seventeen, and it caused a major crisis in my house," remembered one young Guatemalan activist, whose parents had been Communist Party militants during the country's civil war. The document in question was the "Diario Militar," the thick army file smuggled out of military archives listing 183 men and women, with their photographs and identifying details, who had been detained and murdered by army intelligence officers and police detectives. "My mother was extremely upset," he recalled, "because you could just download the Diario from the Internet, and in it appeared all her friends from [the Party]."[52] Without concerted efforts to collect individuals' stories of encounter with digitized documents of this type, broader conclusions about the impact of these experiences cannot be drawn. However, given the push to digitize documentary holdings and the rise in Internet access, one can only assume that such experiences are becoming more and more frequent.

One measure of digital platforms' ability to massively increase the circulation and creative use of print archival materials is the backlash they have incurred from political actors who would prefer to turn the page on the past. In 2018 and 2019, Guatemala saw a targeted campaign to defund, defame, and ultimately dismantle the AHPN, at least partly in revenge for the archives' evidentiary role in convicting four former military "untouchables" for the 1981 forced disappearance of Marco Antonio Molina Thiessen.[53] Interior Minister Enrique Degenhart, who spearheaded the campaign against the archives, reserved particular ire for the AHPN's long-standing collaboration with the University of Texas at Austin—the very collaboration which had yielded the publicly accessible web platform making more than ten million of the police documents freely available online—and for its agreement with the Swiss Federal Archives that the latter institution would safeguard a copy of the AHPN's digitized documentary corpus. Degenhart framed his objections in nationalistic terms, but the true target of his animus was the AHPN's ability to use digital tools to preserve and disseminate the police records. "What we will not permit," he told the Guatemalan press, "is for these archives to keep leaving the country at a massive scale, this we will not allow. There cannot be foreign institutions which hold [copies of] the complete archives."[54] The minister's subtext was clear: there cannot be a safe duplicate of the archives held outside the country, and there cannot be a website where anyone can download evidence of state-sponsored war crimes in the state's own hand.

What unites these diverse applications of archival materials, and the varied attempts to undermine them, is the importance of having citizens, as individuals and communities, gain or regain the ability to generate and control documents in a way that corresponds to their own experiences. In all these instances, people in the Americas are marshaling the documentary record, in a bottom-up fashion, in the service of memory and, in some cases, historical reconstruction. That some of the versions of history that emerge from these bottom-up processes are "thicker" than others, which is to say more layered and complex and problematic and multivocal, is inevitable. That they are frequently private, haphazardly funded initiatives rather than state-supported or state-led ones is of course fraught. However, they represent collective efforts—at times, very risky collective efforts—to democratize access to the archives and records documenting the immense state-sponsored violence of the Cold War period. If the international community is going to generate programmatic statements of principle advising states on their too-often unmet obligations to open the files of their authoritarian or colonial antecedents, so too should it attempt to collate and share best-practices advice, toolkits even, for those civil society groups worldwide who are prepared to use any tool possible—lawsuits, leaks, public campaigns, pressure from abroad—to force their governments to comply. After all, habeas data—you should have the data—is both a statement of fact and a demand.

Conclusion: What Are Human Rights Archives?

This chapter has raised more questions than it can answer, not least because the phrase "human rights archives" around which its discussion has revolved is such an unsatisfying, problematic one. To designate certain records as pertaining to human rights and others not is an arbitrary distinction, one shaped by preconceptions about what counts as a "human rights violation" in the neoliberal discursive space of the post–Cold War period and what does not. In a place like Guatemala, where the international funders of the rescue of the National Police archives consider documents about torture and killing to have a human rights "angle" but see the moldering land records abandoned in the national archives as unworthy of attention, definitions of "human rights" (and, hence, of human rights archives) skew toward the narrow, toward the political and legal rather than the social and economic. Moreover, just as mainstream discussions about human rights violations tend to be directed toward the actors of the Global South (as opposed to, say, members of the George W. Bush administration, or fossil fuel companies), so too do prescriptive discussions about preserving so-called human rights archives from "past repressive regimes," even as major scandals about state secrecy and abuses of power engulf Western polities like the United States (WikiLeaks, the Snowden disclosures) and the United Kingdom (the Hanslope disclosures, the migrated archive) which are almost never referred to in the same kind of language. (As the Quintana report points out, preserving documentation from repressive contexts is more difficult when the institutional heirs of those repressive outfits remain in charge of the documentation, as in the case of colonial powers.) And because the democratization of archival access came to be articulated as a political demand at the same time as transitional justice came to be theorized and practiced, and therefore the primary value of recuperating so-called human rights archives came to be seen as juridical in nature, the kinds of records that have been prioritized for preservation are those most in line with the objectives of lawyers seeking to prosecute cases.

Archivists are trying to change the conversation, proposing a more expansive definition of human rights archives that includes not only the bureaucratic residue of perpetrators but also survivors' oral history testimonies, social movements' records, truth commission records, DNA samples, and any other type of documentary production related to asymmetries of power and violence. "Human rights archives," writes Michelle Caswell, "are those collections of records that document violent and systematic abuses of power," while Anne Gilliland suggests that "all archives are human rights archives."[55] Perhaps so, though a historian might wish for a framing more like Peterson's, which both underscores the importance of all records and also accommodates historical contingency and specificity.[56] What is important, though, is that archives and archival access became key points of contestation between state power and Latin American citizen movements at a particular historical moment in which the language of human rights supplanted revolutionary praxis, with very real consequences. The limitations of transitional justice mechanisms, which have largely privileged legal forms of repair over social and economic ones, have been amply revealed in recent years. Nevertheless, social movements and justice activists have transcended the narrow imagination of the courtroom, engaging records ecologically in the service of social repair. They leverage archives not only to win court cases but to write and disseminate fuller, more multifaceted histories of the recent past, seeking less to invite condemnation than to foster understanding.

Notes

1. Louis Bickford, "The Archival Imperative: Human Rights and Historical Memory in Latin America's Southern Cone," *Human Rights Quarterly* 21:4 (1999), 1097.
2. For the classic account of this rise, see Samuel Moyn, *The Last Utopia: Human Rights in History* (Cambridge, MA: Belknap Press, 2010)—usefully revised, for the purposes of this chapter, in Samuel Moyn, *Not Enough: Human Rights in an Unequal World* (Cambridge, MA: Belknap Press, 2018).
3. On the history of transitional justice, see, for example, Ruti G. Teitel, "Transitional Justice Genealogy," *Harvard Human Rights Journal* 16 (2003): 69–94, as well as her *Transitional Justice* (Oxford: Oxford University Press, 2000) and *Globalizing Transitional Justice: Essays for the New Millennium* (Oxford: Oxford University Press, 2014).
4. Michelle Caswell, "Defining Human Rights Archives," *Archival Science* 14 (2014): 207–213.
5. For example, the truth-seeking effort led by Guatemala's Catholic Church in the late 1990s was titled the Interdiocesan Project for the Recuperation of Historical Memory. The term is widely used throughout the region.
6. To keep the discussion manageable, this chapter will focus on four case studies: Argentina, Chile, El Salvador, and Guatemala.
7. For a survey of the different animating goals and ideas behind truth commissions in different regions and at different times, see Priscilla Hayner, *Unspeakable Truths: Transitional Justice and the Challenge of Truth Commissions* (New York: Routledge, 2010).
8. On the challenges of marshaling these types of records in contexts of political transition, see John D. Ciorciari, "Archiving Memory After Mass Atrocities," Rapoport Center Human Rights Working Paper Series (April 2012), http://papers.ssrn.com/sol3/papers.cfm?abstract_id=2269305, accessed 23 February 2015. See also Ciaran B. Trace, "What is Recorded is Never Simply 'What Happened': Record Keeping in Modern Organizational Culture," *Archival Science* 2:1–2 (2002), 137–159; A. James McAdams, *Judging the Past in Unified Germany* (New York: Cambridge University Press, 2001), Part III; and Katherine Verdery, *Secrets and Truths: Ethnography in the Archives of Romania's Secret Police* (Budapest: Central European University Press, 2014) and *My Life as a Spy: Investigations in a Secret Police File* (Durham, NC: Duke University Press, 2018).
9. On this point, see Laurel E. Fletcher and Harvey M. Weinstein, "Violence and Social Repair: Rethinking the Contribution of Justice to Reconciliation," *Human Rights Quarterly* 24:3 (August 2002), 573–639.
10. Carlota McAllister, "'Terrorism' as an Artifact of Transition in Post-Cold War Latin America," in Claudia Verhoeven and Carola Dietze, eds., *The Oxford*

Handbook on the History of Terrorism, forthcoming; see also Jean Comaroff and John L. Comaroff, *Theory from the South: Or, How Euro-America is Evolving Toward Africa* (Boulder, CO, Paradigm Publishers, 2011), Chap. 6.

11. For example, in Guatemala, where inordinate amounts of effort have been poured into attempting to secure and preserve army and police documents, there has been an eerie silence among justice activists when it comes to the marshaling and preservation of the documents produced and held by guerrilla groups like the Ejército Guerrillero de los Pobres, the Fuerzas Armadas Rebeldes, and the Organización del Pueblo en Armas. A guerrilla organization will necessarily use records (written or otherwise) differently than will a traditional office-based state bureaucracy, but this does not mean there are not records to be found and preserved.

12. Trudy Huskamp Peterson, "Human Rights, Human Wrongs, and Archives," *Arch-e: Revista Andaluza de Archivos* 5 (Jan–Feb 2012), p. 115.

13. Eric Ketelaar, "Archival Temples, Archival Prisons," *Archival Science* 2:3 (2002), 221–238.

14. On the "activating" of archives, see Eric Ketelaar, "Tacit Narratives: The Meaning of Archives," *Archival Science* 1:2 (2001), 131–141; Michelle Caswell, *Archiving the Unspeakable: Silence, Memory, and the Photographic Record in Cambodia* (Madison, WI: University of Wisconsin Press, 2014); and Michelle Caswell and Anne Gilliland, "False Promise and New Hope: Dead Perpetrators, Imagined Documents and Emergent Archival Evidence," *The International Journal of Human Rights* 19:5(2015): 615–27.

15. Gabriel García Márquez, "The Solitude of Latin America," Nobel Lecture, 8 December 1982, available at http://www.nobelprize.org/nobel_prizes/literature/laureates/1982/marquez-lecture.html

16. On the fates of the documents produced by some of these truth commissions, see Trudy Huskamp Peterson, *Final Acts: A Guide to Preserving the Records of Truth Commissions* (Washington, DC: Woodrow Wilson Center Press, 2005).

17. On the particular social and collective torture of forced disappearance, see Carlos Figueroa Ibarra, *Los que siempre estarán en ninguna parte: La desaparición forzada en Guatemala* (Mexico City: CIIDH, 1999), and Kirsten Weld, "Because They Were Taken Alive: Forced Disappearance in Latin America," *Revista: Harvard Review on Latin America* (Fall 2013).

18. R. Andrew Nickson, "Paraguay's Archivo del Terror," *Latin American Research Review* 30:1 (1995), 125–129; Martín Almada, "The Man Who Discovered the Archives of Terror," *The UNESCO Courier* 9 (2009); Mike Ceaser, "Paraguay's Archive of Terror," *BBC News* (11 March 2002).

19. Kirsten Weld, *Paper Cadavers: The Archives of Dictatorship in Guatemala* (Durham, NC: Duke University Press, 2014); Kate Doyle, "The Atrocity Files: Deciphering the Archives of Guatemala's Dirty War," *Harper's Magazine* (December 2007), 52–64.

20. "Tendremos Archivo de la Memoria," *La República,* Uruguay, (12 November 2008).
21. The online service, "Memórias Reveladas," is maintained by Brazil's Arquivo Nacional.
22. Carlos Osorio, "Argentina: Declassification of Military Records on Human Rights," *Freedominfo.org* (14 January 2010); Alexia Richardson, "Lifting the Sentence of Secrecy in Chile," *nacla.org* (25 August 2014). The Chilean declassification campaign is being led by the human rights collective Londres 38.
23. Kathryn Sikkink, *The Justice Cascade: How Human Rights Prosecutions are Changing World Politics* (New York: W. W. Norton, 2011).
24. Stacy Wood et al., "Mobilizing Records: Re-framing Archival Description to Support Human Rights," *Archival Science* 14 (2014), 401.
25. Stefan Berger, "The Role of National Archives in Constructing National Master Narratives in Europe," *Archival Science* 13:1 (2013); Jennifer S. Milligan, "'What is an Archive?' in the History of Modern France," in Antoinette Burton, ed., *Archive Stories: Facts, Fictions, and the Writing of History* (Durham, NC: Duke University Press, 2005): 159–83.
26. On activist self-archiving practices in a different context, see, for example, Kate Eichhorn, *The Archival Turn in Feminism: Outrage in Order* (Philadelphia: Temple University Press, 2013).
27. On habeas data, see Andrés Guadamuz, "Habeas Data Versus the European Data Protection Directive," *Journal of Information Law and Technology* 3 (2001), http://www2.warwick.ac.uk/fac/soc/law/elj/jilt/2001_3/guadamuz/ and Weld, *Paper Cadavers,* 60–61.
28. Quoted in Naomi Roht-Arriaza, *The Pinochet Effect: Transitional Justice in the Age of Human Rights* (Philadelphia: University of Pennsylvania Press, 2006), 102. On the use of habeas data in the context of Paraguay's "Archivos del Terror," see Stella Calloni, "Los Archivos del Horror de Operación Condor" (Madrid: Equipo Nizkor, 1998), http://www.derechos.org/nizkor/doc/condor/calloni.html
29. All quotations in this paragraph from Antonio González Quintana, "Archives of the Security Services of Former Repressive Regimes (Paris: UNESCO, 1997). In 2009, González Quintana issued an updated and revised version of the report, with the new title "Archival Policies in the Protection of Human Rights" (Paris: UNESCO, 2009).
30. Ibid.
31. Louis Joinet, "Principles for the Protection and Promotion of Human Rights through Action to Combat Impunity," UN Commission for Human Rights, E/CN.4/Sub.2/1997/20/Rev.1.z.
32. Diane Orentlicher, "Updated Set of Principles for the Protection and Promotion of Human Rights through Action to Combat Impunity," UN Commission for Human Rights, UN Doc. E/CN.4/2005/102/ADD.1, 8 February 2005.

33. John D. Ciorciari, "Archiving Memory after Mass Atrocities," Rapoport Center Human Rights Working Paper Series 4/2012, downloaded at http://papers.ssrn.com/sol3/papers.cfm?abstract_id=2269305
34. See Ibid., for a helpful summary of these and other measures and initiatives linking archival work to human rights.
35. International Convention for the Protection of All Persons from Enforced Disappearance, G.A. res. 61/177, U.N. Doc. A/RES/61/177 (2006), entered into force 23 December 2010.
36. See Open Society Justice Initiative et al., "*Amicus Curiae* Submission in the Case of *Gomes Lund and Others v. Brazil*," June 2010; Inter-American Court on Human Rights, sentence, *Gomes Lund and Others v. Brazil*, 24 November 2010, both available at www.soros.org/initiatives/justice/litigation/brazil
37. Greg Grandin, "The Instruction of Great Catastrophe: Truth Commissions, National History, and State Formation in Argentina, Chile, and Guatemala," *American Historical Review* 110:1 (February 2005), 46.
38. Cynthia J. Arnson, ed., *El Salvador's Democratic Transition Ten Years After the Peace Accords* (Washington, DC: Woodrow Wilson International Center for Scholars, 2003).
39. Cath Collins, "Human Rights Trials in Chile During and After the 'Pinochet Years'," *International Journal of Transitional Justice* 4 (2010), 72; Naomi Roht-Arriaza, *The Pinochet Effect*.
40. Christian Tomuschat, "Clarification Commission in Guatemala," *Human Rights Quarterly* 23:2 (2001): 233–58.
41. "The Yellow Book: Secret Salvadoran Military Document from the Civil War Catalogued 'Enemies,' Many Killed or Disappeared," National Security Archive Electronic Briefing Book No. 486, 28 September 2014, http://www2.gwu.edu/~nsarchiv/NSAEBB/NSAEBB486/
42. Verne Harris, "Antonyms of our Forgetting," *Archival Science* 14:3–4 (2014), 216.
43. Richardson, "Lifting the Sentence"; Reporters Without Borders, "Intimidation of Journalists Who Investigate Military Dictatorship" (18 December 2012), http://en.rsf.org/chile-break-in-at-home-of-reporter-who-16-12-2012,43799.html
44. Collins, "Human Rights Trials," 86.
45. Fletcher and Weinstein; Verne Harris points out, however, that "community" is no utopia either; "Antonyms of our Remembering," 219.
46. See, for example, Jeannette A. Bastian, *Owning Memory: How a Caribbean Community Lost its Archives and Discovered its History* (Westport, CT: Libraries Unlimited, 2003); Jeannette A. Bastian and Ben Alexander, eds., *Community Archives: The Shaping of Memory* (London: Facet Publishing, 2009); Michelle Caswell, "Toward a survivor-centered approach to records documenting human rights abuse: lessons from community archives," *Archival Science* 14 (2014): 307–22.

47. Lisa Gitelman, *Paper Knowledge: Toward a Media History of Documents* (Durham, NC: Duke University Press, 2014).
48. Museo de la Memoria, *Memoria anual 2014*, http://www.museodelamemoria.cl/memoria_anual/memoria_2014/
49. Wendy M. Duff and Verne Harris, "Stories and Names: Archival Description as Narrating Records and Constructing Meanings," *Archival Science* 2:3 (2002), 272.
50. Weld, *Paper Cadavers*, chaps. 6 and 7.
51. The best chronicler of how DNA collection has impacted Guatemalan communities is the photojournalist James Rodríguez; his photo-essays accompanying exhumations and inhumations in highland Maya communities can be found at mimundo.org.
52. Cited in Weld, *Paper Cadavers*, 65.
53. See Cora Currier, "A Vast Archive Exposed the Secret History of Kidnapping and Assassination in Guatemala. Now It's Under Threat," *The Intercept* (8 June 2019), https://theintercept.com/2019/06/08/guatemala-historical-archive-national-police-jimmy-morales/ and Colum Lynch, "Guatemala Declares War on History," *Foreign Policy* (30 July 2019), https://foreignpolicy.com/2019/07/30/guatemala-declares-war-on-history-dirty-war-archives-jimmy-morales/?fbclid=IwAR10DON2MoU5ze-UPTbjiivogyBCiIITG-5DYwkGVCoXPeuT4L5J7EPQTolI
54. Andrea Orozco and Willian Cunes, "Ministro Degenhart dice que PNC debe participar en manejo del archivo de la Policía Nacional," *Prensa Libre* (27 May 2019), https://www.prensalibre.com/guatemala/justicia/ministro-degenhart-dice-que-archivo-de-la-policia-nacional-debe-pasar-a-manos-de-la-pnc/
55. Both citations from Caswell, "Defining Human Rights Archives," 208–209.
56. See the discussion of land records in Peterson, "Human Rights, Human Wrongs."

12

Globalism, Transparency, and Loss

Maurice S. Lee

It is tempting to say that our information age has entered a period of chastened disenchantment. The social networks that promised democratic springs have ushered in a winter of autocracy. Big Tech, once the next inspiring Big Thing, increasingly feels like Big Brother. Screens menace young minds. AI threatens old jobs. STEM fields crowd out the humanities. We were told that information wants to be free, but it seems everywhere in chains and relentlessly capitalized. More specifically, the digital humanities, as it moves from manifestos and methodological groundwork to more practical applications in the disciplines, is facing the kind of challenges a start-up might face as it reaches corporate maturity: one can value DH's scholarly contributions while continuing to rate it a solid investment and yet still sense that the knowledge it is producing remains more incremental than visionary. Long the subject of utopian dreams, our digital revolution can feel suddenly limited, as if failing to achieve escape velocity from history's gravitational pull.

This should come as no surprise to humanists with a historical bent, for our information age is not so much discovering disenchantment as returning to the realities of constraint. Jerome McGann has recently worried that the digital humanities has been operating under an "attenuated historical sense," while Andrew Piper writes of the humanities and data sciences, "We are talking not only past each other, but also past the past itself."[1] How might such

M. S. Lee (✉)
Boston University, Boston, MA, USA
e-mail: molee@bu.edu

shortcomings be addressed? How can we historicize an information revolution that sometimes sees itself as leaving history behind? How can we grasp not only how digitization increasingly mediates and thereby produces archival knowledge but also how historical archives condition and thereby chasten our informational fantasies?

There are at least two ways in which historical consciousness can sharpen understandings of how archival knowledge works in our information age. The first, which this chapter does not pursue in detail but that forms a necessary background, is to acknowledge that our digital revolution is part of a longer information revolution begun at least as early as the Enlightenment. As developments in print technology, distribution, literacy, and archive management altered informational ecologies, print culture was possessed by dreams and nightmares that remain with us today. Hopes for global interconnectivity, epistemological transparency, and untrammeled access to total knowledge emerged alongside fears of unregulated communications, information overload, and privacy concerns. Robert Darnton has written that "every age was an age of information," and scholars of the subject—from book historians and literary critics to media archeologists and library scientists—have traced how informational disenchantment and anxiety arose centuries before the computer.[2] Viewed from a broad historical vantage, our digital revolution is less an epistemic rupture than an acceleration along established trajectories.

Another way to understand how history impinges on our informational imaginary is to undertake specific historical projects with a self-consciousness about archival mediation, technology, structures, and gaps. That is, rather than take up the history of information, scholars can do history with critical attention to the limits of archival information. This seems to me the case of the three previous chapters, all of which were originally presented as part of "The Global Politics of Archives" panel that I moderated at the Recording Lives: Libraries and Archives in the Digital Age forum at Boston University. The promise of interdisciplinarity (so often more touted than fulfilled) was powerfully borne out in the panel, and what follows attempts to recreate the energy generated between three far-flung papers: Beatriz Jaguaribe's "Nambiquaras in Paris: Archival Images, Appearances and Disappearances"; Kirsten Weld's "Human Rights Archives in Latin America"; and Rudolf Wagner's "Harvesting the Web, Preserving Chinese Voices." Individually and collectively, directly and obliquely, these pieces question utopian ideals of globalism, transparency, and comprehensiveness.

Globalism

From the Internet to the telegraph to newspapers carried by trains and steamships, information revolutions compress time and space, seemingly shrinking the world and cultural differences through the simultaneous experience of shared information. Communication without impedance and circulation without boundaries are the stuff of Habermasian and cosmopolitan dreams in which globalism is characterized by, among other homogenizing forces, the frictionless flow of data and texts. But as Pascale Casanova has grandly narrated in the field of literary studies, and as book and print historians have demonstrated in more granular detail, texts and information spread unevenly along global vectors inflected by histories of conflict, inequality, and exclusion.[3] Information revolutions do not make the world a smaller, smoother, and more uniform sphere; they crumple, as it were, older maps into balls—bringing some regions into nearer proximity but also distorting preexisting relations and representations while rendering some domains less legible.

Beatriz Jaguaribe's account of photographs from the Rondon expeditions in Mato Grosso (1907–1930) testifies to the unevenness of globalized information. Jaguaribe's primary interest is in the visual representation of native peoples, particularly the Nambiquaras, who—despite the relatively progressive thinking of Candido Rondon—were trapped within the period's racialized ideologies (aesthetic, ethnographic, geopolitical). Jaguaribe shows how imperial projects and primitivist discourses obscure the meaning of anonymous Nambiquara subjects, even as subsequent constructions of indigeneity in Brazil give their images a renewed and haunting agency. Crisscrossing Jaguaribe's nuanced critique are tragic ironies of the long information revolution. The Paresis, Terenas, Bororos, and Nambiquaras who appear in her images were included in the Rondon expeditions, not only to support the making of maps but to install telegraph wires across greater Mato Grosso, a mission of incredible scope. Just as cobalt mining in the Congo and Foxconn factories in China compel us to recognize that our wireless devices do not come without strings, Jaguaribe's visual history shows the costs and failures of an information revolution memorably represented by Levi Strauss's witness to the decaying obsolescence of Rondon's telegraph lines. Imperial enterprises always involve the informational labor of gathering data, creating maps, and connecting margins to the metropole. The disenchantments of empire thus also entail the chastening of informational dreams.

And the history of the limits of information endures in the legacies of Jaguaribe's recovered archive. She initially found her images of the Nambiquaras on microfiche in the Paris collections of the Société de Géographie, though the original photographs are housed in the Museu do Índio in Rio de Janeiro, indicating the remediation and global circulation of an archive that has traversed the uneven topographies of history. As Jaguaribe details, the Museu do Índio was originally located in a mansion that had housed the Service for the Protection of Indians (an office created by Rondon himself), and after the museum moved to a new location, the mansion was occupied by homeless indigenous people. With the coming of the 2013 World Cup and 2016 Olympics, the occupants of the mansion were displaced by authorities, with some eventually moving to the new site of the Museu do Índio where they eventually clashed with security forces, damaging the museum and precipitating its closure. As a result, Jaguaribe's photographic archive can only be accessed digitally, on microfiche, or by appointment as the recrudescent cycle of displacement and remediation continues on through the twenty-first century. The Nambiquaras of the Rondon expeditions must be sought through archival objects that do not flow freely across time and space but are impeded by abiding histories of imperialism. Advertisements for the World Cup and Olympics often recur to a trope: a montage of people of different races and nationalities respond diversely as they watch a variety of screens, but they all react to the same event at the same time, as if one single digital feed of a GOAL! can bring the whole world together. This is the global dream of unbounded, simultaneous information that superficially acknowledges—only to disavow—recalcitrant histories of difference. As Jaguaribe's chapter shows, the Rondon expeditions were premised on ideals of global interconnectivity, but their legacy reveals to the open-eyed critic a more jagged and elusive reality.

Transparency

Where does the authority of information lie? What constitutes information as such? Does the meaning and power of archived information come from its content or context, its epistemological status or its practical operations in the world? In its modern incarnations, the authority of information depends in part on a supposed transparency equated with unmediated objectivity. Data speaks for itself, we are sometimes told, and some academic theories and everyday practices align archives and information with veridical facts that serve as the building blocks for knowledge and truth. Yet as Lisa Gitelman and Theodore Porter have shown, data and numbers are never raw, and as Geoffrey Nunberg and N. Katherine Hayles have detailed, information is always already constructed within rhetorical, social, technological, and epistemological systems.⁴ Even the most bureaucratic and informational documents are subject to the contingencies of context. If the graininess of Jaguaribe's Nambiquara images figures the mediation of imperialist histories and the impossibility of frictionless circulation, the Latin American archives studied by Kirsten Weld point toward the power and limits of transparency.

Weld starts with something of a truism in the field of human rights: the opening of archives from oppressive regimes advances the work of truth commissions and the goals of reparative justice. With commanding sweep, Weld traces struggles for archival transparency across the post–Cold War Global South, demonstrating a hard truth for historicist scholars inclined to view archives in only a positive light: the forms of information that support our research and connect the present to the past can also serve as tools of terror, literalized by Guatemala's murderous security unit known as "El Archivo." The documents of civilization are also the documents of barbarism, and Weld shows how the ethical orientation of archives is contingent on their shifting uses. The systems theorist Gregory Bateson once described information as "a difference that makes a difference," which we see when governmental records complicit in past abuses are transformed into human rights archives, even as the differences their information makes do not live up to dreams of transparency.⁵

Weld's chapter demonstrates how theories of transparency work—and do not work—in historical and contemporary social practice. Her comparativist study of efforts to open restricted archives is shadowed by the many obstacles to recovery—from destroyed, sequestered, and dispersed archives, to the sheer volume of documents that require sorting and analysis, to the mixed results of judicial and institutional initiatives, to the challenge of mobilizing citizen actors, to questions about the limits of archival information itself (for instance, what kinds of knowledge and reparative practices are unavailable through the opening of government records?). Weld calls the global Cold War in Latin America "a kind of simultaneous dream and nightmare." One might say something similar about the archives that Weld studies, which in the twenty-first century are changing from documents of terror into manifestations of truth and reparation that have not been (and cannot be) fully realized. The ethical warrant of recovering archives is clear, but their evidentiary authority and social function are less certain. Put differently, people do indeed have a right to their data, but the power of such information—what it might mean and what differences it might make—remains an open question.

In this way, Weld's chapter, especially when considered alongside Jaguaribe's, suggests a distinction in how we think about the limits of transparency. On the one hand, hermeneutics challenges transparency in that the meaning of documents, such as images of the Nambiquara, both requires and resists our interpretive efforts. For scholars committed to interpretation, phenomenology, and critique, no text is ever transparent. On the other hand, social structures also threaten transparency through bureaucratic protocols, legal injunctions, institutional legacies, and outright force. Here transparency is less about interpreting documents and more fundamentally about accessing such documents in the first place. Content and context, epistemology and social practice—these two approaches to thinking about transparency are by no means mutually exclusive and are frequently entangled, though they often entail disparate disciplinary commitments and different scales of analysis. For a hermeneutically inclined literary critic such as myself, Weld's chapter is a vital reminder about the power and even primacy of social systems that govern the accessibility and thus the meaning of our archives.

Comprehensiveness

Another illusion of the digital revolution is the promise of total information—the hope that new technologies will render all data available and even usable at the click of a button. There is something amazing about finding century-old images and dragging secret files into the light of the public sphere, and yet despite (and because) of the emphasis on recovery in the chapters of Jaguaribe and Weld, loss and partiality are conspicuous. The Nambiquaras of the Rondon expeditions remain beyond our reach. The reclamation of documents from Cold War regimes highlights the incompleteness of such efforts. One need not be Borges, Derrida, Pynchon, Saramago, or Foster Wallace to recognize that even the most comprehensive archives are riven with silences, erasures, and gaps that no amount of digital technology can rectify. Jaguaribe encounters such elisions in the past, Weld traces how they might be repaired in the present, and Rudolf Wagner shows how the Digital Archive for Chinese Studies (DACHS) hopes to limit losses of information for future histories.

Under the auspices of the Heidelberg Institute of Chinese Studies, DACHS is remarkably forward looking. Scholars of China have long faced the problem of censorship in the archives, and this is especially true in digital domains, for the Chinese Communist Party goes to great lengths to control Internet resources within the nation and beyond. Whereas Weld's activists work to recover physical records, DACHS preserves digital information in real time, racing to identify and archive at-risk materials before the Chinese government censors them. One might worry about potential hazards—copyright infringement, the use of preserved records to persecute dissidents, and content providers who might want to exercise their right to be forgotten. One might also point out that reducing such risks by making the DACHS archives password protected imposes another, though less objectionable, form of control. Be that as it may, DACHS remains a constructive effort to save knowledge for future scholarly use. As such, it is a curatorial project in which ideals of total information meet the practical challenges of information overload.

Wagner's description of the operations of DACHS outlines a kind of informational triage. By algorithmic protocol, a small number of Chinese newspapers and blogs are automatically preserved, while other items are targeted by DACHS personnel for their cultural relevance and the likelihood of censorship. Short staffed and with limited digital storage, DACHS saves what its operators deem most important—a job made more difficult by the Chinese Communist Party, which not only removes information from the Internet but simultaneously floods the Web with content provided by agents of the state. Information can be lost through elision, but it also goes missing in superabundance. As with the chapters from Jaguaribe and Weld, dreams of the information age meet practical realities as the incompleteness of our archives leaves only partial traces. In the case of DACHS, it is metadata in the form of rotten links, only a small portion of which can be reconstructed. The "net" of the Internet refers to networks, but it can also conjure the work of retrieving and preserving selected materials from an ocean of information. Our archives are necessarily full of holes through which valuable data has slipped.

The chapters of Wagner, Jaguaribe, and Weld all demonstrate what seems to me a critical point for humanists thinking about archives in our digital age. Utopians can hope for a kind of informational accessibility, objectivity, and totality that eliminates the most vital of activities: choice. In a world of global interconnectivity, transparency, and comprehensive information, everyone in theory can have and know it all, but such fantasies do not sufficiently acknowledge the interpretation, exclusion, and triage that define the archives taken up in our three previous chapters. It almost goes without saying that we cannot have and know it all, but our information age, even as it rediscovers disenchantment, may still need reminding from humanists and others that we live under historical limits. This reminder can be chastening and should incline us toward modesty (epistemological, ethical, social). But it can also be heartening, for our limits connect us to a past—a centuries-long information revolution—in which information, partial and contingent as it is, forces us to make pragmatic choices that ground us in reality. What are the limits of your information? How much can you repair it? What can you make—and not make—of your archive, and what difference does it make?

Notes

1. Jerome McGann, *A New Republic of Letters: Memory and Scholarship in the Age of Digital Reproduction* (Cambridge, MA: Harvard University Press, 2014), 14; Andrew Piper, *Enumerations: Data and Literary Study* (Chicago: University of Chicago Press, 2018), 3.
2. Robert Darnton, *The Case for Books: Past, Present, and Future* (New York: PublicAffairs, 2010), 23.
3. Pascale Casanova, *The World Republic of Letters*, trans. M.B. DeBevoise (Cambridge, MA: Harvard University Press, 2004).
4. *Raw Data Is an Oxymoron*, ed. Lisa Gitelman (Cambridge, MA: MIT Press, 2013); Theodore Porter, *Trust in Numbers: The Pursuit of Objectivity in Science and Public Life* (Princeton: Princeton University Press, 1995); Geoffrey Nunberg, "Farewell to the Information Age," *The Future of the Book*, ed. Geoffrey Nunberg (Berkeley: University of California Press, 1996); N. Katherine Hayles, *How We Became Posthuman: Virtual Bodies in Cybernetics, Literature, and Informatics* (Chicago: University of Chicago Press, 1999).
5. Gregory Bateson, *Steps to an Ecology of Mind: Collected Essays in Anthropology, Psychiatry, Evolution, and Epistemology* (Chicago: University of Chicago press, 1972), 230.

Part IV

Digital Practice

13

Building from the Inside Out: Librarians as Nodes in Digital Scholarship Collaboratories

Harriett E. Green

Introduction

Libraries have never been just buildings, but robust hearts that pump blood into the veins and bones of scholarly research processes. Even in their most traditional incarnations, libraries always have been dynamically engaged with scholars: As scholars generate new findings from what they unearth in the stacks and archives—"discoveries" that were actually cataloged by archivists and librarians long before—librarians have been partners, though all too frequently silent ones, in a variety of capacities.

And today in the digital age, libraries have attained new types of prominence with broad digitization of collections, provision of access to new media tools for research, and engagement with diverse populations that now populate university campuses—something that we learn of throughout these other chapters in this collection. But while libraries have built (and continue to build) rapidly growing corpora of data and technical infrastructure to support the dissemination of data, where are the people in this dramatic change?

Scholarship across the disciplines today requires interdisciplinary collaborations, which points to an emergent truth: We must reorient our perspective to recognize librarians as collaborators, and not just as research support staff and collection curators. In this chapter, I aim to highlight the rich diversity of touchstones where librarians—and not just the library as institution—become partners for research, particularly in digital scholarship. What is emerging and

H. E. Green (✉)
Washington University in St. Louis, St. Louis, MO, USA

is still urgently needed are strategies to empower librarians to take on new roles in the research life cycle and adjust their skill sets to meet the data-driven needs of users. Through grasping the significance of librarians as producers of knowledge, we may unearth the potentialities for new, more holistic research ecosystems in higher education.

New Roles for Research Libraries

For all the fanfare of new funding streams, innovative conference themes, and groundbreaking forms of research that has marked digital humanities and digital scholarship over the past couple decades, I think that we are still grappling with the full import of digital tools and content in the research ecosystem.

If we truly want to enable this transformation of research work across humanities and social sciences with the incorporation of digital content and tools, who needs to be at the table? All too often, digital humanities projects are made up of an ad hoc grouping of professionals—scholar, programmer, student assistants, designers, and sometimes librarians—that coalesce around a specific project and then dissipate, a transient type of research process as Lynne Siemens notes in her study of digital humanities researcher practices.[1]

But the foundations of sustainability for digital scholarship lie in a cohesive support system for the digital scholarship itself—a gathering of expertise and infrastructure to ensure that the research work extends and is preserved in ways that contribute to the history and future of scholarship. The Association of Research Libraries declares in its 2014 strategic planning and design report that

> [w]ithin two decades, the research library will have transitioned its focus from its role as a knowledge service provider within a single university to become a collaborative partner within a broader ecosystem of higher education.... Research libraries will be even more intimately engaged in supporting the full life cycle and activity range of knowledge discovery, use, and preservation, as well as the curating and sharing of knowledge in diverse contexts of the university's mission and of society more broadly.[2]

In this spirit, libraries are reconfiguring their infrastructure: Library spaces, services, staff hiring, and administrative portfolios are evolving to encompass educational technology, digital pedagogy, and digital scholarship.

These changes and reconfigurations happening in libraries aren't quite embedded in the identity and working of libraries, however—in many ways, we are in a transitory moment where new types of services and expertise in libraries struggle to realize against the traditional. The Association for Research Libraries' SPEC Kit #350 report on Digital Scholarship in Libraries released in 2016 noted that of the 73 responding libraries, 67% of the digital scholarship library personnel had joined within the past five years and 74% had been doing digital scholarship work in the library for five years or fewer. The report also found that digital scholarship support is frequently distributed across the library, ranging from professional librarians and archivists to administrative staff and student assistants, along with a growing number of technology specialists whose work is stretched beyond standard IT system administration. Individuals conducted a variety of work for areas such as project planning, digitization and creating digital collections, data management, database development, interface and UX, computational text analysis, and digital publishing.[3]

We see brand-new professional organizations springing up in response as well: Groups such as the Digital Scholarship Section of the Association for College and Research Libraries (ACRL) and the Libraries Special Interest Group of the Association for Digital Humanities Organizations (ADHO) are brand-new professional spaces only emerging in the past couple years for librarian communities involved in digital humanities. Therefore, support for digital scholarship in libraries is growing rapidly, but is still nascent and overly concentrated among a relative few.

But the persona of the librarian, and not just the library, is key: The 2017 report from the Coalition of Networked Information (CNI) and EDUCAUSE on "Building Capacity for Digital Humanities" notes that to build capacity for digital scholarship and data science, librarians must be more than support:

> A more mature DH institutional culture is one that recognizes that many forms of DH work—particularly those that involve computationally intensive and/or data-intensive analysis—are most effectively implemented through partnerships between individuals with diverse skill sets. In these cases, the role of librarians and IT professionals is not simply to provide access to resources or to produce code according to predefined specifications. Instead, DH work becomes a partnership that provides access to a different kind of valuable expertise, starting with the project design.[4]

Thus despite these initial advances, there is a matter of people: How can all librarians, from the deeply experienced professionals to the fresh graduates, be empowered to engage in data-driven research in the diverse learning and research environments we encounter both inside and outside of the library?

The systems that librarians have developed to manage information are essential to take into account, as we witness how scholars build their own collaboratories that are dense sociotechnical networks of information, technical infrastructure, and scholarly communications.

What Are Digital Scholarship Collaborations?

I introduce the concept of "collaboratory," because collaboration is the hallmark of digital humanities scholarship, which is made up of partnerships across disciplines, archives, and methods. The standard usage of a "collaboratory" is to refer to a sociotechnical infrastructure that supports a research team (often in the sciences and social sciences) and the virtual research environment developed for the research project, what William Wulf first defined as, "A center without walls, in which researchers can perform their research without regard to physical location-interacting with colleagues, accessing instrumentation, sharing data and computational resources, and accessing information in digital libraries."[5]

But the humanistic ethos that infuses digital humanities scholarship pushes us to consider a collaboratory that isn't simply its standard sociotechnical framework, but the networks of people, an idea proposed in the *Our Cultural Commonwealth* report in describing humanities cyberinfrastructure:

> A cyberinfrastructure for humanities and social sciences must encourage interactions between the expert and the amateur, the creative artist and the scholar, the teacher and the student. It is not just the collection of data—digital or otherwise—that matters: at least as important is the activity that goes on around it, contributes to it, and eventually integrates with it.[6]

This also highlights how the research life cycle of digital scholarship is notably fluid: Rather than the relatively structured steps of scientific method or adherence to a specific theoretical or epistemological framework, digital scholarship is highly interdisciplinary and blends a host of methods and approaches, as outlined by Tanya Clement in *Debates in Digital Humanities,* where she argues that the cross-disciplinary methodological approaches employed by digital humanities research require us to heed the information practices of scholars and the philosophical approaches behind the techniques and methods utilized by different disciplines.[7] In this boundary crossing, we might consider how the interdisciplinary methodologies employed in digital humanities shape our dynamic networks of collaboration in digital scholarship, and in this case, how the ethos and methodological approaches of library information science (LIS) as an academic field and practice factor into the social dynamics of a collaboratory.

Library services have long been about process, database functions, and the order of materials in the stacks. But the disciplinary ethos that motivates our work can and should infuse our research partnerships: Whether the ALA Code of Ethics and Library Bill of Rights, Ranganathan's Five Laws of Library Science, or the perspective of information scientists, librarians' engagement with digital methods and not simply the tools, means that we bring to bear a critical factor that can inflect how researchers approach data and disseminate research.

Digital Cultural Heritage and Care

The valuing by librarians of users and the user experience, the premium placed on sustainability and preservation, and a perspective that extends to encompass the broad scope of communities that engage with information systems—these are fundamental elements that librarians bring to bear to the work of digital scholarship. In this light, I would affirm what Bethany Nowviskie has characterized as an ethics of capacity and care, as well as her call to build "digital cultural heritage communities of practice" that engage in digital spaces in thoughtful and careful ways. In her words, "let's create more cultural heritage platforms that promote an understanding of the vulnerability of the individual person and object. Let our visualization systems more beautifully express the relationship of parts, one to another and to many a greater whole. Let our open data finally be linked."[8] A community of practice is critically about sharing knowledge and expanding that knowledge base through interlinked networks. Librarians as information provisioners intersect with a multitude of communities, and to be effective as individual professionals as well as operate as a holistic institution, librarians must know their users and enact practices of care as they engage with these communities. The extension of practices of care in the library from the traditions of patron privacy and open accessibility to the digital resources and virtual spaces where users now pursue information needs poses opportunities and challenges for libraries as they continue to anchor communities. Thus how can librarians prepare to engage in this digitally inflected community of practice?

Building Research Connections

Through the growth of skills and knowledge, librarians can promote broader integration across the library for digital pedagogy, digital curation, and digital scholarship. There are several areas where librarians can make impacts with researchers to connect them to digital scholarship.

Collections as Data and Digital Curation

Librarians as researchers, not just curators, means that we must reconceptualize our perspective on our collections in their digital materiality as data—and this means engaging not just with tools, but with users and their needs. The British Library just released its Research Data Strategy and their declaration of priorities states a goal of:

> Ensuring users, both onsite and online, are able to discover the data held by the Library (as well as by third parties) and use that data, requires us to develop new tools and skills. We will develop new models of data access, and attempt to widen access to restricted data, to ensure that our users, wherever they are, can make the most of the UK's research data.[9]

In order to frame their collections as data and engage with researchers around the data, they state upfront that the re-skilling of library professionals is critical milestone. As Thomas Padilla observed, "Collections as data entails thinking about ways to increase meaning making capacity by making collections more amenable to use across an expanded set of methods and tools, typically but not exclusively computational in nature," and he argues that this process of developing collections for digital scholarship "entails vigilant attention to *who the work is done for.*"[10]

Thus the incorporation of cultural heritage collections into data science and digital scholarship is not as cut and dried as it may seem: It is not simply the creation of digital surrogates through scanning, imaging, 3D photography, and other digitization approaches; but instead, we must engage with the complexities of the sociotechnical and cultural contexts surrounding our collections. Zeynep Tufekci observes that "Technology alters the landscape in which human social interaction takes place, shifts the power and the leverage between actors, and has many other ancillary effects. It is certainly not the only factor in any one situation, but ignoring it as a factor or assuming that a technology could be used to equally facilitate all outcomes obscures our understanding."[11]

If we think of library collections when digitized as a whole new layer of "meaning making" as Padilla observes, then the effect of technology must be carefully considered when librarians seek to engage users around collections in their new forms and accessible environments. As libraries create these digitized collections and the data surrounding them, the essential next steps are educating users on what it means to interact with these new collections, which means teaching literacies for information architecture and distillation.

Digital Pedagogy and Scholarly Engagement

Digital pedagogy and multimodal learning are about connection: Connecting students to tools that transform and enrich their learning and connecting faculty to tools and approaches that enhance their teaching or catalyze new avenues for achieving disciplinary learning outcomes.

The concept of "metaliteracy" can be a key framework for how librarians engage in digital pedagogy: As defined by Mackey and Jacobson, metaliteracy "promotes critical thinking and collaboration in the digital age, providing a comprehensive framework to effectively participating in social media and online communities." The metaliteracy framework integrates information literacy—a standards-driven approach for educating students to be information literate defined by the Association for College and Research Libraries, among others—with other literacies that have emerged with the rise of digital resources and interdisciplinary research such as media literacy, digital literacy, and visual literacy.[12] In a learning environment guided by principles of metaliteracy, educators provide "an integrated and all-inclusive core for engaging with individuals and ideas in digital information environments." But whether we call it "metaliteracy," "digital literacies," or "media literacy," librarians are an essential part of a reconfigured research ecosystem, where students and faculty alike explore implications of data and computational tools in how they carry out their research. With the incursion of digital content and tools, the research ecosystem is complexly layered with physical and digital artifacts and research resources, and teaching students and scholars to navigate among these requires the emerging approaches of digital pedagogy, or as Jesse Stommel frames it, a "hybrid pedagogy," noting:

> The word "hybrid" has deeper resonances, suggesting not just that the place of learning is changed but that a hybrid pedagogy fundamentally rethinks our

conception of place. So, hybrid pedagogy does not just describe an easy mixing of on-ground and online learning, but is about bringing the sorts of learning that happen in a physical place and the sorts of learning that happen in a virtual place into a more engaged and dynamic conversation.[13]

Libraries sit at this intersection of physical and virtual learning spaces, as a third space beyond the academic classroom and professors' offices that facilitates learning, and increasingly so for digital scholarship. Bonnie Stewart further argues in an analysis of online courses and learning that

> [o]nline is different, in the sense that bringing people fully into an experience requires some explicit scaffolding that face-to-face tends not to. And yet online is no different at all, in the sense that it is teaching and learning for all the same reasons as any other teaching and learning experience, and we need to approach it with our whole selves, not just as mediators of technology.[14]

While the experience of learning and teaching in digital spaces versus face-to-face is oft debated, the inescapable fact of the exponentially expanding mode of online education has required all of us to examine our approaches. In this spirit, librarians can approach the hybrid interactions with users by not simply pointing the ways to technology, but also investing in assisting them and helping users to expand their digital and data literacies.

Digital Literacies

In the same way that librarians have long connected researchers to reference volumes and boxes of materials, we now are increasingly asked to connect them to tools and resources they can directly employ in their research. In my past work as a librarian for digital humanities and digital publishing, I found myself conducting research consultations not dissimilar from a research consultation for English literature: Instead of advising students on research resources for Chaucer, I taught them how to use Scalar and WordPress for digital publishing—but the common through line is teaching how to critically synthesize resources together toward building scholarship.

This critical approach is a valuable factor that we bring to the table when it comes to tool literacies: Libraries subscribe to more and more new tools and databases, we are building data repositories, developing new search interfaces, and even building micropublishing platforms that aim to connect users more rapidly and directly to the data they need. But do we consider the implications of our new technical infrastructure? As library and information professionals advance in skills with methods and approaches for digital scholarship, we can apply our extant skills to expose to learners the assumptions and information environments in which these tools were developed—what does it mean that this text mining tool only takes English-language texts? Why does the tool need metadata parsed in this particular way?

The scholarship generated from these research ecosystems framed by new technical infrastructure, including digital tools and social media platforms, has been defined as "Networked Participatory Scholarship" by Veletsianos and Kimmon. They note that "to participate productively in scholarly networks online, scholars not only need to understand the participatory nature of the Web, they also need to develop the social and digital literacies and skills essential for effective engagement with such networks."[15]

In this framing, there is opportunity and need to challenge researchers to think beyond the black box and engage with the methodological implications of the digital tools and data they aim to use, and librarians are among the most well positioned for this type of engagement.

Pedagogical Approaches to Re-skilling

So how do we re-skill librarians to be equipped for these multitude of demands for the digital age? There are a host of digital humanities workshops and institutes, including well-established programs such as the University of Victoria's Digital Humanities Summer Institute, Digital Humanities at Oxford Summer School (DHOxSS), and the US-based Humanities Intensive Learning and Training (HILT) institute. But these trainings are oriented to faculty, researchers, and graduate students, and do not consistently address the range of concerns and issues that information professionals must grapple with in their engagements with digital scholarship researchers.

Digital scholarship training specifically for librarians has emerged in recent years, including the Data Science and Visualization Institute for Librarians at North Carolina State University Libraries and the Rochester Digital Humanities Institute for Mid-Career Librarians as specific initiatives to train information professionals for digital methods. The future of digital scholarship in libraries is also propelled by projects funded by the National Digital Platform initiative of the Institute of Museum and Library Services (IMLS), which has developed a suite of initiatives to empower librarians to engage with data science skills and build digital access to collections and other research resources.[16] I have experienced firsthand several experiences in teaching and training practical workshops aimed specifically at LIS professionals doing digital scholarship. There are several critical elements that stretch across my experiences in three initiatives: The Hong Kong Data-Driven Scholarship Institute, The ARL Digital Scholarship Institute, and the IMLS-funded project, "Digging Deeper, Reaching Further: Librarians Empower Users to Mine the HathiTrust Digital Library." A brief look at these experiential case studies I engaged in may illuminate some of the opportunities and challenges of inculcating library and information science professionals in digital scholarship.

The Hong Kong Data-Driven Scholarship Institute was held in November 2016 at the Hong Kong University Library, as three colleagues and I taught about digital scholarship methods and approaches to 30 academic librarians from East Asia and the Pacific Rim, including the Philippines, Singapore, Thailand, and China.[17] We quickly saw that the impact of digital scholarship for library and information professionals is rippling across boundaries. Our colleagues the world over are wrestling with the transformations of their work and its changing scope with the emergence of large-scale data and digital approaches.

The Association for Research Libraries (ARL) Digital Scholarship Institute was launched in the summer of 2017, and its workshops focus on introducing a selected cohort of librarians from ARL institutions to an array of approaches and tools in digital scholarship. In the week-long workshop during which ARL colleagues and I taught, attendees explored an array of digital scholarship topics, including GIS, text mining, XML and TEI, digital publishing in Scalar and Omeka, and data visualization. Librarians who were learning digital scholarship for the first time participated in this experience, and we sought to build a cohort of librarians—a community of practice—who could learn from each other as they contributed their interdisciplinary backgrounds and professional perspectives.[18]

An in-depth example of developing infrastructure for digital scholarship training is the grant-funded initiative that I led called "Digging Deeper, Reaching Further: Librarians Empowering Users to Mine HathiTrust Digital Library Resources" (hereafter referred to as DDRF).[19] Led by the University of Illinois at Urbana–Champaign, and involving a collaboration with Indiana University, Northwestern University, Lafayette College, and the University of North Carolina at Chapel Hill, the three-year project was focused on developing and disseminating a train-the-trainer curriculum that educated librarians and LIS professionals in approaches and tools frequently used for text mining research. The anchor of the curriculum was the text data content and resources in the HathiTrust. But given that librarians operate in many different contexts and research areas, we developed a training program with a focus on fundamentals in text data mining and data science skills, such as web scraping, formatting data, and using Python scripts for basic approaches for text analysis. Our project team members conducted a "roadshow" of 18 workshops throughout 2017 and 2018 attended by over 300 library and information professionals at major conferences and key geographic areas, including the American Library Association and the International Federation of Libraries and Associations (IFLA) conferences. We ultimately aimed to build foundational skills for text data mining in librarians through a "train the trainer" approach: Librarians who participated in these workshops gained foundational skills in text data mining and went forth with a full package of instructional resources to teach at their own institutions. The final package of curriculum materials is openly available as an Open Educational Resource "toolkit" hosted in the IDEALS institutional repository.[20] Additionally, forthcoming reports will chronicle the project's research study on curriculum development for digital scholarship and strategies for LIS professional development.

In my experience with these three initiatives, I learned that teaching LIS professionals digital scholarship requires a specific hybrid pedagogical approach that is grounded in the practical and hands-on experimentation, but still imparts theory so librarians can learn the methodology and vocabulary of research disciplines.

As librarians gain the skills to be both learners and teachers of digital scholarship through an ever-expanding number of digital scholarship training initiatives, I believe we will see this community of practice expand: I anticipate that in academic libraries and cultural heritage institutions across the world, we will see the emergence of a networked community of information professionals who share their experiences and approaches as they engage in digital scholarship and the research it generates at their own institutions.

Conclusion

The profession of librarianship has transformed in discomfiting yet exciting ways with the advent of data-driven scholarship: Librarians now advise students and faculty on how to compile archival materials gathered from the University Archives to create a digital publication; how to translate the material from scholarly exhibition into an open digital exhibition for the community; or how to openly share their articles and data with DOIs. Researchers and library users are making, building, and creating dynamic scholarship in these ways and more, and more and more, they are inviting librarians as partners into this research process. Librarians have opportunities to be research partners and contributors as researchers engage in building new forms of digital archives, embed content with new modes of classification and organization, wrestle with copyright and rights concerns, and upend notions of scholarly products and traditional publishing. As Burdick et al. note, "The digital turn in scholarship is bringing into view genres undreamt of in earlier media. As it does this, libraries and publishers will forge alliances that distribute old tasks along new lines as they take on novel responsibilities and forms of engagement unforeseen in an analog world."[21]

As more and more librarians from across specializations—such as research services, technical services, archives, and the like—gain digital scholarship skills, they can and will become leaders who guide students, faculty, and researchers into uncharted pathways opened to us by the digital age. Thus the development of communities of practice is critically important for facilitating this overarching transformation of the roles of librarians in the research ecosystem. We thus must critically examine the roles of librarians as they pivot to support new forms of scholarship:

- How do the infrastructures being developed for supporting digital scholarship adapt and respond to the needs of users and professionals engaged in these systems?
- How do we empower librarians to build the skills needed to respond to new research needs?
- How can librarians build a community of practice that hones our approaches to supporting digital scholarship in effective and ethically aware ways?

I believe that as we expand the research ecosystem to encompass a broad range of partnerships within and beyond the ivory tower, we must attend to how the people at the heart of the systems can be empowered to develop collaborative networks of discovery that acknowledge and incorporate the research from all involved.

Notes

1. Lynne Siemens, "'It's a team if you use Reply All': An Exploration of Research Teams in Digital Humanities Environments," *Literary and Linguistic Computing* 24, no. 2 (2009): 225–234.
2. Association for Research Libraries, *Report of the Association and Research Libraries Strategic Design and Thinking Initiative*, Washington, DC: Association

for Research Libraries, 2014. https://www.arl.org/storage/documents/publications/strategic-thinking-design-full-report-aug2014.pdf
3. Rikk Mulligan, *SPEC Kit 350: Supporting Digital Scholarship*, Washington, DC: Association for Research Libraries, 2016. https://publications.arl.org/Supporting-Digital-Scholarship-SPEC-Kit-350/
4. Kirk Anne, Tara Carlisle, Quinn Dombrowski et al. *Building Capacity for Digital Humanities: A Framework for Institutional Planning*. ECAR Working Group Paper. Washington, DC: EDUCause Center for Analysis and Research, 2017. https://library.educause.edu/resources/2017/5/building-capacity-for-digital-humanities-a-framework-for-institutional-planning
5. William A. Wulf, "The Collaboratory Opportunity," *Science* 13 (1993): 854–855. DOI: https://doi.org/10.1126/science.8346438
6. American Council of Learned Societies, *Our Cultural Commonwealth: The report of the ACLS Commission on Cyberinfrastructure for the Humanities and Social Sciences*. New York: American Council of Learned Societies, 2006. http://www.acls.org/uploadedFiles/Publications/Programs/Our_Cultural_Commonwealth.pdf
7. Tanya Clement, "Where is Methodology in Digital Humanities?" *Debates for Digital Humanities 2016 Edition*, dhdebates.gc.cuny.edu/debates/text/65
8. Bethany Nowviskie, "On Capacity and Care," blog post. http://nowviskie.org/2015/on-capacity-and-care/
9. British Library, *British Research Data Strategy 2017*. http://blogs.bl.uk/digital-scholarship/2017/08/announcing-the-new-british-library-research-data-strategy.html
10. Thomas Padilla, "On Collections as a Data Imperative," *Proceedings from the Library of Congress Collections As Data Forum 2016*. http://digitalpreservation.gov/meetings/dcs16/tpadilla_OnaCollectionsasDataImperative_final.pdf?loclr=blogadm
11. Zeynep Tufekci, *Twitter and Tear Gas: The Power and Fragility of Networked Protest*, New Haven: Yale University Press, 2017.
12. Mackey, T. P. & Jacobson, T.E. (2011). Reframing information literacy as metaliteracy. College & Research Libraries 72(1), 62–78.
13. Jesse Stommel, "What Is a Hybrid Pedagogy?" in *The Urgency of Teachers*, Fredericksburg, VA: Hybrid Pedagogy, Inc., 2018.
14. Bonnie Stewart, "How NOT to Teach Online: A STory in Two Parts," *Hybrid Pedagogy* (2016): http://hybridpedagogy.org/how-not-to-teach-online:-a-story-in-two-parts/
15. Veletsianos, George and Royce Kimmon, "Assumptions and Challenges of Open Scholarship," *The International Review of Research in Open and Distance Learning* 13, no. 4 (2012): 166–189.
16. *IMLS Focus Summary Report: National Digital Platform*, https://www.imls.gov/publications/imls-focus-summary-report-national-digital-platform

17. Hong Kong Data Driven Scholarship Institute, "Digital Scholarship Centers: Building Library Services for Data-Driven Scholarship," https://lib.hku.hk/ddsal/index.html
18. Melton, Sarah, Michelle Dalmau, Nora Dimmock, Dan Tracy, and Erin Glass. "ARL Digital Scholarship Institute." *Proceedings of the DH 2017 Conference*. 2017. https://dh2017.adho.org/abstracts/112/112.pdf
19. Green, Harriett and Eleanor Dickson, "Expanding the Librarian's Tech Toolbox: The 'Digging Deeper, Reaching Further: Librarians Empowering Users to Mine the HathiTrust Digital Library' project," *D-Lib Magazine* 23, no. 5–6 (2017): https://doi.org/10.1045/may2017-green
20. "Digging deeper, reaching further: libraries empowering users to mine the HathiTrust Digital Library resources" curriculum, http://hdl.handle.net/2142/102049
21. Anne Burdick, Johanna Drucker, Peter Lunenfeld, Todd Presner, and Jeffrey Schnapp, *Digital_Humanities*, Cambridge, MA: MIT Press, 2012.

14

On Librarianship and/with Digital Scholarly Practice

Vika Zafrin

A Framing

At its best, digital scholarship in the humanities and social sciences is often marked by a combination of challenge, inspiration, and pragmatism. By its nature inherently collaborative, it benefits from the participation of information management specialists in this politically fraught information age. In higher education, such specialists are often found in libraries.

In the continuing process of situating digital scholarship within higher education institutions, views of library professionals' intellectual contributions to it are often fraught with legacy understandings of what librarians do and by frequent institutionalized inequity between faculty and staff. Widely acknowledged by the fields involved, and largely unacknowledged by institutional structures, is this: what's involved in libraries' digital scholarly work is the creation of new knowledge. We offer expertise on the ethics of knowledge production and access that is unavailable in most other academic sectors. Trained digital humanities practitioners also often work in libraries as an academic career choice. Library professionals are not service providers in this

---

The author is grateful to Carol Chiodo, Quinn Dombrowski, Christina Geuther, Shane Landrum, and Brian Rosenblum for comments on an early draft of this chapter.

V. Zafrin (✉)
Boston University, Boston, MA, USA
e-mail: vzafrin@bu.edu

context; we are collaborators whose unique position at the intersection of knowledges is at the heart of digital scholarship. But by and large, our institutions relegate that creation to the status of things we do *on top of* our work, not *as* our work. In this they are for the most part not yet taking full advantage of libraries' unique position, perspective, and ability to bring together strands of knowledge work in order to gain new perspectives on it.

When academic institutions reframe library work as knowledge work and when libraries have the resources to pursue research alongside our public service functions, we bring essential innovative thinking to the academic pursuit. One area in which notable progress along these lines has been made is digital scholarship in the humanities and social sciences.

Great benefit lies in continuing to shape an understanding of libraries[1] as a locus of knowledge production, in deliberately locating the digital scholarly endeavor within them more frequently and in resourcing that endeavor properly. This chapter outlines some current obstacles to this work and opportunities that lie beyond them. I will begin with some context specific to Boston University (BU), expand to a larger view of the fields and administrative structures involved, and conclude with a proposed reframing of what it means to properly resource digital scholarship in the humanities, in libraries.

But first, a definition—such as it is. Digital scholarship has long eluded a single definition. With good reason: it encompasses all fields of humanistic expertise (which themselves have neither an all-inclusive definition nor clearly defined borders) and layers over them many others. Project management, semantically significant metadata work, archival science, digital collection building, use of geographic information systems, user interface building, grant writing, data modeling—all these skills can be brought to bear on digital scholarly projects which, at their best, are highly collaborative and in themselves constitute ongoing research and discovery into the very frameworks we use to perform and thus shape our work. Digital scholarly pursuits can yield research results both at the level of the original humanistic research question and at the meta-level of how we conduct the research and the ways in which our tool and method choices influence the results.

Over the course of several years, participants from across the globe in the once-annual Day of Digital Humanities (DH) event were asked how they define it. Here are a few responses that bear on the consideration of DH work in this chapter:

> Let's be broad: DH is the self-reflexive, critical practice of humanistic enquiry with computer technology. (Aimée Morrison, University of Waterloo)

I see DH as a set of resources—software, texts, tools, etc.—that contribute [to] building knowledge. A network, a crossroad, a bridge, a meeting point. (Gimena del Rio Riande, Universidad de Buenos Aires)

DH is the use of computing in the humanities, arts, and social sciences; DH is the creation of new computing resources for use in these areas; DH is the study of computing from the perspective of these areas. (Stan Ruecker, University of Illinois)

With some reluctance. (Bethany Nowviskie, Digital Library Federation and University of Virginia)

For the purposes of this chapter, I abbreviate digital scholarship to DH, keeping in mind that humanistic inquiry extends far into all knowledge work; and define it as any nontrivial use of computation (beyond word processing) to create new humanistic knowledge.

A Case Study

Boston University Libraries inaugurated its Digital Scholarship Services (DiSc) department in 2016. Though DiSc has only existed for about three and a half years at the time of this writing, BU Libraries have been building digital collections for about 15 years. Following the launch of our institutional repository OpenBU[2] in 2009, we began thinking about digital collection building more systemically. OpenBU now holds a large variety of materials, including the African Ajami Library created by a team led by Dr. Fallou Ngom and supported by a number of grants. Detailed discussion of this work can be found elsewhere in this volume.

The writings Ngom's team seeks to preserve have been long neglected by the West due in part to colonialist disdain for indigenous African cultural heritage. When Ngom came to us to discuss collaboration, seeking guidance on digitization technologies and preservation standards, he described the original manuscripts as literally rotting in people's houses all over the continent. We have worked as part of Ngom's team since 2012, to help ensure that the photos taken are of preservation quality (resulting in large file sizes) and to provide access in ways that accommodate stringent bandwidth quotas and slow Internet access in world regions where some of our audiences reside. The team has also kept meticulous records of the provenance of these materials, the available stories around their creation and/or significance, and the people involved in making them available more widely as part of this project. All of this, plus the explicit consent of manuscript owners for this work to be performed, is reflected in both collection- and item-level metadata[3] created for the African Ajami Library residing in OpenBU, as well as in video recordings and transcripts of detailed interviews with manuscript owners.

The story that Dr. Ngom tells concerns a set of languages that share not only the Ajami script, but also treatment as Other, deliberate marginalization. When we at Boston University—and in conversation with the British Library, both institutions being agents of cultures that have done irreparable damage to the African continent on top of this marginalization—talk about preservation, we must keep this historical power relationship in mind. On the DiSc side this manifests as an ongoing commitment to viewing ourselves as stewards of someone else's stories, taking our cues regarding their framing from those to whom they belong. In this way, our work with the African Ajami Library project has informed how we think about metadata creation, about working with individuals underrepresented in cultural heritage collections, and about our own place in the hegemonic cultural structures in which we all reside.

Since its creation, DiSc has been examining our work on Dr. Ngom's team with an eye to applying what we have learned more systemically in our digital collections creation work. We have taken to heart Chris Bourg's invocation of libraries as "never neutral," and have begun actively seeking out projects that would allow us to put some part of our scant resources toward evening out the balance of representation in cultural heritage collections. This slight reorientation has quickly led us toward work with some history-rich local resources concerning twentieth-century African American theater and—separately— the city of Roxbury, Massachusetts. Their owners have BU ties and want help preserving them and thinking through the creation of apparatus around them that would encourage both academic and community use.

While it is true that these resources are vulnerable to disappearance or obscurity, we are not here to save them or to empower the communities represented within them—often African American, sometimes poor, demographics whose cultural preservation has often been a low priority for cultural memory agents. We are here to offer infrastructure and knowledge in the domains of preservation and digital humanities that we think can amplify other people's voices and help their histories be told as part of our collective memory. In this, we take our cue from DeRay McKesson, a US grassroots political organizer and civil rights activist with a background in education. On a 2017 episode of his *Pod Save the People* podcast, McKesson said about political organizing: "You can't *give* people power. That's just not how this works. What you can do as an organizer ... is help people remember the power that they already have, and you can help them unlock that power. [...] We're always fighting to make sure structures and systems recognize the power that people should have over their lives, at the structural level, and give that to them. And that is what we think about when we think about empowerment."

DiSc continues to think through how to manifest this in library work as we proceed in conversation with our community partners, working through digitization, metadata, and co-ownership models. Four tenets have already been clarified and are being put into practice. First, our work with resources we do not already physically steward is post-custodial: we digitize physical artifacts belonging to other people, then return those physical artifacts to their owners. In addition to effectively instituting immediate artifact repatriation in a field rife with colonialist tendencies,[4] this practice prompts conversations about ownership, relative responsibility, and eventual use at the very beginning of each digitization project.

Second, we create metadata together with the owners to the extent that they are willing, and metadata are emergent—created through iteration, the process primarily concerned with what stories *should* be told about the artifacts involved, and to whom. This is a radical departure from most library metadata practice. But it is also the logical extension of post-custodial practice, through McKesson's notion of "mak[ing] sure structures and systems recognize the power that people should have over their lives," into co-authorship with artifact owners of the stories told through metadata. We also take our cue from DH projects that, relatively early on in the evolution of digital literary studies, embraced a framing of semantic markup (a type of metadata) not as an objective record of what is, but as a format that can accommodate uncertainty and iteration, and therefore both contain and constitute scholarly argument.[5]

The third tenet flows out of the first two: we must work out some sort of functional co-ownership of every collection of digital artifacts whose physical counterparts are owned by others. Achieving this involves a tricky balance between institutional interests and mission, and the interests and benefit of people represented by or in these collections. Various aspects of agreements made at the outset should, then, be led by one party or the other. For example, the implementation details of a long-term preservation and/or access commitment should be up to the institution. The representative owners should have agency with regard to other aspects: for example, to what groups access is provided, when, and under what reuse conditions.[6] These rights, which we view as moral rights, are nearly identical to copyright; but we are applying them here to people whose relationship to their artifacts is not "author" but "cultural authority." By putting this tenet into practice via conversations with our collaborators, we acknowledge their cultural agency and ourselves as the infrastructure providers for the telling of their stories.

Finally, we talk publicly about our work before it is done. This, too, is a departure from how business is often conducted in the academy—in publications and conference presentations, one usually offers results, not process. Here, too, we see great value in iteration: we offer our work in the hopes of feedback that will allow us to improve it before we are done, sometimes by alerting us early on to pitfalls in our approach.

The Situational Challenge

It is no surprise that this work often happens in libraries, which exist in a charged limbo at the intersection of research and teaching, and of all disciplines, without being wholly a part of any of them. Librarianship itself is a rich convergence of an academic discipline of its own, an organizational crossroads, and a praxis. Libraries are spaces people enter to be alone with their thoughts, or to volley thought processes among a group until they begin to resolve and cohere. They are carefully landscaped mazes that can bring us closer to the knowledge we seek or steer us farther away from it. Properly resourced, they offer a range of programmatic possibilities difficult to imagine elsewhere on an academic campus.

This multiplicity of essence and purpose is often obscured by the most visible and deceptively simple of library functions—objects to be checked out, a circulation desk, public service intermediaries who genially connect seekers to what they're looking for. Behind these service functions is a centuries-long study of how we succeed and fail in organizing existing knowledge. What persists? What falls through the cracks? How do we recognize the biases that lead to these results and do better? The library's vantage point carries great opportunity for insight into our collective knowledge work.

Great peril too: we select, therefore we discard. Knowledge work institutions are here partly to be the memory of humanity, and libraries are the shapers of that memory. Insights are not enough: if memory institutions do not preserve them and make them appropriately discoverable, the world may well forget what was gained. What frightening power, to be able to make us forget selectively.

Libraries and other cultural heritage institutions have a collective history of intermittent success at best when it comes to wielding this power. We have a sordid track record of embedding damaging colonialist practices into the very ways we organize what we preserve. We are in the beginning stages of change in this regard, of which the post-custodial practices discussed earlier are one example.

Related to these are other ethical issues around knowledge production, in which libraries and archives are directly implicated, and which Ellen Cushman touches on in her work elsewhere in this volume. Who owns knowledge and artifacts? Who gets to tell their stories? What are the ethical dimensions of access, not only to the artifacts themselves but to the possibility of weaving a narrative around them? At our core, humanity is the stories that we tell each other about ourselves. Immense power lies in how those stories are told. Who gets to exercise this power? These questions span both librarianship and DH work and speak to a core contribution by librarians to digital scholarship.

I mentioned above legacy understandings of library work, misconceptions based on received stereotypes. We need a radical change in understanding and in approach.

To reiterate my opening framing, echoing Harriett Green's thought in this volume and elsewhere: library work yields new knowledge and new understandings of knowledge work processes. In digital scholarship in particular, librarians are not service providers; we are collaborators whose expertise, at its best, positions us as initiators and/or co-directors of new research. But primary agency in knowledge creation seems to be incompatible with the double whammy that is the perception of libraries as service organizations and a profound misperception of librarianship as relatively esoteric work, inscrutable by and irrelevant to those outside the field. Added to this is the faculty-staff divide: on campuses where librarians do not have faculty status, and even on some campuses where they do, the clear hierarchy between faculty (higher) and staff (lower) plays itself out in overwhelming impressions that new knowledge created by librarians is only useful to the larger organization as a bolster to the real work happening elsewhere, not as insight on its own merits.[7]

But few of us attracted to academic library work want *only* to give books out and reshelve them again, though connecting seekers to information is rewarding in its own right. Questions around knowledge organization quickly dive deep into history—see Buckland—and into questions of how disciplinary boundaries expressed in organizational schemes tend to obscure interdisciplinary knowledge. The library workers at the forefront of engaging with these questions often find themselves making intellectually challenging decisions whose ultimate purpose is as much to fit into existing subject and other classifications as to accurately reflect the work being classified.

Better ways undoubtedly exist to make more of our collective thought accessible to more of us. They are complicated by myriad factors, not least of them the fact that our contemporary audiences differ considerably from even recent ancestors in how they connect strands of thought. Humanity's collective, relentless pursuit of greater understanding of itself in the networked era is inseparable from metacognitive questions around how we organize and reorganize understandings already achieved. And so library work attracts researchers, some of whom have terminal degrees in disciplines other than library and information science. Many of the latter are humanities scholars who have, one way or another, often by way of unconventional academic paths, pursued digital scholarship.

If we reframe academic libraries in this way, as places where new knowledge is created, then they need to be resourced differently—in money, in staff, and in physical space. This is the conclusion higher education institutions are increasingly reaching; many, however, still need to be convinced.

Other Challenges

New possibilities and big dreams are certainly part of the appeal of DH. But everyone needs to eat, teach, attain job stability, and advance some part of their or others' research agenda. And so DH researchers, no matter where they are positioned in the academy, do what they have been trained to do: divide big dreams into manageable parts and formulate more specific research questions that might lead a step or two down the longer path they wish to pursue. They convince others to provide them with the resources to accomplish these things, which, because the collaborative nature of DH work spans vast administrative landscapes, is institutionally tricky on all levels from the local to the international. They—we—continue to chip away at the siloing of disciplinarity, molding new academic identities from well-established ones.

This can threaten scholars who see no benefit in fundamentally changing how they have (successfully!) worked their entire careers. In particular, the visibility of resource use and the primacy of serious commitment of human and monetary resources that DH work requires has led at times to heated conversations regarding a diversion of these resources away from more traditional humanities work, toward what is implicitly or explicitly framed as so much glitz without enough substance to warrant the expense.[8]

Adversarial framings like this set up a false disunion between "digital" and "analog" (or "traditional") humanities. DH does not exist, has never existed, outside of the humanities. The field's research and teaching serves humanistic goals no more imperfectly than all other knowledge work. But one thing is true: the institutionalization of DH has starkly highlighted labor and resourcing issues in the humanities. This presents an opportunity for humanities workers to join forces in continuing to articulate these issues and make proposals for addressing them. Like many of our colleagues in related fields, digital scholarship specialists continue to put a significant part of our effort toward conversations that, with varying success, attempt to reorient the culture of humanists fighting each other for the crumbs that keep us all starving, toward a truly collaborative culture that takes advocacy as part of its work and collectively demands better resourcing from our respective treasuries.

The contention I described earlier and the disquiet underlying it are systemically driven. They arise at least in part from deep-seated institutional anxieties that are substantiated by very real, drastic, and continued under-resourcing of all humanities work. Both the American Academy of Arts and Sciences and Terras et al. make this point starkly: national-level funding for humanities research in the US and Europe is barely a budgetary blip as compared to research funding in other fields. It is not always clear why: widespread agreement exists on the utility of humanistic knowledge, and declining enrollments in humanities courses seem to be driven by misperceptions of the nature of current economic pressures rather than factors pertaining to intrinsic value (Schmidt).

Perhaps the primary driver of humanities resourcing decisions is not actual scarcity, but a combination of privilege given to more tangible-feeling pursuits on the one hand and inaccurate understanding of need on the other. Humanities perceive a resource scarcity because, despite widespread rhetoric acknowledging the centrality of our expertise to all human endeavor, we increasingly experience scarcity, most starkly as continued adjunctification of the faculty and staff workforce. Digital scholarship in the humanities—which inseparably constitutes work in the humanities—has resource requirements that to date have been well addressed by only a handful of institutions. These requirements include types of expertise widely marketable in a variety of fields that more reliably offer job stability, as well as an understanding of administrative higher education structures that benefits from institutional memory. This presents a direct challenge to adjunctification.

Before I delve more deeply into the resource requirements of digital scholarly work, I must also touch on *return on investment* (ROI). I have had baffling conversations with library administrators who have found themselves being asked to articulate libraries' ROI, framed as a monetary gain for the institution. This is a fundamental misunderstanding of value. The value of the libraries, and of the humanities, has been widely discussed elsewhere.[9] Return on investment in both comes down to a deeper understanding of ourselves and, ultimately, different individual and collective choices made. A monetary wealth-based return absolutely follows, but not always directly at the institutional level. The easily recognizable ROI institutions do receive is infrastructure—the logistical and metacognitive scaffolding that enables us to continue creating intellectual frameworks for, and from within, the digital age.

Let's turn back to requirements. All the thought and activity that I described earlier require little resource investment relative to, for example, the setup and operation of a chemistry lab.[10] Why do we need money?

Because these are merely the fundamental conceptual pillars of projects. We can digitize, though not at scale; we can tell stories through metadata, though likewise slowly. We cannot do anything else interesting with these artifacts without further investment of infrastructure, money, and people to engage deeply with questions of use, audience, and design. Even that further investment is pocket change to some of our academic colleagues. But it is essential, and must be made at the institutional level, being fiscally untenable at the level of individual projects. Such funding, provided at a sustainable time scale, is significantly more likely to be allocated if the institution views our work for what it is—the co-creation of new knowledge.

There exists a threshold of combined monetary, human, and time resources below which the return on any investment in humanities work—digital or otherwise—will be negative. The location of this threshold is individual to each institution, factors such as size and the precise nature of research priorities being at play. If all three of these types of resources are allocated appropriately, the return on investment is quite simply better work.

Commitment to humanities research on the part of most US institutions falls below this threshold, and so human infrastructure in particular continues to be used poorly. Under-resourced projects (short-term gains) are prioritized over infrastructure (long-term gains), leading to technical and expertise debt. People churn through positions, positions churn through people, and the operational advancement and preservation of institutional memory associated with continuous development are lost as a result. Being site-specific and still in the early stages of institutionalization, DH work requires sustained, long-term local engagement on the part of individuals who are afforded the time and resources not only to advance individual projects but to build out infrastructure. The expertise of hired digital scholarship specialists is often squandered as institutions place them within contexts with wildly unreasonable expectations relative to the resources made available. In the field these have been ruefully termed miracle worker scenarios and are understood to be neither sustainable nor by themselves a good investment. DH professionals then spend a significant part of our effort job searching and using our collaboration skills to set up informal support networks outside of our institutions, which is detrimental to productivity and systemically fragile.[11] DH work is, then, reflective of the US academic labor force as regards both faculty and staff positions. The lack of resources and subsequent burnout prevalent even in stable positions in the humanities are incompatible with the healthy development of new knowledge production infrastructures.

As I alluded to earlier, technological infrastructure commitments must keep pace with ones concerning human labor. Piecemeal resourcing of money and computing, currently prevalent in institutions supporting DH, is ultimately more expensive than a well thought out, flexible, resilient architecture that accommodates a variety of projects in ways that allow for experimentation and failure, true research and development.[12]

Resources, Again: A Culture Change

Collaboration is tricky at best to institutionalize. Inevitable, hard choices must be made in deciding what skills to represent in a given pool of available labor, to maximize the number of research and teaching projects it can accommodate whose nature is as yet unknown. The pace of technological obsolescence clashes against the long life span of humanistic knowledge, requiring both careful resilient architecture building and profound, continued work on increasing data portability[13] and platform independence even as we take advantage of technological capacities unique to the platforms we use. Finally, collaborative humanities work requires institutional structures that can only arise from existing ones if the extant administrative separations are made more malleable—that is, if we approach higher education administrative structures as serving primarily to address the knowledge-related world issues an institution has decided to take on, not (as often happens) the other way around.

Why did Dr. Ngom come to the libraries in the first place? No more than for a consult on equipment and formats. The benefit of collaboration with DiSc to his projects, however, has extended far beyond the initially intended knowledge transfer about those, and into the deeper humanistic research questions with which he arrived at BU. Our conversations about what to do with these materials beyond digitizing them have yielded new thinking and new approaches to our work both in African Studies and in librarianship. That only some of these are beginning to coalesce into active projects is partly a function of our resourcing, and partly—of slow DH principles (Hyman/Corona) informing processes where realistic expectations, care, and sustainability are paramount.

Why don't more people come to us early in their projects, and how do we get them to start doing so? The simple, difficult answer is: culture change is needed to institutionalize support for the generative work academic libraries do, and to expand our capacity to do it to match existing demand. Many individual academics, particularly those working in the highly collaborative digital scholarship environments, have already witnessed the benefit of collaborating with information management professionals, many of whom are scholars in their own right. Higher education institutions are increasingly recognizing the essential nature of this work and resourcing it at a level where the return on investment as described earlier becomes positive. While this state of affairs cannot yet be considered common, in institutions at the forefront of this strategic movement a virtuous circle is often created, in which DH units create environments for generating humanities scholarship in ways that attract more participants who then generate more scholarship.

Ultimately, where exactly within a college or university such a DH unit is situated is not material. Essential, however, are three related activities: continued situation (as an active verb) of DH infrastructure within academic structures; as part of that process, recognition and productive use of the unique academic position of libraries at the intersection of knowledges where they serve to translate between them; and, recognition that the most effective librarianship is increasingly inseparable from scholarship, followed by the institutionalization (again as an active verb) of personnel structures to enable and encourage both.

Digital scholarly work in the humanities faces a formidable organizational challenge in its need to create enough time and resource allocation flexibility for the human beings involved to be able to pursue it fully. Organizationally speaking, in order to truly innovate, libraries and digital scholarship support infrastructures—whether administratively united or disparate in a given local context—must be able to square our shoulders, take the space and time to breathe, and sit with existing knowledge in order to create something new. Given the opportunity, the new knowledge we create is indispensable to the higher education institutions actively oriented toward bettering the world.

Notes

1. While much of what I write is applicable across the field, the focus of this chapter is academic libraries.
2. http://open.bu.edu

3. Metadata are descriptors of whatever is understood to be primary data in a specific context. Examples of metadata include column headers in a spreadsheet, hashtags and other tags on social media, and information included in a library catalog record, including an item's title, publisher, date of issue, and subject headings.
4. For vivid examples of this history, see Buckland; Christen; and Anderson 2009.
5. Many such digital literary studies exist. I base my writing chiefly on those in which I have personally participated, including the Decameron Web (see "Methodology," Zafrin 2007), Virtual Humanities Lab (Zafrin and Riva), and my doctoral dissertation *RolandHT* (Zafrin 2007).
6. For examples of contexts where these considerations might be relevant, please see Traditional Knowledge Labels, a tool that has conceptual application far beyond indigenous communities (Local Contexts). For more work around these issues, please see cited works by Anderson (2005) and Christen.
7. This situation is exacerbated by the division, within the libraries themselves, between professional staff (typically, those with specialized degrees) and paraprofessional staff (typically, those without such degrees). Despite the fact that the latter often find themselves on the front lines of intellectually challenging decisions, their positions within their respective organizations often lead to perceptions of them as line workers more than knowledge workers.
8. I hesitate to cite Brennan here due to the number of flaws in his analysis. Taken together with the comments on it, however, his article provides a decent and relatively recent point(s)-counterpoint(s) view of the issues involved.
9. For two gripping examples among many, see Hayden and Smith, respectively.
10. I realize that I write from the perspective of a person working, however underresourced, in a wealthy US university. For many of my colleagues, having a four-person team to tackle these complex questions is an unthinkable luxury. But context is everything: most of my colleagues do not work at institutions the size of a small city.
11. In 2016, Columbia's Digital Scholarship Librarian Alex Gil started an informal, Google-hosted spreadsheet titled "Open Directory of Miracle Workers." Currently this directory contains 148 entries, an astonishing number given the still small size of the field.
12. I am grateful to Jonathan Williams, senior web developer at Boston University, for conversations that have clarified for me both the architecture needed and the language to describe it. For more discussion on this, see Anne et al.
13. Data portability is the degree to which produced and/or recorded knowledge is separable from the technologies within which it resides and transferable from one such set of technologies to another.

Bibliography

Anderson, Jane. 2009. (Colonial) Archives and (Copyright) Law. *Nomorepotlucks* 1 (4). nomorepotlucks.org/site/colonial-archives-and-copyright-law/. Accessed 26 Dec 2018.

———. 2005. Access and Control of Indigenous Knowledge in Libraries and Archives: Ownership and Future Use. In *Correcting Course: Rebalancing Copyright for Libraries in the National and International Arena*, ed. American Library Association and The MacArthur Foundation. New York: Columbia University.

Anne, Kirk M., et al. 2017. Building Capacity for Digital Humanities: A Framework for Institutional Planning. ECAR Working Group Paper, May 31. Louisville: ECAR.

Bourg, Chris. 2015. Never Neutral: Libraries, Technology, and Inclusion. *Feral Librarian*. chrisbourg.wordpress.com/2015/01/28/never-neutral-libraries-technology-and-inclusion/. Accessed 26 Dec 2018.

Brennan, Timothy. 2017. The Digital-Humanities Bust. *The Chronicle Review*, October 15. www.chronicle.com/article/The-Digital-Humanities-Bust/241424. Accessed 26 Dec 2018.

Buckland, Hannah. 2017. Decolonizing Catalogs in Tribal College Libraries. *ALCTS Exchange: Embracing the Past, Building the Future*. youtu.be/sUmS2dmngE0

Christen, Kimberly. 2012. Does Information Really Want to Be Free?: Indigenous Knowledge and the Politics of Open Access. *The International Journal of Communication* 6: 2870–2893.

Hayden, Carla. 2018. Accessing a Diverse Collection by a Diverse Library Audience with Dr. Carla Hayden. Information Matters Lecture at the Smithsonian Libraries, July 19. library.si.edu/webcasts/accessing-diverse-collection-dr-carla-hayden. Accessed 26 Dec 2018.

Local Contexts. Traditional Knowledge Labels. localcontexts.org/tk-labels. Accessed 26 Dec 2018.

Mckesson, DeRay. 2017. We Don't Know How This Movie Ends. *Pod Save the People*, September 5. https://crooked.com/podcast/we-dont-know-how-this-movie-ends/. Accessed 26 Dec 2018.

Schmidt, Benjamin. 2018. The Humanities Are in Crisis. *The Atlantic*, August 23. www.theatlantic.com/ideas/archive/2018/08/the-humanities-face-a-crisisof-confidence/567565/. Accessed 26 Dec 2018.

Smith, Martha Nell. 2011. The Humanities Are Not a Luxury: A Manifesto for the Twenty-First Century. *Liberal Education* 97 (1): 48–55.

Terras, Melissa, Ernesto Priego, Alan Liu, Geoffrey Rockwell, Stéfan Sinclair, Christine Henseler, and Lindsay Thomas. 2013. The Humanities Matter! Infographic. 4humanities.org/infographic. Accessed 26 Dec 2018.

The American Academy of Arts and Sciences. Humanities Indicators. www.humanitiesindicators.org. Accessed 26 Dec 2018.

Zafrin, Vika. 2007. Roland^{HT}. PhD Dissertation, Brown University. http://rolandht.org/. Accessed 26 Dec 2018.

Zafrin, Vika, and Massimo Riva. 2008. Presentazione del Virtual Humanities Lab alla Brown University. *Storicamente* 4 (38). https://doi.org/10.1473/stor302. Accessed 26 Dec 2018.

15

Data Moves: Libraries and Data Science Workflows

Alan Liu

Library-based collections and repositories are today advancing well beyond accumulating or creating resources in digital form for the purposes of searching, reading, and other primary access. New approaches to holdings as "always already computational"—to cite the motto of the Always Already Computational: Collections as Data initiative—treat digitized library materials as datasets for advanced data-mining analysis and other kinds of derivative, synthetic, creative, and meta-level data scholarship.[1] Conceived in this way, libraries have a role to play in partnering with today's burgeoning, cross-disciplinary field of "data science," which a pioneering program in the field such as the Division of Data Science and Information at UC Berkeley, originating in 2014, defines for its student majors as methods equipping us "to draw sound conclusions from data in context, using knowledge of statistical inference, computational processes, data management strategies, domain knowledge, and theory" while gaining "a deep appreciation of the human, social, and institutional structures and practices that shape technical work around computing and data."[2]

To hone in on the specific role that libraries may have in supporting data science will require comparing data science workflows across disciplines. The goal of research in this direction will be twofold: to identify common "moves" in data processing and to spot points in the data trajectory that are especially

---

A. Liu (✉)
University of California, Santa Barbara, Santa Barbara, CA, USA
e-mail: ayliu@english.ucsb.edu

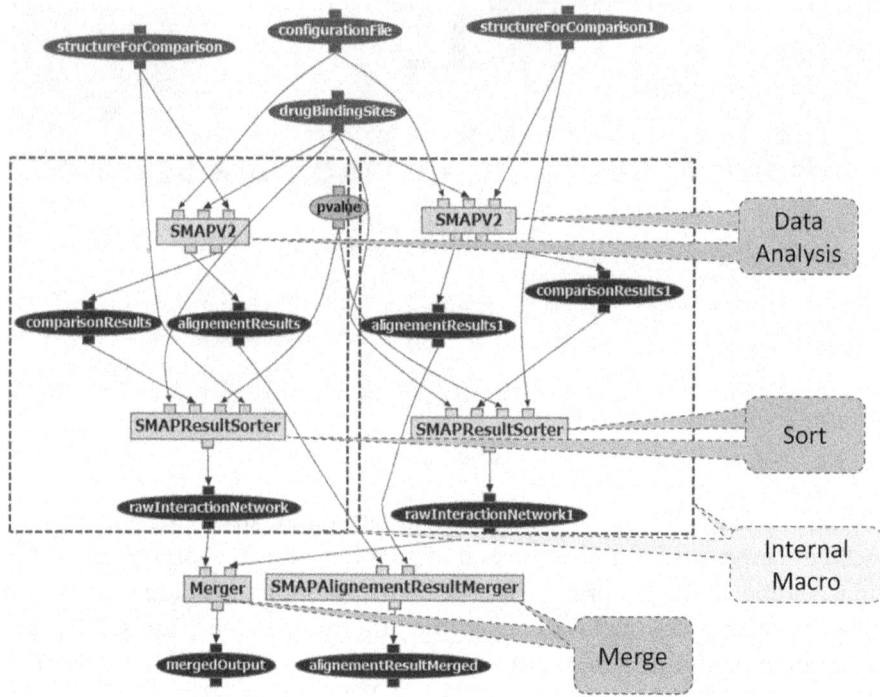

Fig. 15.1 A Wings workflow for a data analysis related to drug discovery. (From Garijo et al., "Common Motifs in Scientific Workflows: An Empirical Analysis"; © 2012 IEEE; reprinted with permission)

in need of library support because—for a variety of technical, social, or ethical reasons—they are brittle.

A methodology for comparative study of the sort I indicate can be borrowed from research on data workflows and data provenance in so-called in silico science. In the past two decades, *scientific workflow management* has become a flourishing area of scholarship and practice, producing integrated systems (such as Wings, Apache Taverna, and Kepler) for describing, visualizing, manipulating, automating, reproducing, and sharing data workflows. These systems typically model workflows as directed, acyclic network graphs in which nodes represent datasets, processes, and algorithms, while edges show causal or logical dependencies (e.g., of source, derivation, transformation, comparison, sorting, or merger) (see Fig. 15.1). As Yolanda Gil et al. explain in "Examining the Challenges of Scientific Workflows,"

> Each step in a workflow specifies a process or computation to be executed (for instance, a software program or Web service). The workflow links the steps according to the data flow and dependencies among them. The representation

of these computational workflows contains many details required to carry out each analysis step, including the use of specific execution and storage resources in distributed environments ... Workflow systems exploit these explicit representations of complex computational processes at various levels of abstraction to manage their life cycle and automate their execution. In addition to automation, workflows can provide the information necessary for scientific reproducibility, result derivation, and result sharing among collaborators.[3]

Correspondingly, *data provenance* (or *data lineage* as it is also called) complements scientific data workflow systems through standards and tools for describing data in evolving states of production, transformation, and dissemination. Important data provenance frameworks, for example, include the Open Provenance Model (OPM) and the W3C (World Wide Web Consortium) PROV model. As the W3C's overview document about PROV defines, "provenance is information about entities, activities, and people involved in producing a piece of data or thing, which can be used to form assessments about its quality, reliability or trustworthiness."[4] Linked data provenance models have also been proposed for understanding the relation of "actors, executions, and artifacts" behind data creation and access.[5]

Besides their practical purposes in helping control and reproduce data analysis, the methods of scientific data workflow and provenance now offer intriguing avenues toward meta-analysis of workflow and provenance. In a 2012 article, for instance, Daniel Garijo et al. inspect 177 workflows in the Wings and Apache Taverna systems to classify high-level data workflow patterns.[6] The study catalogs these patterns as *data-oriented motifs* (common steps or designs of data retrieval, preparation, movement, cleaning/curation, analysis, visualization, etc.) and *workflow-oriented motifs* (common steps or designs of "stateful/asynchronous" and "stateless/synchronous" processes, "internal macros," "human interactions versus computational steps," or "composite workflows"). Then it compares the proportions of these motifs in workflows from different scientific disciplines to observe, for instance, that data-input augmentation is an overwhelmingly important motif in astronomy, while data sorting is a prevalent motif in drug discovery research.

Since the special usage of the word *motifs* in the article by Garijo et al. is unfamiliar, I suggest using the more common, etymologically related word *moves* to speak of "data moves" or "workflow moves." A *move* connotes a combination of *step* and *form*. That is, it is a step implemented not just in any way but in some common way or form. In this regard, the formalist notion of a "move" (in the Russian: *xod*) as deployed by Vladimir Propp and the Russian formalists nicely backs up the choice of the word *move* to mean a common-

> THE TALE AS A WHOLE   93
>
> a text containing one tale from a text containing two or more,
> let us see by what methods the moves are combined, regardless
> of the number of tales in a text.
>   The combination of moves may be as follows:
>
> 1. One move directly follows another. An approximate scheme
>   of such combinations is:
>
>   I. A_____W*
>   II. A_____W²
>
> 2. A new move begins before the termination of the first one.
>   Action is interrupted by an episodic move. After the comple-
>   tion of the episode, the completion of the first move follows
>   as well. The scheme is:
>
>   I. A_____G.............K_____W*
>   II. a_____K
>
> 3. An episode may also be interrupted in its turn, and in this
>   case fairly complicated schemes may result.
>
>   I._____............._____.............._____
>   II._____..............._____
>   III._____
>
> 4. A tale may begin with two villainies at once, of which the
>   first one may be liquidated completely before the other is.
>   If the hero is killed and a magical agent is stolen from him,
>   then first of all the murder is liquidated, and then the theft
>   is liquidated also.
>
>   A₂¹⁴ { I._____K⁹
>   { II. ...._____K¹
>
> 5. Two moves may have a common ending.
>
>   I._____...............}
>   II._____   } _____
>
> 6. Sometimes a tale contains *two* seekers (see No. 155, "The
>   Two Iváns, Soldier's Sons"). The heroes part in the middle
>   of the first move. They usually part with omens at a road
>   marker. This road marker serves as a *disuniting* element.
>   (Parting at a road marker we shall designate by the sign <.

Fig. 15.2 Combinations of "moves" or "motifs" in folk narratives from Vladimir Propp, *Morphology of the Folktale*, 2d ed., translated by Laurence Scott, revised and edited with a preface by Louis A. Wagner, University of Texas Press, 1968; reprinted with permission. (Original work published in 1928)

place data step/form. Indeed, Propp's diagrammatic analyses of "moves" in folk narratives (see Fig. 15.2) look a lot like scientific workflows. We might even bridge between scientific and humanistic contexts and say, in the spirit of Propp, that "workflows" are actually narratives. Scientists, social scientists, and humanists do not just process data; they tell data stories. Indeed, one of the latest developments in the scientific data workflow field is the automatic generation of prose narratives of data processing. Yolanda Gil and Daniel Garijo's article titled "Towards Automating Data Narratives," for instance, includes such computer-generated "narratives" of data steps as the following,

15 Data Moves: Libraries and Data Science Workflows 215

which are told from what in narrative theory would be called different points of view:

> Data view – The term-topic matrix visualization results have been derived from the Reuters_R8_train and English_Stopwords datasets.
>
> Functionality view – The method Detect Topics performs a single main type of analysis on the input dataset through the Topic Detection step. First, the input data is filtered by, Stop Words and Small Words, followed by Format Dataset (a type of transformation step), and Topic Detection (a type of Analysis step). The final results are produced by Plot Topics (a type of Visualization step).
>
> Dependency view – The topic modeling method has five steps. The first one, Stop words step, uses an input dataset and a words dataset to produce a filtered result. Next, the Small words step consumes that output to produce another filtered result. The next step is the Format dataset a reformatting step which adapts the result for the Train topics step. Next, the TrainTopics step produces an output topics dataset. Finally the Plot topics step is [sic] takes the output topics dataset to create the term-topic matrix visualization.[7]

The takeaway from all the above is that a general comparative study of data workflow and provenance across disciplines—including the sciences, social sciences, humanities, arts, and the library and archive fields themselves—conducted using workflow modeling tools could help identify high-priority "data moves" for a library-based "always already computational" framework. Such a study could be made even more general through adding other methodologies—for example, ethnographical, science-technology studies (STS), historical, social science, or cultural critical studies of what happens when scholars work with data in academic institutions that today, precisely because of the omnipresence of data, interact in unstable relations of similarity and difference with other major social institutions practicing data science (business, government, journalism, sports, etc.). Or studies could be tailored more narrowly for local contexts. An individual university and its library, for instance, could realistically conduct a comparative data workflow study of projects in three or four areas of data-science strength on campus. At my own university, for instance, the digital humanities, digital arts, and new media studies would need to be in the mix of such a study alongside strong STEM (science, technology, engineering, mathematics) and social science computational fields.

Whether general or local, a comparative study of data workflows could help guide libraries in developing digital collection, curation, metadata, standards, storage, subscription purchasing, open-access, access, and other strategies to support "data moves" of several classes. One important class consists of very common data moves. For example, imagine that a comparative study showed that, in a sample of data analysis projects, over 40% of the data moves involved Python- or R-based processing using common code libraries implemented in similar sequences (perhaps concatenated in Jupyter data notebooks), and, moreover, that among these moves a key subset was common across multiple disciplinary sectors (e.g., science, digital social science, and digital humanities). Then these are clearly data moves to prioritize in planning "always already computational" resources, formats, and access frameworks and standards.

Equally important is another class of data moves (or, more accurately in this case, immobilities) that creates brittle points in workflows where humans have to intervene manually or ad hoc. One example is repetitive, low-level preprocessing to overcome messy, missing, or incompatible data that is often easier to fix through manual kludges than by devoting time and resources to programing a computational process. Another example is the simple exercise of citing data of inconsistent kinds, in varying states, for different dissemination targets (e.g., journals in various fields). And yet another example is overcoming the friction involved in moving or repurposing data when technical, format, or contractual barriers intervene. For instance, researchers at different universities collaborating on a project may be collecting data from the "same" proprietary database but find that they are prevented from sharing working references to the original data because links generated through their different institutions' access to the databases are different or cannot be distributed. Brittle points in data workflows of these kinds identified through comparative study would be high-value targets for "always already computational" provisioning in libraries, whether by means of standards, ingest and access methods, or tools. Not all pain points of the kind I mention can be solved by standard means, of course. But identifying very common pain points (e.g., Unicode character encoding problems in digital texts intended to be used in data workflows) sets a target.

Finally, another class of high-priority data moves deserves attention from libraries for a combination of practical and ethical issues. Many scenarios of data science research involve generating transient data products, meaning data that has been transformed at one or more steps of remove from the original dataset but that are not the final output. A comparative workflow study could identify common kinds of transient data forms that require holding by libraries for reasons of research replication or as supporting evidence for research publications. In addition, because some datasets cannot safely be held in human-readable form due to intellectual property issues or sensitive IRB ("institutional review board," "human subjects research") constraints, so-called nonconsumptive use datasets such as texts converted into "bags of words," extracted features, or anonymized and aggregated materials become important as holdings, even though in normal workflows they would be merely transient products. A comparative data workflow study could identify high-value kinds of such holdings that need the support of "always already computational" library frameworks and standards.

Envisioned most generally, it seems to me, libraries in the digital age are partners with scholarship in new ways because storage, curation, metadata creation, finding, circulation, publication, and similar functions now blur together as tributaries of the broader river of data science. Increasingly a part of mainstream scholarship, data science is not *universal knowledge* in the older sense of the liberal arts. Neither is it just *specialist* and subsequently *interdisciplinary knowledge* into which universal knowledge transmuted in the modern academy. Today, it is a transformation of both universal and specialist/interdisciplinary knowledge paradigms that we do not yet know how best to describe. It is none and all of the following: a reduction, sampling, parameterizing, modeling, analysis, synthesis, and simulation of knowledge. Libraries need to work with data science to carry it past its pain points of emergence while not glossing over the reasons for all that pain in the first place: the original social and historical reasons behind messy, incompatible, or missing data that are part of the human, and not just data, narrative that the liberal arts arose to tell.

Notes

1. From 2016 to 2018, the Always Already Computational: Collections as Data initiative (principal investigator: Thomas Padilla) aimed to advance "approaches to developing cultural heritage collections that support computationally-driven research and teaching" (Collections as Data, "Always Already Computational"). The initiative continued after 2018 with a Andrew W. Mellon Foundation grant under the project name Collections as Data: Part to Whole.

    This chapter is a revised and expanded version of my position statement for the Always Already Computational: Collections as Data forum held at the University of California, Santa Barbara, on March 1–3, 2017. My original position statement, titled "Assessing Data Workflows for Common Data 'Moves' Across Disciplines," appeared online in a compilation of statements by forum participants ("Always Already Computational: Library Collections as Data: National Forum Position Statements"). A previous version of that position statement, less revised than this chapter, appeared under its original title on my blog on 6 May 2017 (https://liu.english.ucsb.edu). See also the related discussion of scientific data workflows and data provenance in my *Friending the*

Past (129–139), which in part draws on some of the same examples of workflow and provenance systems discussed in this chapter to make a different argument about what I call "network archaeology."
2. UC Berkeley Division of Data Science and Information, "Data Science Major," 2019, https://data.berkeley.edu/academics/undergraduate-programs/data-science-major
3. Yolanda Gil et al., "Examining the Challenges of Scientific Workflows," 24.
4. W3C (World Wide Web Consortium). "PROV-Overview: An Overview of the PROV Family of Documents."
5. See Olaf Hartig, "Provenance Information in the Web of Data."
6. Daniel Garijo et al., "Common Motifs in Scientific Workflows: An Empirical Analysis."
7. Yolanda Gil and Daniel Garijo, "Towards Automating Data Narratives," quoted from their figure 5.

Bibliography

Always Already Computational. 2017. Always Already Computational: Library Collections as Data: National Forum Position Statements. March. https://github.com/collectionsasdata/collectionsasdata.github.io/raw/master/aac_position-statements.pdf
———. 2019. Collections as Data. Home page. https://collectionsasdata.github.io/
Apache Taverna, v. 3.1.0. Home page ("Taverna Workflow System"). 2014–18. Apache Software Foundation. https://taverna.incubator.apache.org/. Accessed 9 Apr 2018.
Garijo, Daniel, Pinar Alper, Khalid Belhajjame, Oscar Corcho, Yolanda Gil, and Carole Goble. 2012. Common Motifs in Scientific Workflows: An Empirical Analysis. In *2012 IEEE 8th International Conference on E-Science (e-Science)*, https://doi.org/10.1109/eScience.2012.6404427. http://ieeexplore.ieee.org/document/6404427/
Gil, Yolanda, and Daniel Garijo. 2017. Towards Automating Data Narratives. *Proceedings of the Twenty-Second ACM International Conference on Intelligent User Interfaces, Limassol, Cyprus, February 2017*. Limassol: ACM. https://doi.org/10.1145/3025171.3025193. https://dl.acm.org/citation.cfm?id=3025193
Gil, Yolanda, Ewa Deelman, Mark Ellisman, Thomas Fahringer, Geoffrey Fox, Dennis Gannon, Carole Goble, Miron Livny, Luc Moreau, and Jim Myers. 2007. Examining the Challenges of Scientific Workflows. *Computer* 40 (12): 24–32. https://doi.org/10.1109/MC.2007.421. http://ieeexplore.ieee.org/document/4404805/
Hartig, Olaf. 2009. Provenance Information in the Web of Data. In *Proceedings of the WWW2009 Workshop on Linked Data on the Web*, ed. Christian Bizer, Tom Heath, Tim Berners-Lee, and Kingsley Idehen, April 20. http://ceur-ws.org/Vol-538/ldow2009_paper18.pdf

Kepler, v. 2.5. Home page. n.d.. https://kepler-project.org/

Liu, Alan. 2017. Assessing Data Workflows for Common Data 'Moves' Across Disciplines. *Alan Liu*, May 6. https://doi.org/10.21972/G21593. https://liu.english.ucsb.edu/data-moves/

———. 2018. *Friending the Past: The Sense of History in the Digital Age*. Chicago: University of Chicago Press.

Open Provenance Model (OPM). 2018. Home page. King's College London. http://openprovenance.org/

Propp, Vladímir. 1968. *Morphology of the Folktale*. 2nd ed. Trans. Laurence Scott and Ed. Louis A. Wagner. Austin: University of Texas Press.

PROV. [See "PROV-Overview" under W3C (World Wide Web Consortium).]

W3C (World Wide Web Consortium). 2013. PROV-Overview: An Overview of the PROV Family of Documents. April 30. https://www.w3.org/TR/prov-overview/

Wings. 2016. Home page. May 8. http://www.wings-workflows.org/

———. n.d. Description. Accessed 2 Feb 2017. http://www.wings-workflows.org/about.html

Index[1]

A

Abu Bakr al-Siddiq, 99
Accessibility, 2, 18, 79, 148, 176, 177, 185
Acculturation, 112, 117, 133
Activists, 76, 113, 153, 159, 162, 165, 167n11, 176
Advocacy, 73, 74, 80, 160, 203
African Ajami Library (AAL, Boston University), 9, 94, 100, 198
Africanus, Leo, 83, 87
Ajami literacy, 88–90, 94, 96, 104n47
Ajami poetry, 98
Ajami script, 83–85, 87–90, 92–96, 98, 99, 198
Alexandria, *see* Library at Alexandria
Allende, Salvador, 152, 163
Amaral, Tarsila do, 120
American Convention on Human Rights, 156
Andrade, Oswald de, 120
Anticommunism, 152
Application Programming Interface (API), 23, 31, 33

Appropriations, 7, 118, 120, 133, 135, 137n10
Arabic script, 6, 83, 88, 89, 91–93, 99
Aramaic script, 92
Archives New Zealand, 76
Argentina, 7, 21, 35–41, 152–155, 158–160, 162
Asma'u, Nana, 87

B

Bamba, Ahmadu, 87, 98
Bopp, Raul, 120
Boston Public Library (BPL), 1, 2, 19, 25n1, 32
Botelho, Amilcar, 126, 127
Bourdieu, Pierre, 15
Bureaucracy, 39–40, 167n11

C

Cannibalism, 120, 137n10
Cavaignac, 127, 129
Censorship, 7, 36, 42, 144, 176, 177

---

[1] Note: Page numbers followed by 'n' refer to notes.

222　Index

Central Nacional de Informaciones, 153
Cherokee Nation, 57, 59, 60, 64
　See also Sequoyan syllabry
Ch'ien-lung, see Qianlong, Emperor of China
Chinese Communist Party (CCP), 176, 177
Citizen actors, 175
　See also Volunteers
Citizen movements, 165
Civic education, 39
Classical Arabic literature, 88, 89
Collaboration, 8, 70, 71, 163, 181, 184–185, 187, 190, 197, 204, 205
Collaboratory, 8, 9, 117, 181–192, 196, 200, 201, 213
Collective memory, 58, 72, 76, 80, 198
Colonial expeditions, 115
Community archives, 6, 34, 47, 69–81
Community Archives and Heritage Group (UK), 75, 76, 79
Community Archive, The (New Zealand), 75
Community-based activism, 71
Community involvement, 33, 77, 79
Comte, Achille, 123
Condorcet, 4, 16
Contreras, Manuel, 153
Copyright, 5, 18, 23, 24, 33, 34, 46, 146, 176, 192, 199
Counter-narratives, 74, 80
Creative Commons, 24, 33
CrossAsia platform, 145
Culturally sensitive materials, 5, 53
Cultural Revolution, 143

D

Data-driven scholarship, 191
Day of Digital Humanities (event), 196
Data-oriented motifs, 213
Data portability, 205, 207n13

Data science, 171, 183, 186, 189, 190, 211–214
Data science skills, 189, 190
Data stories, 214
Data Visualization Institute (North Carolina State University Libraries), 189
de Andrade, Mario, 120
de Andrade, Oswald, 120, 137n10
De Carvalho, Fernando Setembrino (General), 121
Decolonial translation, 5, 53–66
Deng Xiaoping, 143
Diario Militar, 159, 163
Diderot, 17
Digital Commonwealth, 32
Digital humanities, see Digital scholarship
Digital Humanities at Oxford Summer School, 189
Digital Humanities Summer Institute (University of Victoria), 189
Digital pedagogy, 182, 186–188
Digital Public Library of America (DPLA), 3, 4, 13, 19–24, 29–34
Digital revolution, 44, 171, 172, 176
Digital scholarship, 9, 171, 181–192, 195–198, 201–204, 206, 215, 216
　training, 189–191
Digital Scholarship Institute (Association for Research Libraries), 190
Dirección de Inteligencia Nacional, 153
Disruptive technologies, 43, 49
Documentary Heritage Communities program (Canada), 75
Dom Pedro II, 117

E

El Archivo, see Estado Mayor Presidencial
Elsevier, 17, 18, 46

Endangered Archives Programme (EAP, British Library), 94
Epistemology, 5, 55, 56, 58, 64, 176
Esquivel, Adolfo Perez, 154
Estado Mayor Presidencial, 152, 175
Europeana, 20, 33
European Center for Digital Resources in Chinese Studies, 145
Exoticization, 115, 127

F

Fair Access to Science And Technology Research Act (FASTR), 18
Farabundo Martí National Liberation Front, 152
Ferrez, Marc, 117
Francisco Jaguaribe Gomes de Mattos, 111
Freedom of Information Act (United States), 162

G

Gaddafi, Muammar, *see* Qaddafi, Muammar
Gay and Lesbian Archive (GALA, South Africa), 76
Gomes Lund v. Brazil, 157
Grandmothers of the Plaza de Mayo (Argentina), 162
Grassroots organizations, *see* Community archives
Guatemalan Forensic Anthropology Foundation (FAFG), 162, 163

H

Habeas data, 154, 164, 168n28
Harvard University Libraries, 13, 14
Hausa society, 90, 91
Higgins, Olga, 127, 128
Hong Kong Data-Driven Scholarship Institute, 190

Hu Yaobang, 141
Humanities cyberinfrastructure, *see* Collaboratory
Humanities Intensive Learning and Training (HILT), 189
Human rights, 8, 76, 80, 149–161, 164–165, 175
Hunwick, John, 88, 90
Hyper-reading, 48, 49

I

Ibn Battuta, 83
Implied censorships, 42
Indigenous identities, 113, 133, 134
Indigenous language documents, 53, 54, 56
Indigenous portraits, 122
Intellectual property legislation, 46
Inter-American Court of Human Rights (IACHR), 156, 157
Interdisciplinarity, 172
International Council on Archives, 155
International Covenant for the Protection of All Persons from Enforced Disappearance, 157
International Day for the Right to the Truth Concerning Gross Human Rights Violations and for the Dignity of Victims, 156

J

Jaguaribe, Francisco, 117, 136n6, 136n7
Jarpa, Voluspa, 163
Jefferson, Thomas, 4, 16
Joinet, Louis, 156

K

Ka, Muusaa, 95, 97
Kayre, Moor, 87, 88

L

Language perseverance, 57–59, 65
Language preservation, 5, 60
La Referencia, 20
Leigh, Gustavo, 161
Lesbian Herstory Archives, 74, 78, 81n10
Levi-Strauss, Claude, 118, 130, 131, 173
Librarians
   and faculty status, 201
   librarians as collaborators, 181
Libraries and Archives Canada, 75
Library at Alexandria, 14, 37
Library of Congress, 2, 4, 24, 43–45
Link rot, 145
Literacy, 6, 60, 83–92, 94, 96, 98, 104n47, 144, 172, 187–189
Literacy rates, 84, 86
Louro, José, 118, 127–129
Lula de Silva, Luiz Inacio, 153
Lustration committees, see Special transitional bodies

M

Magalhaes, Amilcar Botelho, 126, 127
Marginalized groups, 74, 80
Market editions, 90
Mato Grosso, 111–114, 117, 118, 121, 129, 131, 132, 134, 136n4, 173
   maps of, 111, 114, 117
Maya, 152, 170n51
Mbakke, Soxna May, Jr., 87
Mbakke, Soxna May, Sr., 87
Metaliteracy, 187
Mooney, James, 55, 56
Moore, Francis, 83
Motifs/moves, 9, 44, 54, 81, 120, 137n10, 158, 171, 211–214
Muhammad al-Wazzan al-Zayyati, Hasan B., see Africanus, Leo
Muhammad, Sayyida Raliya, 90
Multimodal learning, 187
Musee de l'homme, 117, 131, 133
Museo de la Memoria (Santiago, Chile), 161
Museo de la Palabra y laImagen (MUPI, San Salvador, El Salvador), 161
Museu do Indio (Rio de Janeiro), 7, 113, 115, 131–133, 135n1, 174
Museum Maguta, 134
Museum of the Indian, see Museu do Indio (Rio de Janeiro)
Museums of ethnology, 115, 131
Music-derived literacy, 96, 98

N

Nambiquaras, 6, 111–135, 172–176
Narratives, 9, 47, 54, 56, 69, 70, 79, 80, 113, 114, 119, 120, 124, 130, 134, 143, 144, 150, 201, 214, 215, 217
National Archive of Remembrance, 153
National Archives and Records Administration (NARA), 45, 47
National archives (Australia), 76
National Digital Platform initiative (Institute for Museum and Library Services), 189
National Institutes of Health, 18
National Police (Guatemala), 153, 161, 162, 164
National Reorganization Process (el Proceso), 152
National Security Archive (United States), 162
Network model, 29

O

Occom Digital archive, 55
Online education, see Digital pedagogy
Open access, 3, 4, 17–19, 24, 27–34, 50n9, 79, 94, 215
Open government data, 45

Oral traditions, 6, 84, 86
Orentlicher, Diane, 156
Oxford University, 15

P

Park, Mongo, 83
Partner institutions, 29
PBS, 31
Photographs, 7, 22, 32, 78, 112–119, 123–125, 128, 129, 131, 133, 137n12, 161, 163, 173, 174
Pickering, John, 55
Pinochet, Augusto, 152–154, 158, 161
Pinto, Roquette, 120
Platform independence, 205
Positivism, 111
Primary source sets, 30, 31
Project Save, 78, 79
Propaganda, 48, 115, 126, 142, 144, 145
Provenance, 64, 73, 78, 80, 81n8, 197, 212, 213, 215, 217–218n1
Publisher business models, 46

Q

Quintana, Antonio Gonzalez, 155, 156, 168n29
Quintana report, 155, 156, 159, 165
Quranic education, 88–90, 96

R

Reading, 4, 5, 7, 16, 38–41, 48, 49, 57, 59, 70, 78, 83, 84, 113–116, 126, 135, 137n9, 137n10, 137n11, 211
Reparations commissions, *see* Special transitional bodies, 155
Return on investment (ROI), 203, 204, 206
Reyes v. Chile, 156

Ribeiro, Darcy, 131–133
Rivet, Paul, 117, 118, 131–133
Rochester Digital Humanities Institute for Mid-Career Librarians, 189
Romero, Oscar, 156
Rondon, Candido, 7, 111–114, 117, 120–125, 127, 129–132, 134, 135n2, 135–136n3, 136n4, 136n5, 136n6, 173, 174, 176
Rondon Commission, 6, 7, 111–121, 123–127, 129, 133, 135, 136n7, 137n12
Rondon-Roosevelt expedition (1913–1914), 113

S

Scientific workflow management, 212
Self-documentation, 154
Self-identification, 72
Sequoyan syllabry, 59, 61
Serre, Paul, 117
Service hubs, 21, 22, 29
Service of the Protection of the Indian (Brazil), 117
Silences, 167n11, 176
Sistema Nacional de Repositorios Digitales (SNR, Argentina), 21
Smartphones, 32
Social justice, 36, 40, 71, 73, 74, 76, 77, 80, 154, 162
Social repair, 8, 149, 151, 157, 160, 162, 165
Société de Géographie, 6, 112, 113, 115–117, 119, 121, 122, 129, 174
South African History Archive (SAHA), 76
South East Asian American Digital Archives (SAADA), 78, 79
Special transitional bodies, 155
Stiftung Preussischer Kulturbesitz, 145
Sub-Saharan Africa, 6, 83, 84, 86–90, 95, 96, 100

T

Taxmiis bub Wolof, 95
Terror Archives (Paraguay), 153
Thomaz Reis, Luiz, 112, 114, 118, 123–127, 136n5
Timbuktu, 86–88
Transatlantic slavery, 99
Transcribe Yale project, 55
Transitional justice, 7, 149, 150, 153, 157, 158, 165
Translation practices, 54, 56, 59, 64
Transparency, 171–177
Trove (Australia national digital library), 34
Truth commissions, 150, 152, 153, 156, 159, 161, 165, 166n7, 175

U

United Nations Commission on Human Rights (UNCHR), 156

V

Vázquez, Tabaré, 153
Vicaria de la Solidaridad, 154
Villa-Lobos, Heitor, 120
Virtual research environment, *see* Collaboratory
Volunteers, 22, 23, 40, 71, 73, 75, 77, 162
   See also Citizen actors, 162

W

War crimes, 153, 164
West African Research Center (WARC, Senegal), 94, 147
Wikipedia, 17, 47
Worcester, Samuel Austin, 55
Wright, Richard, 14

X

Xi Jinping, 142
Xingu National Park, 132, 136n4

GPSR Compliance
The European Union's (EU) General Product Safety Regulation (GPSR) is a set of rules that requires consumer products to be safe and our obligations to ensure this.

If you have any concerns about our products, you can contact us on

ProductSafety@springernature.com

In case Publisher is established outside the EU, the EU authorized representative is:

Springer Nature Customer Service Center GmbH
Europaplatz 3
69115 Heidelberg, Germany

www.ingramcontent.com/pod-product-compliance
Lightning Source LLC
LaVergne TN
LVHW022039260326
834688LV00061B/935